HISTORY AS IT

ARAB SPRING
THEN AND NOW

FROM HOPE TO DESPAIR

The ✦INDEPENDENT

Mango Publishing Group
Miami
in collaboration with
The Independent

First edition published by Mango Publishing Group.

This is a work of non-fiction adapted from articles and content by journalists of The Independent and published with permission.

For permission requests, please contact the publisher at:
Mango Publishing Group
2850 Douglas Road, 3rd Floor
Coral Gables, FL 33134 USA
info@mango.bz

For special orders, quantity sales, course adoptions and corporate sales, please email the publisher at sales@mango.bz. For trade and wholesale sales, please contact Ingram Publisher Services at customer.service@ingramcontent.com or +1.800.509.4887.

Library of Congress Cataloging
Names: Fisk, Robert; Cockburn, Patrick; Sengupta, Kim
Title: Arab Spring Then and Now / by Robert Fisk, Patrick Cockburn, and Kim Sengupta
Library of Congress Control Number: 2016919560
ISBN 9781633534933 (paperback), ISBN 9781633534926 (eBook)
BISAC Category Code: POL059000 POLITICAL
SCIENCE/World/Middle East

Front Cover Image: ValeStock/Shutterstock.com
Back Cover Image: The Independent

ARAB SPRING THEN AND NOW *From Hope to Despair*
ISBN: 978-1-63353-493-3

Printed in the United States of America

"Several experts on the Middle East concur that the Middle East cannot be democratized."

–Recep Tayyip Erdogan,
President of Turkey

Editor's Note

The wave of demonstrations, protests, riots, coups and civil wars that engulfed North Africa and the Middle East, known as the *Arab Spring,* was touched off on 17 December 2010 in Tunisia. Bloody civil wars followed in Iraq, Libya, Syria, and Yemen and major uprisings broke out in Bahrain and Egypt. Countries that experienced large and small street demonstrations and protests included Algeria, Iran, Lebanon, Jordan, Kuwait, Morocco, Oman, Sudan, Djibouti, Mauritania, Saudi Arabia, Somalia, Western Sahara, and the Palestinian territories. The initial wave faded by mid-2012, morphing into what some have called *Arab Winter* – large scale conflicts or a return to authoritarianism. Only the Tunisian uprising resulted in a form of constitutional democracy.

This book seeks to capture and contrast events in six countries (Tunisia, Egypt, Libya, Bahrain, Yemen, and Syria) during two moments in time – THEN (*Arab Spring* - 2011) and NOW (*Arab Winter* - 2016). The events are reported and interpreted by three of *The Independent's* distinguished and widely acclaimed foreign affairs journalists who have specialized in coverage of the Middle East for many years – Robert Fisk, Patrick Cockburn, and Kim Sengupta.

TABLE OF CONTENTS

FOREWORD

ONE MAN WHO CHANGED THE WORLD IN 2011

In truth, Mohammed Bouazizi only survived a few days into 2011. On 4 January, in a coma and swathed in bandages that covered his terrible burns, he died in a hospital near Tunis, aged just 26. He was an ordinary man, just a humble fruit vendor trying to make an honest living and support his family.

On 17 December 2010, however, after one routine petty harassment too many from the authorities, something inside his long-suffering soul snapped. He dowsed himself in petrol and set himself ablaze. In doing so he lit a fire across the Arab world that blazes to this day.

His act of self-immolation stirred protests in his home town of Sidi Bouzid, that quickly spread across all Tunisia. In a bid to save his regime, President Zine El Abidine Ben Ali, who had ruled the country for the previous 23 years, paid a visit to Bouazizi's bedside a few days before he died. But on 14 January, Ben Ali was swept from power.

The 'Arab Spring' had started. The protests spread first to Egypt, where President Hosni Mubarak would be ousted on 11 February, then to Libya, Yemen, Bahrain and Syria. Some regimes made reforms, some resisted, and some were toppled. But not a single one was unaffected.

Anyone familiar with the Arab world had long known that sooner or later its problems - corrupt regimes that tolerated no independent political movements, feeble economies and mass unemployment in populations in which two-thirds were aged under 25 - would explode. But no one knew when or where the spark would come, still less that it would be provided by Mohammed Bouazizi.

His father died when he was aged three, and though his mother remarried, his stepfather was in poor health and unable to earn. The son attended secondary school, but left to become the main provider for his family, selling fruit and vegetables from a barrow in Sidi Bouzid's market. The young Mohammed was liked by everyone. He was honest and hardworking, trying to give his younger siblings the chance to stay at school. "My sister was the one in university - he would pay for her," his sister Samia said, "and I am still a student and he would spend money on me."

Bouazizi tried to join the army, but was turned down. Efforts to find a regular civilian job met a similar fate. So he was stuck with being a street vendor; every day, he went to the market and bought produce, before pushing his barrow to the local souk. The day's work done, he went back to his family, trying to forget the police who would often make his life a misery because he didn't have the money to bribe them off. And so life went on. Until 17 December, 2010.

That day, he was harassed again, and hauled before a more senior police official, Faida Hamdi, who confiscated his cart and scales. According to Bouazizi's family, either she or her subordinate officers slapped him and insulted his dead father. That this humiliation was directly or indirectly inflicted by a woman only made it worse. He tried to complain to Hamdi's superiors, but they wouldn't see him. Despairing, Bouazizi bought a can of petrol, returned to the municipal building and set himself on fire.

In 17 days, he was dead. The authorities tried to keep the funeral private, but 5,000 people attended. Today, Bouazizi is a symbol of the quest of people throughout the region for human dignity and freedom. The main square in Tunis has been renamed after him; the European Parliament posthumously awarded him its Andrei Sakharov Prize.

The story has not a happy ending. Syria's agony continues, while Egypt's 'caretaker' military has dragged its heels on giving up power; repressive autocracy could yet return in another guise. Back in Sidi Bouzid the mood is sour, too. A few months after his death, Bouazizi's family moved to Tunis, prompting some neighbours to accuse them of turning their backs on their home town, to cash in on their fame. There were even rumours that he hadn't meant to set himself on fire, that he had been drunk.

Nonsense, his friend Mohammed Amri told reporters, almost a year after Bouazizi's death. He was "a serious man who had one dream - to work, buy a car and build a house", he added. Modest goals, but in an Arab world denied them for decades, enough to spur a revolution.

Rupert Cornwell

Editor's Note: Mohammed Bouazizi was one of the ten best "People who changed the world" in 2011, nominated by writers of The Independent.

INTRODUCTION

EARTHQUAKE

The Middle East earthquake of the past five weeks has been the most tumultuous, shattering, mind-numbing experience in the history of the region since the fall of the Ottoman empire. For once, "shock and awe" was the right description. The docile, supine, unregenerative, cringing Arabs of Orientalism have transformed themselves into fighters for the freedom, liberty and dignity which we Westerners have always assumed it was our unique role to play in the world. One after another, our satraps are falling, and the people we paid them to control are making their own history - our right to meddle in their affairs (which we will, of course, continue to exercise) has been diminished forever.

The tectonic plates continue to shift, with tragic, brave - even blackly humorous - results. Countless are the Arab potentates who always claimed they wanted democracy in the Middle East. King Bashar of Syria is to improve public servants' pay. King Bouteflika of Algeria has suddenly abandoned the country's state of emergency. King Hamad of Bahrain has opened the doors of his prisons. King Bashir of Sudan will not stand for president again. King Abdullah of Jordan is studying the idea of a constitutional monarchy. And al-Qa'ida are, well, rather silent.

Who would have believed that the old man in the cave would suddenly have to step outside, dazzled, blinded by the sunlight of freedom rather than the Manichean darkness to which his eyes had become accustomed. Martyrs there were aplenty across the Muslim world - but not an Islamist banner to be seen. The young men and women bringing an end to their torment of dictators were mostly Muslims, but the human spirit was greater than the desire for death. They are Believers, yes - but they got there first, toppling Mubarak while Bin Laden's henchmen still called for his overthrow on outdated videotapes.

But now a warning. It's not over. We are experiencing today that warm, slightly clammy feeling before the thunder and lightning break out. Gaddafi's final horror movie has yet to end, albeit with that terrible mix of farce and blood to which we are accustomed in the Middle East. And his impending doom is, needless to say, throwing into ever-sharper perspective the vile fawning of our own potentates. Berlusconi - who in many respects is already a ghastly mockery of Gaddafi himself - and Sarkozy, and Lord Blair of Isfahan are turning out to look even shabbier than we believed. Those faith-based eyes blessed Gaddafi the murderer. I did write at the time that Blair and Straw had forgotten the "whoops" factor, the reality that this weird light bulb was absolutely bonkers and would undoubtedly perform some other terrible act to shame our masters. And sure enough, every journalist is now going to have to add "Mr Blair's office did not return our call" to his laptop keyboard.

Everyone is now telling Egypt to follow the "Turkish model" - this seems to involve a pleasant cocktail of democracy and carefully controlled Islam. But if this is true, Egypt's army will keep an unwanted, undemocratic eye on its people for decades to come. As lawyer Ali Ezzatyar has pointed out, "Egypt's military leaders have spoken of threats to the "Egyptian way of life"... in a not so subtle reference to threats from the Muslim Brotherhood. This can be seen as a page taken from the Turkish playbook." The Turkish army turned up as kingmakers four times in modern Turkish history. And who but the Egyptian army, makers of Nasser, constructors of Sadat, got rid of the ex-army general Mubarak when the game was up?

And democracy - the real, unfettered, flawed but brilliant version which we in the West have so far lovingly (and rightly) cultivated for ourselves - is not going, in the Arab world, to rest happy with Israel's pernicious treatment of Palestinians and its land theft in the West Bank. Now no longer the "only democracy in the Middle East", Israel argued desperately - in company with Saudi Arabia, for heaven's sake - that it was necessary to maintain Mubarak's tyranny. It pressed the Muslim Brotherhood button in Washington and built up the usual Israeli lobby fear quotient to push Obama and La Clinton off the rails yet again. Faced with pro-democracy protesters in the lands of oppression, they duly went on backing the oppressors until it was too late. I love "orderly transition". The "order" bit says it all. Only Israeli journalist Gideon Levy got it right. "We should be saying 'Mabrouk Misr!'," he said. Congratulations, Egypt!

Yet in Bahrain, I had a depressing experience. King Hamad and Crown Prince Salman have been bowing to their 70 per cent (80 per cent?) Shia population, opening prison doors, promising constitutional reforms. So I asked a government official in Manama if this was really possible. Why not have an elected prime minister instead of a member of the Khalifa royal family? He clucked his tongue. "Impossible," he said. "The GCC would never permit this." For GCC - the Gulf Co-operation Council - read Saudi Arabia. And here, I am afraid, our tale grows darker.

We pay too little attention to this autocratic band of robber princes; we think they are archaic, illiterate in modern politics, wealthy (yes, "beyond the dreams of Croesus", etc), and we laughed when King Abdullah offered to make up any fall in bailouts from Washington to the Mubarak regime, and we laugh now when the old king promises $36bn to his citizens to keep their mouths shut. But this is no laughing matter. The Arab revolt which finally threw the Ottomans out of the Arab world started in the deserts of Arabia, its tribesmen trusting Lawrence and McMahon and the rest of our gang. And from Arabia came Wahabism, the deep and inebriating potion - white foam on the top of the black stuff - whose ghastly simplicity appealed to every would-be Islamist and suicide bomber in the Sunni Muslim world. The Saudis fostered Osama bin Laden and al-Qa'ida and the Taliban. Let us not even mention that they provided most of the 9/11 bombers. And the Saudis will now believe they are the only Muslims still in arms against the brightening world. I have an unhappy suspicion that the destiny of this pageant of Middle East history unfolding before us will be decided in the kingdom of oil, holy places and corruption. Watch out.

But a lighter note. I've been hunting for the most memorable quotations from the Arab revolution. We've had "Come back, Mr President, we were only kidding" from an anti-Mubarak demonstrator. And we've had Saif el-Islam el-Gaddafi's Goebbels-style speech: "Forget oil, forget gas - there will be civil war." My very own favourite, selfish and personal quotation came when my old friend Tom Friedman of The New York Times joined me for breakfast in Cairo with his usual disarming smile. "Fisky," he said, "this Egyptian came up to me in Tahrir Square yesterday, and asked me if I was Robert Fisk!" Now that's what I call a revolution.

Robert Fisk

PART 1

ARAB SPRING

Tuesday, 22 March 2011

FREEDOM IS NOW A PROSPECT

In the dying days of the Ottoman empire, American diplomats - US consuls in Beirut, Jerusalem, Cairo and other cities - NGOs across the region and thousands of American missionaries, pleaded with the State Department and with President Wilson to create one modern Arab state stretching from the shores of Morocco to the borders of Mesopotamia and Persia. This, they believed, would bring a large part of the Muslim world into the democratic orbit of Europe and the West.

Of course, the Sykes-Picot agreement which had already secretly carved up the Middle East, a dying Woodrow Wilson and America's lurch into isolationism put paid to any such fanciful ideas.

Besides, who knows if some Arabs might have preferred the "civilisation" of Rome and, just over a decade later, of Madrid and Berlin, to the supposedly decadent democracies elsewhere in Europe? In the end, the Second World War scarred Tunisia, Libya, Egypt and Lebanon and left the rest comparatively unscathed. But this is the moment to recall the might-have-beens of history. For it is now just possible to recognise a future world in which we may be able to travel from Morocco to the Iraq-Iran border without a visa in our passports. Whether Arabs will be able to do this as speedily, of course, is another matter.

What is not in doubt is the extraordinary tempest passing through the region, the spectacular break-up of the Arab world which most of us have known for most of our lives and which most Arabs have known for most of their lives. From the mildewed, corrupted dictatorships - the cancer of the Middle East - is emerging a people reborn. Not without bloodshed, and not without much violence in front of them as well as behind them. But now at last the Arabs can hope to march into the bright sunlit uplands. Every Arab friend of mine has said exactly the same thing to me over the past weeks: "Never did I believe I would ever live to see this."

We have watched these earthquake tremors turn to cracks and the cracks into crevasses. From Tunisia to Egypt to Libya, to Yemen - perhaps only 48 hours from freedom - to Morocco and to Bahrain and, yes, even now to Syria, the young and the brave have told the world that they want freedom. And freedom, over the coming weeks and months, they will undoubtedly obtain. These are happy words to write, but they must be said with the greatest caution.

Despite all the confidence of D Cameron, Esq, I am not at all sure that Libya is going to end happily. Indeed, I'm not sure I know how it is going to end at all, although the vain and preposterous US attack on Gaddafi's compound - almost identical to the one that was staged in 1986 and took the life of Gaddafi's adopted daughter - demonstrated beyond any doubt that the intention of Obama is regime liquidation. I'm not certain, either, that Bahrain is going to be an easily created

democracy, especially when Saudi Arabia - the untouchable chalice almost as sacred from criticism as Israel - is sending its military riff-raff
across the border bridge.

I have noticed, of course, the whinging of the likes of Robert
Skidelsky who believes that the Bush-Blair fantasy "liberation" of Iraq
- which has ended up with the country effectively controlled from
Tehran - led to the street uprisings today "But Western democracies"
combination of freedom and order... is the product of a long history
that cannot be replicated in short order," he has been saying. "Most
non-Western peoples rely upon the ruler's personal virtues, not insti-
tutional limits on his power, to make their lives tolerable." I get the
point. Arabs cannot be trusted with democracy - indeed they aren"t
ready for it like we smug Westerners are and, er, the Israelis of course.
This is a bit like Israel saying - as it does say - that it is the only democracy in the Middle East, and then trying to ensure it stays that way by
pleading for the Americans to keep Mubarak in power. Which is exactly what happened in January.

But Israel is a case worth examining. Usually capable of considerable forethought, its government and diplomats and overseas
supporters have been hopelessly lazy and cackhanded in their response to the events thundering across the Arab world. Instead of
embracing a new and democratic Egypt, they are sullenly warning of
its volatility. For Israel"s government, it now appears, the fall of dictators whom they have many times compared to Hitler is even worse
than the dictators" preservation. We can see where the problem lies.
A Mubarak would always obey orders - via Washington - from Israel.
A new president will be under no such pressure. Voters in Egypt do
not like the siege of Gaza. They are outraged by the theft of Arab land
for Israeli colonies in the West Bank. No matter how big the bribes
from Washington, no elected Egyptian president is going to be able to
tolerate this state of affairs for long.

Talking of bribes, of course, the biggest of all was handed out last
week - in promissory notes, to be sure - by the Saudi monarch, who is
disbursing almost $150bn (£104bn) around his merry kingdom in the
hope of being spared the wrath of his people. Who knows, it may work
for a time.

But as I always say, watch Saudi Arabia. And don"t take your
eyes off it.

The epic we can afford to forget, however, is the "war on terror". Scarcely a squeak from Osama's outfit for months. Now isn't that strange? The only thing I heard from "al-Qaeda" about Egypt was a call for the removal of Mubarak - a week after he had been deposed by people power. The latest missive from the man in the cave has urged the heroic peoples of the Arab world to remember that their revolutions have Islamic roots; which must come as a surprise to the people of Egypt, Tunisia, Libya, Yemen, Bahrain et al. For they all demanded freedom and liberation and democracy. And there, in a sense, is the answer to Skidelsky. Does he believe they are all lying? And if so, why? As I said, there is much blood still to flow. And many a meddling hand to turn new democracies into time-serving dictatorships. But for once - just once - the Arabs can see the broad sunlit uplands.

Robert Fisk

CHAPTER 1

TUNISIA SPRING

Saturday, 15 January 2011

IS IT A REAL REVOLUTION?

Is it a real revolution in Tunisia or will another member of the ruling elite succeed in replacing President Zine el-Abidine Ben Ali who took flight yesterday? It is a crucial question for the rest of the Arab world where other corrupt police states face the same political, social and economic problems as Tunisia.

A striking feature of the whole Middle East for more than 30 years has been the unpopularity of the regimes combined with their depressing ability to stay in power. Most have found ways of preventing revolutions or military coup d'etats through ferocious security services protecting rickety state machines that mainly function as a source of jobs and patronage.

In Tunisia, Mr Ben Ali, along with other Arab leaders, presented himself as an opponent of Muslim fundamentalism and therefore won tolerance if not plaudits in Western capitals.

But the revolution that is brewing across the Middle East is of a traditional model springing from high unemployment, particularly among better educated young men, and a ruling class unable to resolve any of their countries' economic problems. The most obvious parallel with Tunisia is Egypt where the sclerotic regime of President Hosni Mubarak clings to power.

Will the present so-called "soft coup" work whereby Prime Minister Mohamed Ghannouchi takes power and calms down protesters by promises of reform and elections? It does not look very likely. The declared State of Emergency is not working.

There is not reason to suppose that a political leader so closely associated with the old regime will have any credibility with people in the streets.

Conditions vary across the Arab world but there is plenty in common between the situation in Tunisia and that in Algeria, Jordan and Egypt. Economic and political stagnation is decades old. In some states this is made more tolerable by access to oil revenues, but even this is not enough to provide jobs for educated youths who see their path blocked by a corrupt elite.

There are echoes of the Tunisian crisis in other countries. In Jordan the security forces have been battling rioters in Maan, a traditional site of unrest in the past where the government has difficulty coping. In Kuwait there was an attack by security forces in December on academic and members of parliament. Food prices have been going up.

Yet all these regimes that are now in trouble had a carefully cultivated image in the west of being "moderate" and antifundamentalist. In the aftermath of the invasion of Iraq, President George Bush and Tony Blair made much of their democratic agenda for the Middle East, but when one of the few democratic elections to take place in the region produced victory for Hamas among the Palestinians of Gaza and the West Bank, the US did everything to thwart the outcome of the poll.

The Middle East still has a reputation for coups but a striking feature of the region since the early 1970s is how few of the regimes have changed. The forces behind the Tunisian events are not radically new but they are all the more potent for being so long suppressed.

Western governments have been caught on the hop because explosions of social and economic frustration have been long predicted but have never happened. The extent of the uprising is yet to be defined and the Tunisian army evidently hopes that the departure of Mr Ben Ali may be enough for the government to restore its authority. The generals could be right, but the shootings over the last month failed to work. There is no particular reason why the same tactics should start to work now.

Patrick Cockburn

Monday, 17 January 2011

DEMOCRACY, BUT NOT TOO MUCH DEMOCRACY

The end of the age of dictators in the Arab world? Certainly they are shaking in their boots across the Middle East, the well-heeled sheikhs and emirs, and the kings - including one very old one in Saudi Arabia and a young one in Jordan, and presidents - another very old one in Egypt and a young one in Syria, because Tunisia wasn't meant to happen.

Food price riots in Algeria, too, and demonstrations against price increases in Amman. Not to mention scores more dead in Tunisia, whose own despot sought refuge in Riyadh - exactly the same city to which a man called Idi Amin once fled.

If it can happen in the holiday destination Tunisia, it can happen anywhere, can't it? Tunisia was feted by the West for its "stability" when Zine el-Abdine Ben Ali was in charge. The French and the Germans and the Brits, dare we mention this, always praised the dictator for being a "friend" of civilised Europe, keeping a firm hand on all those Islamists.

Tunisians won't forget this little history, even if we would like them to. The Arabs used to say that two thirds of the entire Tunisian population - seven million out of 10 million, virtually the whole adult population - worked in one way or another for Ben Ali's secret police.

They must have been on the streets too, then, protesting at the man we loved until last week.

But don't get too excited. Yes, Tunisian youth have used the internet to rally each other - in Algeria, too - and the demographic explosion of youth (born in the Eighties and Nineties with no jobs to go to after university) is on the streets.

But the "unity" government is to be formed by Mohamed Ghannouchi, a satrap of Ben Ali's for almost 20 years, a safe pair of hands who will have our interests - rather than his people's interests - at heart.

For I fear this is going to be the same old story. Yes, we would like a democracy in Tunisia - but not too much democracy. Remember how we wanted Algeria to have a democracy back in the early Nineties? Then, when it looked like the Islamists might win the second round of voting, we supported its military-backed government in suspending elections and crushing the Islamists and initiating a civil war in which 150,000 died. No, in the Arab world, we want law and order and stability. Even in Hosni Mubarak's corrupt and corrupted Egypt, that's what we want. And we will get it.

The truth, of course, is that the Arab world is so dysfunctional, sclerotic, corrupt, humiliated and ruthless - and remember that Ben Ali was calling Tunisian protesters "terrorists" only last week - and so totally incapable of any social or political progress, that the chances of a series of working democracies emerging from the chaos of the Middle East stand at around zero per cent. The job of the Arab potentates will be what it has always been - to "manage" their people, to control them, to keep the lid on, to love the West and to hate Iran.

Indeed, what was Hillary Clinton doing last week as Tunisia burned? She was telling the corrupted princes of the Gulf that their job was to support sanctions against Iran, to confront the Islamic republic, to prepare for another strike against a Muslim state after the two catastrophes the United States and Britain have already inflicted in the region.

The Muslim world - at least, that bit of it between India and the Mediterranean - is a more than sorry mess. Iraq has a sort-of government that is now a satrap of Iran, Hamid Karzai is no more than the mayor of Kabul, Pakistan stands on the edge of endless disaster, Egypt has just emerged from another fake election (a friend called me from Cairo yesterday because she knew what I wanted to know - "No, we won't," she said). And Lebanon... Well, poor old Lebanon hasn't even got a government. Southern Sudan - if the elections are fair - might be a tiny candle, but don't bet on it.

It's the same old problem for us in the West. We mouth the word "democracy" and we are all for fair elections - providing the Arabs vote for whom we want them to vote for. In Algeria 20 years ago, they didn't. In "Palestine" they didn't.

And in Lebanon, because of the so-called Doha accord, they didn't. So we sanction them, threaten them and warn them about Iran and expect them to keep their mouths shut when Israel steals more Palestinian land for its colonies on the West Bank.

There was a fearful irony that the police theft of an ex-student's fruit produce - and his suicide in Tunis - should have started all this off, not least because Ben Ali made a failed attempt to gather public support by visiting the dying youth in hospital. For years, this wretched man had been talking about a "slow liberalising" of his country. But all dictators know they are in greatest danger when they start freeing entrapped countrymen from their chains.

And the Arabs behaved accordingly.

No sooner had Ben Ali flown off into exile than Arab newspapers which have been stroking his fur and polishing his shoes and receiving his money for so many years were vilifying the man. "Misrule", "corruption", "authoritarian reign", "a total lack of human rights", their journalists are saying now. Rarely have the words of the Lebanese poet Khalil Gibran sounded so painfully accurate: "Pity the nation that welcomes its new ruler with trumpetings, and farewells him with hootings, only to welcome another with trumpetings again." Mohamed Ghannouchi, perhaps? Of course, everyone is lowering their prices now - or promising to. Cooking oil and bread are the staples of the masses. So prices will come down in Tunisia and Algeria and Egypt and Jordan. But why should they be so high in the first place? Algeria should be as rich as Saudi Arabia - it has the oil and gas - but it has one of the worst unemployment rates in the Middle East, no social security, no pensions, nothing for its people because its generals have salted their country's wealth away in Switzerland.

And police brutality. The torture chambers will keep going. We will maintain our good relations with the dictators. We will continue to arm their wretched armies and tell them to seek peace with Israel. And they will do what we want. Ben Ali has fled. The search is now on for a more pliable dictator in Tunisia - a "benevolent strongman" as the news agencies like to call these ghastly men. And the shooting will go on - as it did yesterday in Tunisia - until "stability" has been restored.

No, on balance, I don't think the age of the Arab dictators is over. We will see to that.

Robert Fisk

Friday, 21 January 2011

'I AM PROUD OF WHAT HE DID'

The street vendor who set himself alight, sparking an uprising which swept away 23 years of dictatorship in Tunisia and triggered protests across North Africa, had been beaten down by years of poverty and oppression by the authorities, his family told *The Independent* last night.

Mohamed Bouazizi - whose desperate act, copied in countries including Algeria and Egypt, has become a symbol of injustice and oppression - had lost his land, his living and had been humiliated by local officials.

In an interview yesterday at his home, his mother Mannoubia said she was proud of her son and of his role in changing the regime. His cries for help had been ignored by banks and officials, his family said. "The government drove him to do what he did; they never gave him a chance. We are poor and they thought we had no power," his mother said. "My son is lost, but look what is happening, how many people are now getting involved."

What made Mr Bouazizi's desperation and sense of hopelessness so real to those who were to rise up afterwards was that it mirrored many of their experiences. The 26-year-old lived in Sidi Bouzid, in the poor interior of the country, which is economically and culturally different from the capital Tunis and the northern coastal areas where then president Zine al-Abidine Ben Ali, his wife Leila Trabelsi and their venal courtiers enjoyed a life of opulence.

Mr Bouazizi had passed his baccalaureate but had found no skilled job in a region suffering from chronic underinvestment; the family land had been taken back by the bank, and his only source of income, from selling fruit and vegetables from a cart, was about to be

lost because he could not get the required permit from the local council. The act which drove Mr Bouazizi over the edge, it is claimed, was
the humiliation of being slapped on the face in public by a female official of the municipality, Feyda Hamdi, during an altercation when she
had attempted to impound his cart. Leila, 24, one of Mohamed's six
siblings, acknowledged that the blow from an official, especially a
woman, had undoubtedly shamed his brother. But what happened
was the culmination of a series of events which had made him, and the
family, feel they were the victims of a cruel and unfeeling system.

"It was always difficult. The worst thing was what happened to
the land," she said. "We owned it with our neighbours and we grew
olives and almonds. It was earning good money, but then things
turned bad for a lot of people, our sales went down and the bank
seized our land. I went with Mohamed, we appealed to the bank, we
appealed to the governor, but no one listened. Other families had the
same problem; people just ignored us."

Asma Gharbi, a hydraulic engineer who lives nearby, said: "Just
look at this town, how everything is falling apart, there is no money. I
have lived in Tunis and I can tell you the high-up people there don't
care. Everyone is fed-up here, but Mohamed did something that forced
people to take notice."

At the municipality headquarters, a junior official, Hassan Raidi,
admitted shortcomings of the past. "But we were all afraid of Ben Ali
and his people. So no one could make any criticism. Now things will
change."

After his argument with Ms Hamdi, Mr Bouazizi walked off, came
back with a can of patrol and set himself alight in front of the regional
governor's residence.

That was on 17 December. There were protests locally, unheeded
calls for an investigation and for officials to be held to account. But
there was very little wider publicity in Tunisia's censored and cowed
media.

"The unions got involved, teachers, lawyers, doctors, all sections
of civil society, and set up a Popular Resistance Committee to back the
people of Sidi Bouzid and back the uprising. The uprising continued
for 10 days in Sidi Bouzid, but with no support from outside," said La-
zhar Gharbi, a head teacher. But then the news of the self-immolation
by the fruit seller began to spread through the online social network -
Facebook, Twitter and blogs, raising an outcry unexpected in scale for

some-thing that happened in a small town. Mr Bouazizi was moved to a hospital in Tunis. Among the visitors was the president, who declared an inquiry would be held. He said Sidi Bouzid and surrounding areas would get grants and jobs. But the mood in the area was one of anger, fuelled by aggressive action by the police. After Mr Bouazizi died on 4 January, his funeral was attended by several hundred people chanting "Farewell Mohamed, we will avenge you. We weep for you today, others will weep tomorrow for what they did to you."

Since then Tunisia has changed, with Ben Ali forced into exile by protesters, many of whom cried out the name of Mohamed Bouazizi. He has been mentioned in blogs written by some of the others who burned themselves to death in Algeria, Egypt and Mauritania. Street clashes continue between protesters and police, as the country faces an uncertain future.

Sitting at the family home, a three roomed house, surrounded by her children, 48-year-old Mannoubia talked about how her son's death has politicised her: "I now know how Ben Ali had been stealing from the country. How the relations of Leila Trabelsi have been stealing. We do not want them back. But the situation is not just bad in Tunisia. I remember my husband used to talk about Libya, poor people there suffered as well. She continued: "I have a lot of people who come up to me now to say it is not just me who has lost a son, but the whole village that has lost a son. I am proud of what he did. I would like to go up to Tunis and take a look at these demonstrations. It is good to know that my son had played a part in changing things."

Whether any real changes come to Tunisia through the "Jasmine Revolution" remains to be seen. In Sidi Bouzid's central square a group of young men sit around on a wall with no job to go to.

Walid Ben Sanai, who trained as an engineer, sees no change for the better in sight. "Ben Ali has gone, but the government ministers are still the same. We are not seeing any real improvement, and unless there is some real improvement there will be real trouble. "But we think about Mohamed Bouazizi. I hope he will be remembered."

Kim Sengupta

FIRST DESPOT TO FLEE

The ousted Tunisian President Zine al-Abidine Ben Ali was convicted in absentia on embezzlement and other charges yesterday after £16.6 million in jewels and public funds were found in one of his palaces.

Mr Ben Ali and his wife were both sentenced to 35 years each in prison, and fined 50 million dinars (£22m) and 41 million dinars respectively.

The conviction of Mr Ben Ali and Leila Trabelsi followed a day-long trial before the Tunis criminal court. Mr Ben Ali, 74, vigorously denied the charges in a statement through his French lawyer, calling the proceedings a "shameful masquerade of the justice of the victorious".

The trove of jewels, some which the court said had "historic value," and the money were found in a palace in the picturesque town of Sidi Bou Said, outside Tunis, following Mr Ben Ali's departure in the face of widespread demonstrations and riots against him and his extended family over allegations of corruption and abuse of power. Further details of that departure were revealed yesterday, as Mr Ben Ali said through his lawyers that he had been tricked into leaving his country.

In his first detailed account of how he hurriedly left Tunisia on 14 January for Saudi Arabia, where he is in exile after 23 years in power, Mr Ben Ali claimed he only went there to bring his family to safety after being told of an assassination plot against him by a "friendly" foreign intelligence service. He was persuaded into taking his wife and children to Jeddah but had intended to return immediately.

Mr Ben Ali denied that he had deliberately fled the country. A statement by his lawyer said: "He boarded the plane with his family after ordering the crew to wait for him in Jeddah. But after his arrival in Jeddah, the plane returned to Tunisia, without waiting for him, contrary to his orders."

Mr Ben Ali's story shows how his former allies, such as the US, were eager to get him out of the country without a confrontation between him and the hundreds of thousands of demonstrators who were demanding he step down. His flight, the first of the Arab despots in charge of police states to flee at the start of the Arab Spring, was followed by popular uprisings in Egypt, Libya, Bahrain, Yemen and Syria.

The trial of Mr Ben Ali is the beginning of a process by the Tunisian government to punish those responsible for killings and torture under the old regime. It is also the start of an attempt to gain control of the 30 to 40 per cent of the Tunisian economy estimated to have fallen under the sway of Mr Ben Ali's family and that of his wife, Leila Trabelsi, whom he married in 1992.

Hatred of the Ben Ali regime was fuelled by tales of their unbridled greed and gargantuan wealth. In US embassy cables released by Wiki-Leaks, the American ambassador expressed shock at how Mr Ben Ali's extended family was a "quasi-mafia" and the "nexus of Tunisian corruption".

The ambassador gives an account of having dinner at the villa of one of the Ben Ali's daughters, Nesrine and her husband, Sakhr el-Meteri, where frozen yogurt was flown in from St Tropez, and four chickens a day were fed to a pet tiger. Not only did the Ben Ali and Trabelsi families take over profitable businesses, but they made it impossible for anybody else to do business without cutting them in for a share. One entrepreneur who went to see Mr Ben Ali with his plan to start a university was told by him "OK, but its 50:50" according to a report in The Wall Street Journal. The entrepreneur dropped his proposal.

One of the President's brothers-in-law, Belhassen Trabelsi, suggested to a car importer, who intended to import Citroën cars, that he join him in a partnership. When the importer turned him down he was promptly subjected to 17 tax inspections and his cars were stopped at customs for having 10 seats. "There is no such thing as a 10-seat car," the importer told the newspaper.

Mr Ben Ali, who came to power in a coup in 1987, ran a tightly controlled police state similar to that in other parts of the Arab world. The ruling family cherry-picked the most profitable enterprises and bought up privatised businesses at rock-bottom prices. Mr Trabelsi's business interests included the Bank of Tunisia, Karthago Airlines and radio and television companies.

Mr Ben Ali, born in 1936, had made his career in the Tunisian military and was a graduate of American and French military training schools. In Tunisia he was head of national security from 1977 and was well placed to take over from his ageing predecessor President

Habib Bourguiba He always revelled in the costly trappings of office and ignored the way in which the pervasive corruption and creeping economic domination of the ruling families fuelled furious resentment among all classes of Tunisians. This exploded last December after a 26-year-old street vendor burnt himself to death when his vegetable cart was confiscated by the police because he did not have the required licence. Mr Ali is likely to face a further trial by military tribunal, the date for which has not been set, at which he will be charged with ordering the police to open fire on protesters, hundreds of whom were killed. Tunisia was typical of the era of Arab police states which developed from the 1970s and were very similar, regardless of whether or not they were republics or monarchies. Absolute power was held through multi-layered security agencies, tight censorship and control of information and communications, and state domination of all independent organisations such as trade unions and political parties. The wave of privatisations of public property became plundering expeditions for predatory ruling families.

In Tunisia popular loathing for Leila Trabelsi, a former hairdresser, was particularly acute. No part of the economy was immune from seizure or interference by the ruling families. They took over banks, insurance companies, tourist venture, property, distribution and agencies of big foreign firms. As Mr Ben Ali was being toppled, the cars and villas of his relatives and in-laws were ransacked by angry crowds. It is not known how much of their assets had been moved abroad.

Such was the grip of "The Family" on the economy that government officials say they are moving cautiously in dealing with their many businesses and, instead of closing them down, the courts have appointed managers.

Patrick Cockburn

Tuesday, 9 July 2011

A DICTATOR'S TRIAL

How do you defend a dictator who's been around for years and years and years when he's accused of - well, being a dictator for years and years and years? When I mention the "trials" of Zine el-Abidine Ben Ali, the former Tunisian autocrat's lawyer throws his hands in the air, an expression of cynicism and laughter on his face. "These weren't judgements, they weren't even real cases - they were a joke," Akram Azoury says of the Tunis courts which last month, after just one-and-a-half hours of deliberations, sentenced Ben Ali and his wife Leila Traboulsi to 35 years' imprisonment and the equivalent of £48m in fines, and then, this week, to another 15-and-a-half years. "The speed of the first trial - the length of time between the opening of the trial and the judgement - was closer to a Formula One race than to a classical judicial procedure."

Oddly, Ben Ali's first farcical trial - with no witnesses and no lawyers chosen by the defendant - enraged both his lawyer and the ex-dictator's most vehement opponents. They wanted charges of high treason and crowds of tortured ex-prisoners to testify to the brutality of the Ben Ali regime. Azoury, a Lebanese Christian who acted for Ben Ali with his French colleague Jean-Yves Le Borgne and who runs a family legal practice in Beirut - his two daughters are also lawyers - wanted a fair trial. "No lawyers were invited to the court," Azoury says with quiet fury. "I had power of attorney, certified by the Tunisian embassy in Beirut. I applied for a visa - but I was not granted a visa. I applied to the Tunisian Bar for authorisation - and I was not granted authorisation." In the end, the Tunisian Bar appointed two lawyers of its own to "defend" Ben Ali.

"This trial, it violates each and every criteria of the 1966 Fair Trial pact that preceded the pact of civil rights of the European Union," Azoury says.

"After 1966, the Human Rights Committee was set up in Geneva. This court hearing in Tunis was not eligible to qualify as a trial - so the verdict is not a verdict. No European country can extradite Ben Ali to Tunisia based on this verdict. Should he be free in France, England, Germany, especially if he was in England and the Tunisians wanted to extradite him, no court in England would accept to do this." I forbear to suggest that no immigration officer in England - let alone France - would allow Ben Ali or his wife to enter the country, although Mr Azoury does believe his client should leave Saudi Arabia.

"Ben Ali described the judgements as 'the wording of the justice of the victors'. Don't forget that the mere fact that President..." - and here I note Azoury can still call his client 'President' - "...Ben Ali hired me as his lawyer is a precedent in this part of the world. It means he wants to play by the rules. He doesn't care about a political trial. He governed Tunisia for 25 years and it's the right of the Tunisian people to judge him. In his opinion, these accusations are not made innocently. If you look at the substance of these accusations, they are shameful. They want to kill him morally. Don't forget that all this stuff in the second trial - the drugs and weapons - were 'found' in his official residence two or three months after Ben Ali left. After seven months now, you might 'find' nuclear weapons in his residence!" The second "trial" of Ben Ali this week - for possession of drugs and illegal weapons - also added another fine of £50,000. Even his Tribunal Bar-appointed lawyers objected that the hearing was unfair. "The only purpose," Azoury says, "was to brand President Ben Ali as a drugs dealer and weapons dealer before the Tunisian elections."

But why did the old dictator hire a Lebanese lawyer to act for him? Azoury has an interesting legal pedigree. In 2000, he defended Lebanese petroleum minister Barsoumian and secured his acquittal before the courts after 11 months of imprisonment; in 2003, he prosecuted board members of the Medina Bank; in 2005, he represented General Jamil Sayed of the Lebanese General Security when he was accused by the UN tribunal of possible involvement in the assassination of ex-prime minister Rafiq Hariri. After four years of false imprisonment, Sayed was released by the UN who admitted it had no evidence against him.

"A lawyer can only perform his job in a court of law," Azoury says. "Law and politics cannot be present at the same time. My job was to take the politics out of the courtroom. Because if they wanted a political judgement in Tunis, it has already been issued and executed. The guy (Ben Ali) is not going to Tunisia any more. I respect this. But if the Tunisian authorities want to start a real judicial process, they should abide by the principles of a fair trial."

But Akram Azoury is no patsy. "It is an excellent thing to judge heads of state," he says suddenly.

"It will help to implement a culture of justice - because the responsibility of the new regime in Tunisia is also to implement due process of law. If these rulers were that bad, there should be no difficulty in convicting them after a fair trial." Azoury lived in Tunis for a month in 1989 when he was consultant to the company building the new Arab League headquarters, but never met Ben Ali. "I wasn't involved in politics," he says.

But he clearly thinks a lot about it. When we talked of the Tunisian revolution, Azoury spoke of the street vendor Mohamed Bouazizi - whose death by self-immolation started the revolt against Ben Ali - in words that I am still pondering. "The body of Bouazizi will either be a light in this part of the world," Azoury says. "Or he will be the fire that will consume it."

Robert Fisk

CHAPTER 2

EGYPT SPRING

Cairo's Tahrir Square, 22 November 2011.

Friday, 28 January 2011

'DAY OF WRATH' AND DAYS OF RAGE

A day of prayer or a day of rage? All Egypt was waiting for the Muslim Sabbath today - not to mention Egypt's fearful allies - as the country's ageing President clings to power after nights of violence that have shaken America's faith in the stability of the Mubarak regime.

Five men have so far been killed and almost 1,000 others have been imprisoned, police have beaten women and for the first time an office of the ruling National Democratic Party was set on fire. Rumours are as dangerous as tear gas here. A Cairo daily has been claiming that one of President Hosni Mubarak's top advisers has fled to London with 97 suitcases of cash, but other reports speak of an enraged President shouting at senior police officers for not dealing more harshly with demonstrators.

Mohamed ElBaradei, the Nobel prize-winning former UN official, flew back to Egypt last night but no one believes - except perhaps the Americans - that he can become a focus for the protest movements that have sprung up across the country.

Already there have been signs that those tired of Mubarak's corrupt and undemocratic rule have been trying to persuade the ill-paid policemen patrolling Cairo to join them. "Brothers! Brothers! How much do they pay you?" one of the crowds began shouting at the cops in Cairo. But no one is negotiating - there is nothing to negotiate except the departure of Mubarak, and the Egyptian government says and does nothing, which is pretty much what it has been doing for the past three decades.

People talk of revolution but there is no one to replace Mubarak's men - he never appointed a vice-president - and one Egyptian journalist yesterday told me he had even found some friends who feel sorry for the isolated, lonely President. Mubarak is 82 and even hinted he would stand for president again - to the outrage of millions of Egyptians.

The barren, horrible truth, however, is that save for its brutal police force and its ominously docile army - which, by the way, does not look favourably upon Mubarak's son Gamal - the government is powerless. This is revolution by Twitter and revolution by Facebook, and technology long ago took away the dismal rules of censorship.

Mubarak's men seem to have lost all sense of initiative. Their party newspapers are filled with self-delusion, pushing the massive demonstrations to the foot of front pages as if this will keep the crowds from the streets - as if, indeed, that by belittling the story, the demonstrations never happened.

But you don't need to read the papers to see what has gone wrong. The filth and the slums, the open sewers and the corruption of every government official, the bulging prisons, the laughable elections, the whole vast, sclerotic edifice of power has at last brought Egyptians on to their streets.

Amr Moussa, the head of the Arab League, spotted something important at the recent summit of Arab leaders at the Egyptian resort of Sharm el-Sheikh. "Tunisia is not far from us," he said. "The Arab men are broken." But are they? One old friend told me a frightening story about a poor Egyptian who said he had no interest in moving the corrupt leadership from their desert gated communities. "At least we now know where they live," he said. There are more than 80 million people in Egypt, 30 per cent of them under 20. And they are no longer afraid.

And a kind of Egyptian nationalism - rather than Islamism - is making itself felt at the demonstrations. January 25 is National Police Day - to honour the police force who died fighting British troops in Ishmaelia - and the government clucked its tongue at the crowds, telling them they were disgracing their martyrs. No, shouted the crowds, those policemen who died at Ishmaelia were brave men, not represented by their descendants in uniform today.

This is not an un-clever government, though. There is a kind of shrewdness in the gradual freeing of the press and television of this ramshackle pseudodemocracy. Egyptians had been given just enough air to breathe, to keep them quiet, to enjoy their docility in this vast farming land. Farmers are not revolutionaries, but when the millions thronged to the great cities, to the slums and collapsing houses and universities, which gave them degrees and no jobs, something must have happened.

"We are proud of the Tunisians - they have shown Egyptians how to have pride," another Egyptian colleague said yesterday. "They were inspiring but the regime here was smarter than Ben Ali in Tunisia. It provided a veneer of opposition by not arresting all the Muslim Brotherhood, then by telling the Americans that the great fear should be Islamism, that Mubarak was all that stood between them and 'terror' - a message the US has been in a mood to hear for the past 10 years."

There are various clues that the authorities in Cairo realised something was afoot. Several Egyptians have told me that on 24 January, security men were taking down pictures of Gamal Mubarak from the slums - lest they provoke the crowds. But the vast number of arrests, the police street beatings - of women as well as men - and the near-collapse of the Egyptian stock market bear the marks of panic rather than cunning.

And one of the problems has been created by the regime itself; it has systematically got rid of anyone with charisma, thrown them out of the country, politically emasculating any real opposition by imprisoning many of them. The Americans and the EU are telling the regime to listen to the people - but who are these people, who are their leaders? This is not an Islamic uprising - though it could become one - but, save for the usual talk of Muslim Brotherhood participation in the demonstrations, it is just one mass of Egyptians stifled by decades of failure and humiliation.

But all the Americans seem able to offer Mubarak is a suggestion of reforms - something Egyptians have heard many times before. It's not the first time that violence has come to Egypt's streets, of course. In 1977, there were mass food riots - I was in Cairo at the time and there were many angry, starving people - but the Sadat government managed to control the people by lowering food prices and by imprisonment and torture. There have been police mutinies before - one ruthlessly suppressed by Mubarak himself. But this is something new.

Interestingly, there seems no animosity towards foreigners. Many journalists have been protected by the crowds and - despite America's lamentable support for the Middle East's dictators - there has not so far been a single US flag burned. That shows you what's new. Perhaps a people have grown up - only to discover that their ageing government are all children.

Who Could Succeed Hosni Mubarak?

Gamal Mubarak — Protesters on the streets of Egypt aren't just rallying against the 30-year-reign of President Hosni Mubarak, they are also taking aim at his son Gamal Mubarak, 47, an urbane former investment banker who has scaled the political ladder, prompting speculation that he is being groomed for his father's post.

The youngest son of Mr Mubarak and his half-Welsh wife, Suzanne, Gamal was educated at the elite American University in Cairo, going on to work for the Bank of America.

He entered politics about a decade ago, quickly moving up to become head of the political secretariat of his father's National Democratic Party (NDP). He was heavily involved in the economic liberalisation of Egypt, which pleased investors but provoked the ire of protesters, who blame the policies for lining the pockets of the rich while the poor suffered.

Although he has always denied having an eye on his father's throne, a mysterious campaign sprung up last year, with posters plastered across Cairo calling for Gamal to stand for president in elections scheduled for later this year. His 82-year-old father has not yet declared his candidacy.

Certainly the protesters appeared unhappy with the chosen son, chanting "Gamal, tell your father Egyptians hate you" and tearing up his picture.

Mohamed ElBaradei — Protests in Egypt today will be different from the others that have swept the Middle East in recent weeks in one important way. Mohamed ElBaradei, former head of the International Atomic Energy Agency (IAEA), landed at Cairo airport last night to lead rallies against Hosni Mubarak's rule.

The 68-year-old was born in the Egyptian capital, from where he launched a legal career. He joined the IAEA in the 1980s, becoming head of the UN body in 1997.

The 2003 invasion of Iraq thrust Mr ElBaradei into the public consciousness. He demurred on the US rationale for attacking Saddam Hussein, describing the war as "a glaring example of how, in many cases, the use of force exacerbates the problem rather than solving it". The award, jointly with the IAEA, of the 2005 Nobel Peace Prize further rankled with the Bush administration .

He has long been urged to challenge the 82-year-old President, but hitherto has bided his time, insisting first on electoral reform, but his participation in today's protests indicate he is ready. Recent speeches, including recently at Harvard, when he joked that he was "looking for a job" have done nothing to dissuade his supporters, but at 68 his presidency would surely be only a short-term fix to Egypt's problems.

Robert Fisk

Saturday, 29 January 2011

SHOWERS OF TEAR GAS

It might be the end. It is certainly the beginning of the end. Across Egypt, tens of thousands of Arabs braved tear gas, water cannons, stun grenades and live fire yesterday to demand the removal of Hosni Mubarak after more than 30 years of dictatorship.

And as Cairo lay drenched under clouds of tear gas from thousands of canisters fired into dense crowds by riot police, it looked as if his rule was nearing its finish. None of us on the streets of Cairo yesterday even knew where Mubarak - who would later appear on television to dismiss his cabinet - was. And I didn't find anyone who cared.

They were brave, largely peaceful, these tens of thousands, but the shocking behaviour of Mubarak's plainclothes battagi - the word does literally mean "thugs" in Arabic - who beat, bashed and assaulted demonstrators while the cops watched and did nothing, was a disgrace. These men, many of them expolicemen who are drug addicts, were last night the front line of the Egyptian state. The true representatives of Hosni Mubarak as uniformed cops showered gas on to the crowds.

At one point last night, gas canisters were streaming smoke across the waters of the Nile as riot police and protesters fought on the great river bridges. It was incredible, a risen people who would no longer take violence and brutality and prison as their lot in the largest Arab nation. And the police themselves might be cracking: "What can we do?" one of the riot cops asked us. "We have orders. Do you think we want to do this? This country is going downhill." The government imposed a curfew last night as protesters knelt in prayer in front of police.

How does one describe a day that may prove to be so giant a page in Egypt's history? Maybe reporters should abandon their analyses and just tell the tale of what happened from morning to night in one of the world's most ancient cities. So here it is, the story from my notes, scribbled amid a defiant people in the face of thousands of plainclothes and uniformed police.

It began at the Istikama mosque on Giza Square: a grim thoroughfare of gaunt concrete apartment blocks and a line of riot police that stretched as far as the Nile. We all knew that Mohamed ElBaradei would be there for midday prayers and, at first, the crowd seemed small. The cops smoked cigarettes. If this was the end of the reign of Mubarak, it was a pretty unimpressive start.

But then, no sooner had the last prayers been uttered than the crowd of worshippers, perched above the highway, turned towards the police. "Mubarak, Mubarak," they shouted. "Saudi Arabia is waiting for you." That's when the water cannons were turned on the crowd - the police had every intention of fighting them even though not a stone had been thrown. The water smashed into the crowd and then the hoses were pointed directly at ElBaradei, who reeled back, drenched.

He had returned from Vienna a few hours earlier and few Egyptians think he will run Egypt - he claims to want to be a negotiator - but this was a disgrace. Egypt's most honoured politician, a Nobel prize winner who had held the post of the UN's top nuclear inspector, was drenched like a street urchin. That's what Mubarak thought of him, I suppose: just another trouble maker with a "hidden agenda" - that really is the language the Egyptian government is using right now.

And then the tear gas burst over the crowds. Perhaps there were a few thousand now, but as I walked beside them, something remarkable happened. From apartment blocks and dingy alleyways, from neighbouring streets, hundreds and then thousands of Egyptians swarmed on to the highway leading to Tahrir Square. This is the one tactic the police had decided to prevent. To have Mubarak's detractors in the very centre of Cairo would suggest that his rule was already over. The government had already cut the internet - slicing off Egypt from the rest of the world - and killed all of the mobile phone signals. It made no difference.

"We want the regime to fall," the crowds screamed. Not perhaps the most memorable cry of revolution but they shouted it again and again until they drowned out the pop of tear gas grenades. From all over Cairo they surged into the city, middle-class youngsters from Gazira, the poor from the slums of Beaulak al-Daqrour, marching steadily across the Nile bridges like an army - which, I guess, was what they were.

Still the gas grenades showered over them. Coughing and retching, they marched on. Many held their coats over their mouths or queued at a lemon shop where the owner squeezed fresh fruit into their mouths. Lemon juice - an antidote to tear gas - poured across the pavement into the gutter.

This was Cairo, of course, but these protests were taking place all over Egypt, not least in Suez, where 13 Egyptians have so far been killed. The demonstrations began not just at mosques but at Coptic churches. "I am a Christian, but I am an Egyptian first," a man called Mina told me. "I want Mubarak to go." And that is when the first bataggi arrived, pushing to the front of the police ranks in order to attack the protesters. They had metal rods and police truncheons - from where? - and sharpened sticks, and could be prosecuted for serious crimes if Mubarak's regime falls. They were vicious. One man whipped a youth over the back with a long yellow cable. He howled with pain. Across the city, the cops stood in ranks, legions of them, the sun glinting on their visors. The crowd were supposed to be afraid, but the police looked ugly, like hooded birds. Then the protesters reached the east bank of the Nile.

A few tourists found themselves caught up in this spectacle - I saw three middle-aged ladies on one of the Nile bridges (Cairo's hotels had not, of course, told their guests what was happening) - but the police decided that they would hold the east end of the flyover. They opened their ranks again and sent the thugs in to beat the leading protesters. And this was the moment the tear-gassing began in earnest, hundreds upon hundreds of canisters raining on to the crowds who marched from all roads into the city. It stung our eyes and made us cough until we were gasping. Men were being sick beside sealed shop fronts.

Fires appear to have broken out last night near Mubarak's rubber-stamp NDP headquarters. A curfew was imposed and first reports spoke of troops in the city, an ominous sign that the police had lost control. We took refuge in the old Café Riche off Telaat Harb Square, a tiny restaurant and bar of blue-robed waiters; and there, sipping his coffee, was the great Egyptian writer Ibrahim Abdul Meguid, right in front of us. It was like bumping into Tolstoy taking lunch amid the Russian revolution. "There has been no reaction from Mubarak!" he exalted. "It is as if nothing has happened! But they will do it - the people will do it!" The guests sat choking from the gas. It was one of those memorable scenes that occur in movies rather than real life.

And there was an old man on the pavement, one hand over his stinging eyes. Retired Colonel Weaam Salim of the Egyptian army, wearing his medal ribbons from the 1967 war with Israel - which Egypt lost - and the 1973 war, which the colonel thought Egypt had won. "I am leaving the ranks of veteran soldiers," he told me. "I am joining the protesters." And what of the army? Throughout the day we had not seen them. Their colonels and brigadiers and generals were silent. Were they waiting until Mubarak imposed martial law?

The crowds refused to abide by the curfew. In Suez, they set police trucks on fire. Opposite my own hotel, they tried to tip another truck into the Nile. I couldn't get back to Western Cairo over the bridges. The gas grenades were still soaring off the edges into the Nile. But a cop eventually took pity on us - not a quality, I have to say, that was much in evidence yesterday - and led us to the very bank of the Nile. And there was an old Egyptian motorboat, the tourist kind, with plastic flowers and a willing owner. So we sailed back in style, sipping Pepsi. And then a yellow speed boat swept past with two men making victory signs at the crowds on the bridges, a young girl standing in the back, holding a massive banner in her hands. It was the flag of Egypt.

Egypt's Day Of Crisis

President Mubarak's regime called in the army and imposed a curfew after tens of thousands of protesters took to the streets demanding an end to his rule.

Large numbers of protesters defied the curfew in Cairo to storm the state TV building and the Foreign Ministry.

The headquarters of the ruling National Democratic Party were set alight.

Protesters chased riot police away from Cairo's main square. Some police are reported to have removed their uniforms to join the demonstrators. Tanks and troops were ordered to retake the square.

At least 20 people were killed in violent clashes in Egyptian cities.

Nobel Peace laureate Mohamed ElBaradei was put under house arrest after being hosed by water cannon.

Mobile phone and internet services were disrupted to prevent social networking sites such as Facebook being used to orchestrate protests.

Mr Mubarak announced he will form a new government this morning. He has asked his cabinet to resign.

US President Barack Obama made a televised address in which he revealed that he told Mr Mubarak he must deliver on reforms.

Robert Fisk

Sunday, 30 Janurary 2011

MUHARAK, IT IS OVER!

The Egyptian tanks, the delirious protesters sitting atop them, the flags, the 40,000 protesters weeping and crying and cheering in

Freedom Square and praying around them, the Muslim Brotherhood official sitting amid the tank passengers. Should this be compared to the liberation of Bucharest? Climbing on to an American-made battle tank myself, I could only remember those wonderful films of the liberation of Paris. A few hundred metres away, Hosni Mubarak's black-uniformed security police were still firing at demonstrators near the interior ministry. It was a wild, historical victory celebration, Mubarak's own tanks freeing his capital from his own dictatorship.

In the pantomime world of Mubarak himself - and of Barack Obama and Hillary Clinton in Washington - the man who still claims to be president of Egypt swore in the most preposterous choice of vice-president in an attempt to soften the fury of the protesters - Omar Suleiman, Egypt's chief negotiator with Israel and his senior intelligence officer, a 75-yearold with years of visits to Tel Aviv and Jerusalem and four heart attacks to his credit. How this elderly apparatchik might be expected to deal with the anger and joy of liberation of 80 million Egyptians is beyond imagination. When I told the demonstrators on the tank around me the news of Suleiman's appointment, they burst into laughter.

Their crews, in battledress and smiling and in some cases clapping their hands, made no attempt to wipe off the graffiti that the crowds had spray painted on their tanks. "Mubarak Out - Get Out", and "Your regime is over, Mubarak" have now been plastered on almost every Egyptian tank on the streets of Cairo. On one of the tanks circling Freedom Square was a senior member of the Muslim Brotherhood, Mohamed Beltagi. Earlier, I had walked beside a convoy of tanks near the suburb of Garden City as crowds scrambled on to the machines to hand oranges to the crews, applauding them as Egyptian patriots. However crazed Mubarak's choice of vice-president and his gradual appointment of a powerless new government of cronies, the streets of Cairo proved what the United States and EU leaders have simply failed to grasp. It is over.

Mubarak's feeble attempts to claim that he must end violence on behalf of the Egyptian people - when his own security police have been responsible for most of the cruelty of the past five days - has elicited even further fury from those who have spent 30 years under his sometimes vicious dictatorship. For there are growing suspicions that much of the looting and arson was carried out by plainclothes cops - including the murder of 11 men in a rural village in the past 24 hours

- in an attempt to destroy the integrity of the protesters campaigning to throw Mubarak out of power. The destruction of a number of communications centres by masked men - which must have been coordinated by some form of institution - has also raised suspicions that the plainclothes thugs who beat many of the demonstrators were to blame.

But the torching of police stations across Cairo and in Alexandria and Suez and other cities was obviously not carried out by plainclothes cops. Late on Friday, driving to Cairo 40 miles down the Alexandria highway, crowds of young men had lit fires across the highway and, when cars slowed down, demanded hundreds of dollars in cash. Yesterday morning, armed men were stealing cars from their owners in the centre of Cairo.

Infinitely more terrible was the vandalism at the Egyptian National Museum. After police abandoned this greatest of ancient treasuries, looters broke into the red-painted building and smashed 4,000-year-old pharaonic statues, Egyptian mummies and magnificent wooden boats, originally carved - complete with their miniature crews - to accompany kings to their graves. Glass cases containing priceless figurines were bashed in, the black-painted soldiers inside pushed over. Again, it must be added that there were rumours before the discovery that police caused this vandalism before they fled the museum on Friday night. Ghastly shades of the Baghdad museum in 2003. It wasn't as bad as that looting, but it was a most awful archeological disaster.

In my night journey from 6th October City to the capital, I had to slow down when darkened vehicles loomed out of the darkness. They were smashed, glass scattered across the road, slovenly policemen pointing rifles at my headlights. One jeep was half burned out. They were the wreckage of the anti-riot police force which the protesters forced out of Cairo on Friday. Those same demonstrators last night formed a massive circle around Freedom Square to pray, "Allah Alakbar" thundering into the night air over the city.

And there are also calls for revenge. An al-Jazeera television crew found 23 bodies in the Alexandria mortuary, apparently shot by the police. Several had horrifically mutilated faces. Eleven more bodies were discovered in a Cairo mortuary, relatives gathering around their bloody remains and screaming for retaliation against the police.

Cairo now changes from joy to sullen anger within minutes. Yesterday morning, I walked across the Nile river bridge to watch the ruins of Mubarak's 15-storey party headquarters burn. In front stood a vast poster advertising the benefits of the party - pictures of successful graduates, doctors and full employment, the promises which Mubarak's party had failed to deliver in 30 years - outlined by the golden fires curling from the blackened windows of the party headquarters. Thousands of Egyptians stood on the river bridge and on the motorway flyovers to take pictures of the fiercely burning building - and of the middle-aged looters still stealing chairs and desks from inside.

Yet the moment a Danish television team arrived to film exactly the same scenes, they were berated by scores of people who said that they had no right to film the fires, insisting that Egyptians were proud people who would never steal or commit arson. This was to become a theme during the day: that reporters had no right to report anything about this "liberation" that might reflect badly upon it. Yet they were still remarkably friendly and - despite Obama's pusillanimous statements on Friday night - there was not the slightest manifestation of hostility against the United States. "All we want - all - is Mubarak's departure and new elections and our freedom and honour," a 30-year-old psychiatrist told me. Behind her, crowds of young men were clearing up broken crash barriers and road intersection fences from the street - an ironic reflection on the well-known Cairo adage that Egyptians will never, ever clean their roads.

Mubarak's allegation that these demonstrations and arson - this combination was a theme of his speech refusing to leave Egypt - were part of a "sinister plan" is clearly at the centre of his claim to continued world recognition. Indeed, Obama's own response - about the need for reforms and an end to such violence - was an exact copy of all the lies Mubarak has been using to defend his regime for three decades. It was deeply amusing to Egyptians that Obama - in Cairo itself, after his election - had urged Arabs to grasp freedom and democracy. These aspirations disappeared entirely when he gave his tacit if uncomfortable support to the Egyptian president on Friday. The problem is the usual one: the lines of power and the lines of morality in Washington fail to intersect when US presidents have to deal with the Middle East. Moral leadership in America ceases to exist when the Arab and Israeli worlds have to be confronted.

And the Egyptian army is, needless to say, part of this equation. It receives much of the $1.3bn of annual aid from Washington. The commander of that army, General Tantawi - who just happened to be in Washington when the police tried to crush the demonstrators - has always been a very close personal friend of Mubarak. Not a good omen, perhaps, for the immediate future.

So the "liberation" of Cairo - where, grimly, there came news last night of the looting of the Qasr al-Aini hospital - has yet to run its full course. The end may be clear. The tragedy is not over.

Robert Fisk

Monday, 31 January 2011

'WE WILL NEVER BE AFRAID AGAIN'

The old lady in the red scarf was standing inches from the front of an American-made M1 Abrams tank of the Egyptian Third Army, right on the edge of Tahrir Square. Its soldiers were paratroops, some in red berets, others in helmets, gun barrels pointed across the square, heavy machine guns mounted on the turrets. "If they fire on the Egyptian people, Mubarak is finished," she said. "And if they don't fire on the Egyptian people, Mubarak is finished." Of such wisdom are Egyptians now possessed.

Shortly before dusk, four F-16 Falcons - again, of course, manufactured by President Barack Obama's country - came screaming over the square, echoes bouncing off the shabby grey buildings and the giant Nasserist block, as the eyes of the tens of thousands of people in the square stared upwards. "They are on our side," the cry went up from the crowds. Somehow, I didn't think so. And those tanks, new to the square, 14 in all that arrived with no slogans painted on them, their soldiers sullen and apprehensive, had not come - as the protesters fondly believed - to protect them.

But then, when I talked to an officer on one of the tanks, he burst out with a smile. "We will never fire on our people - even if we are ordered to do so," he shouted over the roar of his engine. Again, I was not so sure. President Hosni Mubarak - or perhaps we should now say "president" in quotation marks - was at the military headquarters, having appointed his new junta of former military and intelligence officers. The rumour went round the square: the old wolf would try to fight on to the end. Others said it didn't matter. "Can he kill 80 million Egyptians?"

Anti-American sentiment was growing after Mr Obama's continued if tepid support for the Mubarak regime. "No, Obama, not Mubarak," posters read. And Mr Mubarak's face appeared with a Star of David superimposed over his face. Many of the crowd produced stun-gun cartridge cases fired last week with "Made in the USA" stamped on the bottom. And I noticed the lead tank's hull bore markings beginning "MFR" - at this point a soldier with a rifle and bayonet fixed was ordered to arrest me so I ran into the crowd and he retreated - but could "MFR" stand for the US Mobile Force Reserve, which keeps its tanks in Egypt? Was this tank column on loan from the Americans? You don't need to work out what the Egyptians make of all this.

Yet there were extraordinary scenes earlier in the day between protesters and tank crews of another unit (this time, the machines were older American M-60 Pattons of Vietnam vintage), which appeared to be about to protect a unit of water cannons sent to clear the streets. Hundreds of young men overwhelmed one tank, and when a lieutenant in sun glasses began firing into the air, he was pushed back against his armoured vehicle and had to climb on top to avoid the men. Yet the crowd quickly became good natured, posed for pictures on the tank and handed the soldiers fruit and water.

When a long line of troops assembled across the road, a very old, hunch-backed man sought and gained permission to approach them. I followed him as he embraced the lieutenant and kissed him on both cheeks and said: "You are our sons. We are your people." And then he walked down the row of troops and kissed each one and embraced each one and told each one that he was his son. You need a heart of stone not to be moved by such scenes and yesterday was replete with them.

At one point, a group of protesters brought a man they said was a thief - of which Cairo seems full at the moment - and he was trussed up and handed to the soldiers. "You are here to protect us," they chanted. When one of the soldiers hit the man in the face, his officer slapped him. Then the soldier sat down, shaking his head in despair. All day, an Egyptian Mi-25 helicopter - this time a relic of Soviet ordnance - circled the crowds, six rockets in the pods, but did nothing. Later a French-built Gazelle of the Egyptian air force flew low over the crowds, and the people waved at the place and the pilot could be seen waving back.

And all the time Egyptians walked up to foreigners - and a grey-haired Englishman doesn't look very Egyptian - and insisted that a people who had lost their fear could never be reinjected with fear.

"We will never be afraid again," a young woman shouted at me as the jets screamed over again. And a former cop now claiming to be a liaison man between the demonstrators and the army said that "the army will be with us because they know Mubarak must go". Again, I am not so sure.

And the looting and burning go on. The former policeman - who should know - told me that many of the looters are members of a group which belonged to Mr Mubarak's National Democratic Party, whose previous role had been to bully Egyptians to go to polling stations and vote for their beloved leader. So why, we all wonder now, are these men trying to loot and burn, crimes which are being blamed on all those who demand that Mr Mubarak leave the country? Those demands, incidentally, now include the expulsion of Omar Suleiman, his former top spy, who is Vice-President.

Across Egypt, and on almost every street in Cairo, there are now vigilantes - not Mubarak men, but ordinary civilians who are tired of the semi-official gangs who are robbing their own people at night-time. To get back to my hotel last night, I had to pass through eight checkpoints of men, young and old - one was stooped, with a walking stick in one hand and an old British .303 Lee Enfield rifle in the other - who are now attacking thieves and handing them to the army. But this is no Dad's Army.

In the early hours of yesterday morning, a group of armed men turned up at the Children's Cancer Hospital near the old Roman aqueduct.

They wanted to take the medical equipment, but within minutes, local people ran down the road and threatened the men with knives. They retreated at once. Dr Khaled el-Noury, the chief operating officer at the hospital, told me that the armed visitors were disorganised and apparently frightened of being harmed.

They were right. The reception clerk at the children's hospital showed me the kitchen knife he kept on his desk for protection. Further proof of fighting power lay outside the gate where men appeared holding clubs and sticks and pokers. A boy - perhaps eight years old -

appeared brandishing an 18-inch butcher's knife, slightly more than half his height. Other men holding knives of equal length came to shake hands with the foreign journalist.

They are no third force. And they believe in the army. Will the soldiers go into the square? And does it matter if Mr Mubarak goes anyway?

Robert Fisk

Wednesday, 2 February 2011

SPEEDING EVENTS

It was a victory parade - without the victory. They came in their hundreds of thousands, joyful, singing, praying, a great packed mass of Egypt, suburb by suburb, village by village, waiting patiently to pass through the "people's security" checkpoints, draped in the Egyptian flag of red, white and black, its governess eagle a bright gold in the sunlight. Were there a million? Perhaps. Across the country there certainly were. It was, we all agreed, the largest political demonstration in the history of Egypt, the latest heave to rid this country of its least-loved dictator. Its only flaw was that by dusk - and who knew what the night would bring - Hosni Mubarak was still calling himself "President" of Egypt.

Later, indeed, he was expected to tell us that he will hang on until the next election - a promise that will not be accepted by the people he claims to love. The people of Egypt were originally told this was to be "the march of the million" to the Kuba Palace, Mubarak's official state pile, or to the man's own residence in Heliopolis. But so vast was the crowd that the organisers, around 24 opposition groups, decided the danger of attacks from the state security police were too great. They claimed later they had discovered a truck load of armed men close to Tahrir Square. All I could find were 30 Mubarak supporters shouting their love of Egypt outside the state radio headquarters under the guard of more than 40 soldiers.

The cries of loathing for Mubarak are becoming familiar, the posters ever more intriguing. "Neither Mubarak, nor Suleiman, and we don't need you Obama - but we don't dislike USA," one of them announced generously. "Out - all of you, including your slaves," announced another. I did actually find a decaying courtyard covered in rectangular sheets of white cloth where political scribes could spray-paint their own slogans for 40 pence a time. The tea-houses behind Talat Harb's statue were crammed with drinkers, discussing Egypt's new politics with the passion of one of Delacroix's orientalist paintings. You could soak this stuff up all day, revolution in the making. Or was this an uprising? Or an "explosion", as one Egyptian journalist described the demonstration to me?

There were several elements about this unprecedented political event that stood out. First was the secularism of the whole affair. Women in chadors and niqabs and scarves walked happily beside girls with long hair flowing over their shoulders, students next to imams and men with beards that would have made Bin Laden jealous. The poor in torn sandals and the rich in business suits, squeezed into this shouting mass, an amalgam of the real Egypt hitherto divided by class and regime-encouraged envy. They had done the impossible - or so they thought - and, in a way, they had already won their social revolution.

And then there was the absence of the "Islamism" that haunts the darkest corners of the West, encouraged - as usual - by America and Israel. As my mobile phone vibrated again and again, it was the same old story. Every radio anchor, every announcer, every newsroom wanted to know if the Muslim Brotherhood was behind this epic demonstration. Would the Brotherhood take over Egypt? I told the truth. It was rubbish. Why, they might get only 20 per cent at an election, 145,000 members out of a population of 80 million.

A crowd of English-speaking Egyptians crowded round me during one of the imperishable interviews and collapsed in laughter so loud that I had to bring the broadcast to an end. It made no difference, of course, when I explained on air that Israel's kindly and human Foreign Minister, Avigdor Lieberman - who once said that "Mubarak can go to hell" - might at last get his way, politically at least. The people were overwhelmed, giddy at the speed of events.

So was I. There I was, back on the intersection behind the Egyptian Museum where only five days ago - it feels like five months - I choked on tear gas as Mubarak's police thugs, the baltigi, the drug addict ex-prisoner cops, were slipped through the lines of state security policemen to beat, bludgeon and smash the heads and faces of the unarmed demonstrators, who eventually threw them all out of Tahrir Square and made it the Egyptian uprising. Back then, we heard no

Western support for these brave men and women. Nor did we hear it yesterday.

Amazingly, there was little evidence of hostility towards America although, given the verbal antics of Barack Obama and Hillary Clinton these past eight days, there might have well been. One almost felt sorry for Obama. Had he rallied to the kind of democracy he preached here in Cairo six months after his investiture, had he called for the departure of this third-rate dictator a few days ago, the crowds would have been carrying US as well as Egyptian flags, and Washington would have done the impossible: it would have transformed the now familiar hatred of America (Afghanistan, Iraq, the "war on terror", etc) into the more benign relationship which the US enjoyed in the balmy 1920s and 1930s and, indeed, despite its support for the creation of Israel, into the warmth that existed between Arab and American into the 1960s.

But no. All this was squandered in just seven days of weakness and cowardice in Washington - a gutlessness so at odds with the courage of the millions of Egyptians who tried to do what we in the West always demanded of them: to turn their dust-bowl dictatorships into democracies. They supported democracy. We supported "stability", "moderation", "restraint", "firm" leadership (Saddam Hussein-lite) soft "reform" and obedient Muslims.

This failure of moral leadership in the West - under the false fear of "Islamisation" - may prove to be one of the greatest tragedies of the modern Middle East. Egypt is not anti-Western. It is not even particularly anti-Israeli, though this could change. But one of the blights of history will now involve a US president who held out his hand to the Islamic world and then clenched his fist when it fought a dictatorship and demanded democracy.

This tragedy may continue in the coming days as the US and Europe give their support to Mubarak's chosen successor, the chief spy and Israeli negotiator, Vice-President Omar Suleiman. He has called, as we all knew he would, for talks with "all factions" - he even contrived to sound a bit like Obama. But everyone in Egypt knows that his administration will be another military junta which Egyptians will again be invited to trust to ensure the free and fair elections which Mubarak never gave them. Is it possible - is it conceivable - that Israel's favourite Egyptian is going to give these millions the freedom and democracy they demand?

Or that the army which so loyally guarded them today will give such uncritical support to that democracy when it receives $1.3bn a year from Washington? This military machine, which has not fought a war for almost 38 years, is under-trained and over-armed, with largely obsolete equipment - though its new M1A1 tanks were on display yesterday - and deeply embedded in the corporation of big business, hotels and housing complexes, all rewards to favourite generals by the Mubarak regime.

And yesterday, what were the Americans doing? Rumour: US diplomats were on their way to Egypt to negotiate between a future President Suleiman and opposition groups. Rumour: extra Marines were being drafted into Egypt to defend the US embassy from attack. Fact: a further evacuation of US families from the Marriott Hotel in Cairo, escorted by Egyptian troops and cops, heading for the airport, fleeing from a people who could so easily be their friends.

Robert Fisk

Thursday, 3 February 2011

EGYPTIAN AGAINST EGYPTIAN

President" Hosni Mubarak's counter-revolution smashed into his opponents yesterday in a barrage of stones, cudgels, iron bars and clubs, an all-day battle in the very centre of the capital he claims to rule between tens of thousands of young men, both - and here lies the most dangerous of all weapons - brandishing in each other's faces the banner of Egypt. It was vicious and ruthless and bloody and well planned, a final vindication of all Mubarak's critics and a shameful indictment of the Obamas and Clintons who failed to denounce this faithful ally of America and Israel.

The fighting around me in the square called Tahrir was so terrible that we could smell the blood. The men and women who are demanding the end of Mubarak's 30-year dictatorship - and I saw young women in scarves and long skirts on their knees, breaking up the paving stones as rocks fell around them - fought back with an immense courage which later turned into a kind of terrible cruelty.

Some dragged Mubarak's security men across the square, beating them until blood broke from their heads and splashed down their clothes. The Egyptian Third Army, famous in legend and song for crossing the Suez Canal in 1973, couldn't - or wouldn't - even cross Tahrir Square to help the wounded.

As thousands of Egyptians shrieking abuse - and this was as close to civil war as Egypt has ever come - swarmed towards each other like Roman fighters, they simply overwhelmed the parachute units "guarding" the square, climbing over their tanks and armoured vehicles and then using them for cover.

One Abrams tank commander - and I was only 20 feet away - simply ducked the stones that were bouncing off his tank, jumped into the turret and battened down the hatch. Mubarak's protesters then climbed on top to throw more rocks at their young and crazed antagonists.

I guess it's the same in all battles, even though guns have not (yet) appeared; abuse by both sides provoked a shower of rocks from Mubarak's men - yes, they did start it - and then the protesters who seized the square to demand the old man's overthrow began breaking stones to hurl them back.

By the time I reached the "front" line - the quotation marks are essential, since the lines of men moved back and forth over half a mile - both sides were screaming and lunging at each other, blood streaming down their faces. At one point, before the shock of the attack wore off, Mubarak's supporters almost crossed the entire square in front of the monstrous Mugamma building - relic of Nasserite endeavour - before being driven out.

Indeed, now that Egyptians are fighting Egyptians, what are we supposed to call these dangerously furious people? The Mubarakites? The "protesters" or - more ominously - the "resistance"? For that is what the men and women struggling to unseat Mubarak are now calling themselves.

"This is Mubarak's work," one wounded stone-thrower said to me. "He has managed to turn Egyptian against Egyptian for just nine more months of power. He is mad. Are you in the West mad, too?"

I can't remember how I replied to this question. But how could I forget watching - just a few hours earlier - as the Middle East "expert" Mitt Romney, former governor of Massachusetts, was asked if Mubarak was a dictator. No, he said, he was "a monarchtype figure".

The face of this monarch was carried on giant posters, a printed provocation, to the barricades. Newly distributed by officers of the National Democratic Party - they must have taken a while to produce after the party's headquarters was reduced to a smouldering shell after Friday's battles - many were held in the air by men carrying cudgels and police batons. There is no doubt about this because I had driven into Cairo from the desert as they formed up outside the foreign ministry and the state radio building on the east bank of the Nile. There were loudspeaker songs and calls for Mubarak's eternal life (a very long presidency indeed) and many were sitting on brand-new motorcycles, as if they had been inspired by Mahmoud Ahmadinejad's thugs after the 2009 Iranian elections. Come to think of it, Mubarak and Ahmadinejad do actually have the same respect for elections.

Only when I had passed the radio building did I see the thousands of other young men pouring in from the suburbs of Cairo. There were women, too, mostly in traditional black dress and white-and-black scarves, a few children among them, walking along the flyover behind the Egyptian Museum. They told me that they had as much right to Tahrir Square as the protesters - true, by the way - and that they intended to express their love of their President in the very place where he had been so desecrated.

And they had a point, I suppose. The democrats - or the "resistance", depending on your point of view - had driven out the security police thugs from this very square on Friday. The problem is that the Mubarak men included some of the very same thugs I saw then, when they were working with armed security police to baton and assault the demonstrators. One of them, a yellow-shirted youth with tousled hair and bright red eyes - I don't know what he was on - carried the very same wicked steel stick he had been using on Friday. Once more, the defenders of Mubarak were back. They even sang the same old refrain - constantly reworked to take account of the local dictator's name - "With our blood, with our soul, we dedicate ourselves to you."

As far away as Giza, the NDP had rounded up the men who controlled voting at elections and sent them hollering their support as they marched along a stinking drainage ditch. Not far away, even a camel-owner was enjoined to say that "if you don't know Mubarak, you don't know Allah" - which was, to put it mildly, a bit much.

In Cairo, I walked beside Mubarak's ranks and reached the front as they began another charge into Tahrir Square. The sky was filled with rocks - I am talking of stones six inches in diameter, which hit the ground like mortar shells. On this side of the "line", of course, they were coming from Mubarak's opponents. They cracked and split apart and spat against the walls around us. At which point, the NDP men turned and ran in panic as the President's opponents surged forward.

I just stood with my back against the window of a closed travel agency - I do remember a poster for a romantic weekend in Luxor and "the fabled valley of the tombs".

But the stones came in flocks, hundreds of them at a time, and then a new group of young men were beside me, the Egyptian demonstrators from the square. Only no longer in their fury were they shouting "Down with Mubarak" and "Black Mubarak" but Allahu Akbar - God is Great - and I would hear this again and again as the long day progressed. One side was shouting Mubarak, the other God. It hadn't been like that 24 hours ago.

I hared towards safe ground where the stones no longer hissed and splintered and suddenly I was among Mubarak's opponents .

Of course, it would be an exaggeration to say that the stones cloaked the sky, but at times there were a hundred rocks soaring through the sky. They wrecked an entire army truck, smashing its sides, crushing its windows. The stones came soaring out of side roads off Champollion Street and on Talaat Harb. The men were sweating, headbands in red, roaring their hatred. Many held white cloth to wounds. Some were carried past me, sloshing blood all over the road.

And an increasing number were wearing Islamist dress, short trousers, grey cloaks, long beards, white head caps. They shouted Allahu Akbar loudest and they bellowed their love of God, which was not supposed to be what this was all about. Yes, Mubarak had done it. He had brought the Salafists out against him, alongside his political enemies. From time to time, young men were grabbed, their faces fist-pulped, screaming and fearful of their lives, documentation found on their clothes to prove they worked for Mubarak's interior ministry.

Many of the protesters - secular young men, pushing their way through the attackers - tried to defend the prisoners. Others - and I noticed an awful lot of "Islamists" among them, complete with obligatory beards - would bang their fists on these poor men's heads, using big rings on their fingers to cut open their skin so that blood ran down their faces. One youth, red T-shirt torn open, face already bloated with pain, was rescued by two massive men, one of whom put the now half-naked prisoner over his shoulder and pushed his way through the crowd.

Thus was saved the life of Mohamed Abdul Azim Mabrouk Eid, police security number 2101074 from the Giza governorate - his security pass was blue with three odd-looking pyramids stamped on the laminated cover. Thus was another man pulled from the mob, squealing and clutching his stomach. And behind him knelt a squadron of women, breaking stones .

There were moments of farce amid all this. In the middle of the afternoon, four horses were ridden into the square by Mubarak's supporters, along with a camel - yes, a real-life camel that must have been trucked in from the real dead pyramids - their apparently drugged riders hauled off their backs. I found the horses grazing gently beside a tree three hours later. Near the statue of Talaat Harb, a boy sold agwa - a peculiarly Egyptian date-bread delicacy - at 4 pence each - while on the other side of the road, two figures stood, a girl and a boy, holding identical cardboard trays in front of them. The girl's tray was filled with cigarette packets. The boy's tray was filled with stones.

And there were scenes that must have meant personal sorrow and anguish for those who experienced them. There was a tall, muscular man, wounded in the face by a slice of stone, whose legs simply buckled beside a telephone junction box, his face sliced open yet again on the metal. And there was the soldier on an armoured personnel carrier who let the stones of both sides fly past him until he jumped on to the road among Mubarak's enemies, putting his arms around them, tears coursing down his face.

And where, amid all this hatred and bloodshed, was the West? Reporting this shame every day, you suffer from insomnia. Sometime around 3am yesterday, I had watched Lord Blair of Isfahan as he struggled to explain to CNN the need to "partner the process of change" in the Middle East. We had to avoid the "anarchy" of the "most extreme elements". And - my favourite, this - Lord Blair spoke of "a government that is not elected according to the system of democracy that we would espouse". Well, we all know which old man's "democracy" he was referring to.

Street rumour had it that this man - Mitt Romney's "monarch-type figure" - might actually creep out of Egypt on Friday. I'm not so

sure. Nor do I really know who won the Battle of Tahrir Square yesterday, though it will not remain long unresolved. At dusk, the stones
were still cracking on to the roads, and on to the people. After a while,
I started ducking when I saw passing birds.

Robert Fisk

Friday, 4 February 2011

TAHRIR SQUARE

From the House on the Corner, you could watch the arrogance
and folly yesterday of those Egyptians who would rid themselves of
their "President". It was painful - it always is when the "good guys"
play into the hands of their enemies - but the young prodemocracy
demonstrators on the Tahrir Square barricades carefully organised
their Cairo battle, brought up their lorryloads of rocks in advance, tel-
ephoned for reinforcements and then drove the young men of Hosni
Mubarak back from the flyovers behind the Egyptian Museum. Maybe
it was the anticipation that the old man will go at last today. Maybe it
was revenge for the fire-bombing and sniper attacks of the previous
night. But as far as the "heroes" of Egypt are concerned, it was not
their finest hour.

The House on the Corner was a referee's touchline, a house of late
18th century stucco with outer decorations of stone grapes and
wreaths and, in the dank and derelict interior, a broken marble staircase, reeking cloth wallpaper and wooden floors, groaning under bag
after bag of stones, all neatly broken into rectangles to hurl at the accursed Mubarakites. It was somehow typical that no one knew the
history of this elegant, sad old house on the corner of Mahmoud Basounee Street and Martyr Abdul Menem Riad Square. It even had a
missing step on the gloomy second floor with a 30ft drop that immediately brought to mind the staircase in Stevenson's Kidnapped, and
its vertiginous drop illuminated by lightning. But from its crumbling
balconies, I could watch the battle of stones yesterday and the brave,
pathetic attempts of the Egyptian army to contain this miniature civil
war, preceding, as it does, another Sabbath day of prayers and anger
and - so the protesters happily believe yet again - the very final hours
of their accursed dictator.

The soldiers manoeuvred through the field of rocks on the highway below, trying to position two Abrams tanks between the armies of stone throwers, four soldiers waving their hands above their heads - the Egyptian street sign for "cease fire".

It was pathetic. The army needed 4,000 troops here to stop this battle. They had only two tank crews, one officer and four soldiers. And the forces of democracy - yes, we have to introduce a little cynicism here - cared nothing for the forbearance of the soldiers they have been trying to woo. They formed in phalanxes across the road outside the Egyptian Museum, each holding a shield of corrugated iron, many of them shouting "God is Great", a mockery of every Hollywood Roman legion, T-shirts instead of breastplates, clubs and the police night-sticks of Mubarak's hated cops instead of swords. Outside the House on the Corner - cheerfully telling me it belonged to anyone - stood a man holding (believe me, reader) a 7ft steel trident. "I am the devil," he cheerfully roared at me. This was almost as bad as the horse and camel attack by the Mubarakites on Wednesday.

Five soldiers from another unit seized a tray of Molotov cocktails from the house next door - Pepsi bottles are clearly the container of choice - but that constituted the entire military operation to disarm this little freedom militia. "Mubarak will go tomorrow," they screeched; and then, between the two tanks, at their enemies 40ft away, "Your old man is leaving tomorrow." They had been encouraged by all the usual stories; that Barack Obama had at last called time on Mubarak, that the Egyptian army - recipients of an annual $1.3bn aid - was tired of being humiliated by the President, infuriated by the catastrophe that Mubarak had unleashed on his country for a mere nine more months of power.

This may be true. Egyptian friends with relatives among the officer corps tell me that they are desperate for Mubarak to leave, if only to prevent him issuing more orders to the military to open fire on the demonstrators.

But yesterday, it was Mubarak's opponents who opened "fire", and they did so with a now-familiar shock of stones and iron hub-caps. They crashed on to the Mubarak men (and a few women) on the flyover, ricocheted off the top of the tanks. I watched their enemies walk - just a few of them - into the road, the rocks crashing around them, waving their arms above their heads in a sign of peace. It was no use.

By the time I climbed down that dangerous staircase, a lone Muslim imam in a white turban and long red robe and an absolutely incredible - distinguished may be the correct word - neatly combed white beard appeared amid the stones. He held a kind of whip and used it to beat back the demonstrators. He, too, stood his ground as the stones of both sides broke around him. He was from those who would rid themselves of their meddlesome President but he, too, wanted to end the attack. A young protester was hit on the head and collapsed to the ground.

So I scampered over to the two tanks, hiding behind one of them as it traversed its massive gun-barrel 350 degrees, an interesting - if pointless - attempt to show both sides that the army was neutral. The great engines blasted sand and muck into the eyes of the stone throwers, the whining of the electrical turbine controlling the turret adding a state-of-the-art addition to the medieval crack of rocks. And then an officer did jump from the turret of one behemoth and stood with the imam and the lead Mubarakites and also waved his arms above his head. The stones still clanged off the highway signs on the flyover (turn left for Giza) but several middle-aged men held out their arms and touched each other's hands and offered each other cigarettes.

Not for long, of course. Behind them, in the square called Tahrir, men slept beneath the disused concrete Metro vents or on the mouldy grass or in the stairwells of shuttered shops. Many wore bandages round their heads and arms. These wounds would be their badges of heroism in the years to come, proof they fought in the "resistance", that they struggled against dictatorship. Yet not one could I find who knew why this square was so precious to them.

The truth is as symbolic as it is important. It was Haussmann, brought to Egypt by Ismail under notional Ottoman rule, who built the square as an Etoile modelled on its French equivalent, laid over the swamps of the regularly flooded Nile plain. Each road radiated like a star (much to the chagrin, of course, of the present-day Egyptian army). And it was on the Nile side of "Ismailia" square - where the old Hilton is currently under repair - that the British later built their vast military Qasr el-Nil barracks. Across the road still stands the pseudo-Baroque pile in which King Farouk maintained his foreign ministry - an institution which faithfully followed British orders.

And the entire square in front of them, from the garden of the Egyptian Museum to the Nile-side residence of the British ambassador, was banned to all Egyptians. This great space - the area of Tahrir Square today - constituted the forbidden zone, the land of the occupier, the centre of Cairo upon which its people could never set foot. And thus after independence, it became "Freedom" - "Tahrir" - Square; and that is why Mubarak tried to preserve it and that is why those who want to overthrow him must stay there - even if they do not know the reason.

I walked back last night, the people around me hopeful they could endure the next night of fire-bombs, that today will bring the elusive victory. I met a guy called Rami (yes, his real name) who brightly announced that "I think we need a general to take over!" He may get his wish.

As for the House on the Corner, well, Mahmoud Basounee Street is named after an Egyptian poet. And the stonebattered sign for the Martyr Abdul Menem Riad attached to the House on the Corner honours a man whose ghost must surely be watching those two tanks under the flyover. Riad commanded the Jordanian army in the 1967 Six Day War and was killed in an Israeli mortar attack two years later. He was chief of staff of the Egyptian Army.

Robert Fisk

Saturday, 5 February 2011

ENVISIONING A NEW GOVERNMENT

Caged yesterday inside a new army cordon of riot-visored troops and coils of barbed wire - the very protection which Washington had demanded for the protesters of Tahrir Square - the tens of thousands of young Egyptians demanding Hosni Mubarak's overthrow have taken the first concrete political steps to create a new nation to replace the corrupt government which has ruled them for 30 years.

Sitting on filthy pavements, amid the garbage and broken stones of a week of street fighting, they have drawn up a list of 25 political personalities to negotiate for a new political leadership and a new constitution to replace Mubarak's crumbling regime.

They include Amr Moussa, the secretary general of the Arab League - himself a trusted Egyptian; the Nobel prize-winner Ahmed

Zuwail, an Egyptian-American who has advised President Barack Obama; Mohamed Selim Al-Awa, a professor and author of Islamic studies who is close to the Muslim Brotherhood; and the president of the Wafd party, Said al-Badawi.

Other nominees for the committee, which was supposed to meet the Egyptian Vice-President, Omar Suleiman, within 24 hours, are Nagib Suez, a prominent Cairo businessman (involved in the very mobile phone systems shut down by Mubarak last week); Nabil al-Arabi, an Egyptian UN delegate; and even the heart surgeon Magdi Yacoub, who now lives in Cairo.

The selection - and the makeshift committee of Tahrir Square demonstrators and Facebook and Twitter "electors" - has not been confirmed, but it marks the first serious attempt to turn the massive street protests of the past seven days into a political machine that provides for a future beyond the overthrow of the much-hated President.

The committee's first tasks would be to draw up a new Egyptian constitution and an electoral system that would prevent the president-for-life swindle which Mubarak's fraudulent elections have created. Instead, Egyptian presidents would be limited to two consecutive terms of office, and the presidential term itself would be reduced from six to four years.

But no one involved in this initiative has any doubts of the grim future that awaits them if their brave foray into practical politics fails. There was more sniping into Tahrir Square during the night - an engineer, a lawyer and another young man were killed - and plainclothes police were again discovered in the square. There were further minor stone-throwing battles during the day, despite the vastly increased military presence, and most of the protesters fear that if they leave the square they will immediately be arrested, along with their families, by Mubarak's cruel state security apparatus.

Already, there are dark reports of demonstrators who dared to return home and disappeared. The Egyptian writer Mohamed Fadel Fahmy, who is involved in the committee discussions, is fearful for himself. "We're safe as long as we have the square," he said to me yesterday, urging me to publish his name as a symbol of the freedom he demands. "If we lose the square, Mubarak will arrest all the opposition groups - and there will be police rule as never before. That's why we are fighting for our lives."

The state security police now have long lists of names of protesters who have given television interviews or been quoted in newspapers, Facebook postings and tweets.

The protesters have identified growing divisions between the Egyptian army and the thugs of the interior ministry, whose guards exchanged fire with soldiers three days ago as they continued to occupy the building in which basement torture chambers remain undamaged by the street fighting. These were the same rooms of horror to which America's "renditioned" prisoners were sent for "special" treatment at the hands of Mubarak's more sadistic torturers - another favour which bound the Egyptian regime to the United States as a "trusted" ally.

Another young man involved in the committee selections admitted he didn't trust Omar Suleiman, the former spy boss and Israeli-Palestinian negotiator whom Mubarak appointed this week. Suleiman it is, by the way, who has been trying to shuffle responsibility for the entire crisis on to the foreign press - a vicious as well as dishonest way of exercising his first days of power. Yet he has cleverly outmanoeuvred the demonstrators in Tahrir Square by affording them army protection. Indeed, yesterday morning, to the shock of all of us standing on the western side of the square, a convoy of 4x4s with blackened windows suddenly emerged from the gardens of the neighbouring Egyptian Museum, slithered to a halt in front of us and was immediately surrounded by a praetorian guard of red-bereted soldiers and massive - truly gigantic - security guards in shades and holding rifles with telescopic sights. Then, from the middle vehicle emerged the diminutive, bespectacled figure of Field Marshal Mohamed Hussein Tantawi, the chief of staff of the Egyptian army and a lifelong friend of Mubarak, wearing a soft green military kepi and general's cross-swords insignia on his shoulders.

Here was a visitor to take the breath away, waving briefly to the protesters who crowded the military cordon to witness this extraordinary arrival. The crowd roared. "The Egyptian army is our army," they shouted in unison. "But Mubarak is not ours." It was a message for Tantawi to take back to his friend Mubarak, but his visit was itself a powerful political symbol. However much Mubarak may rave about "foreign hands" behind the demands for his overthrow, and however many lies Suleiman may tell about foreign journalists, Tantawi was showing that the army took its mission to protect the demonstrators seriously. The recent military statement that it would never fire on those who wish to dethrone Mubarak, since their grievances were "legitimate", was authorised by Tantawi.

Hence the demonstrators' belief - however naïve and dangerous - in the integrity of the military.

Crucially missing from the list of figures proposed for the committee are Mohamed ElBaradei, the former UN arms inspectors and Nobel laureate, and members of the Muslim Brotherhood, the "Islamist" spectre which Mubarak and the Israelis always dangled in front of the Americans to persuade them to keep old Mubarak in power. The Brotherhood's insistence in not joining talks until Mubarak's departure - and their support for ElBaradei, whose own faint presidential ambitions (of the "transitional" kind) have not commended themselves to the protesters - effectively excluded them. Suleiman has archly invited the Brotherhood to meet him, knowing that they will not do so until Mubarak has gone.

But al-Awa's proposed presence on the committee - and that of the Islamist intellectual Ahmed Kamel Abu Magd - will ensure that their views are included in any discussions with Suleiman. These talks would also cover civil and constitutional rights and a special clause to allow Suleiman to rule Egypt temporarily because "the President is unable to perform his duties".

Mubarak would be allowed to live privately in Egypt providing he played no part - publicly or covertly - in the political life of the country. He is regarded as a still-fierce opponent who will not hesitate to decapitate the opposition should he hang on to power. "He is one of the old school, like Saddam and Arafat, who in the last two days has shown his true face," another committee supporter said yesterday.

"He is the man behind the attacks on us and the shooting deaths." Mohamed Fahmy knows what this means. His own father has been in exile from Egypt for seven years - after proposing identical protests to those witnessed today to get rid of the Mubarak empire.

Robert Fisk

MUBARAK IS GOING

The old man is going. The resignation last night of the leadership of the ruling Egyptian National Democratic Party - including Hosni Mubarak's son Gamal - will not appease those who want to claw the President down. But they will get their blood. The whole vast edifice of power which the NDP represented in Egypt is now a mere shell, a propaganda poster with nothing behind it.

The sight of Mubarak's delusory new Prime Minister Ahmed Shafiq telling Egyptians yesterday that things were "returning to normal" was enough to prove to the protesters in Tahrir Square - 12 days into their mass demand for the exile of the man who has ruled the country for 30 years - that the regime was made of cardboard. When the head of the army's central command personally pleaded with the tens of thousands of pro-democracy demonstrators in the square to go home, they simply howled him down.

In his novel *The Autumn of the Patriarch*, Gabriel Garcia Marquez outlines the behaviour of a dictator under threat and his psychology of total denial. In his glory days, the autocrat believes he is a national hero. Faced with rebellion, he blames "foreign hands" and "hidden agendas" for this inexplicable revolt against his benevolent but absolute rule. Those fomenting the insurrection are "used and manipulated by foreign powers who hate our country". Then - and here I use a precis of Marquez by the great Egyptian author Alaa Al-Aswany - "the dictator tries to test the limits of the engine, by doing everything except what he should do. He becomes dangerous. After that, he agrees to do anything they want him to do. Then he goes away".

Hosni Mubarak of Egypt appears to be on the cusp of stage four - the final departure. For 30 years he was the "national hero" - participant in the 1973 war, former head of the Egyptian air force, natural successor to Gamal Abdel Nasser as well as Anwar Sadat - and then, faced with his people's increasing fury at his dictatorial rule, his police state and his torturers and the corruption of his regime, he blamed the dark shadow of the country's fictional enemies (al-Qa'ida, the Muslim Brotherhood, al-Jazeera, CNN, America). We may just have passed the dangerous phase.

Twenty-two lawyers were arrested by Mubarak's state security police on Thursday - for assisting yet more civil rights lawyers who were investigating the arrest and imprisonment of more than 600 Egyptian protesters. The vicious anti-riot cops who were mercifully driven off the streets of Cairo nine days ago and the drugaddled gangs paid by them are part of the wounded and dangerous dictator's remaining weapons. These thugs - who work directly under ministry of interior orders - are the same men now shooting at night into Tahrir Square, killing three men and wounding another 40 early on Friday morning. Mubarak's weepy interview with Christiane Amanpour last week - in which he claimed he didn't want to be president but had to carry on for another seven months to save Egypt from "chaos" - was the first hint that stage four was on the way.

Al-Aswany has taken to romanticising the revolution (if that is what it truly is). He has fallen into the habit of holding literary mornings before joining the insurrectionists, and last week he suggested that a revolution makes a man more honourable - just as falling in love makes a person more dignified. I suggested to him that a lot of people who fall in love spend an inordinate amount of time eliminating their rivals and that I couldn't think of a revolution that hadn't done the same. But his reply, that Egypt had been a liberal society since the days of Muhammad Ali Pasha and was the first Arab country (in the 19th century) to enjoy party politics, did carry conviction.

If Mubarak goes today or later this week, Egyptians will debate why it took so long to rid themselves of this tin-pot dictator. The problem was that under the autocrats - Nasser, Sadat, Mubarak and whomever Washington blesses next - the Egyptian people skipped two generations of maturity. For the first essential task of a dictator is to"infantilise" his people, to transform them into political six-year-olds, obedient to a patriarchal headmaster. They will be given fake newspapers, fake elections, fake ministers and lots of false promises. If they obey, they might even become one of the fake ministers; if they disobey, they will be beaten up in the local police station, or imprisoned in the Tora jail complex or, if persistently violent, hanged.

Only when the power of youth and technology forced this docile Egyptian population to grow up and stage its inevitable revolt did it become evident to all of these previously "infantilised" people that the government was itself composed of children, the eldest of them 83 years old. Yet, by a ghastly process of political osmosis, the dictator had for 30 years also "infantilised" his supposedly mature allies in the West. They bought the line that Mubarak alone remained the iron wall holding back the Islamic tide seeping across Egypt and the rest of the Arab world. The Muslim Brotherhood - with genuine historical roots in Egypt and every right to enter parliament in a fair election - remains the bogeyman on the lips of every news presenter, although they have not the slightest idea what it is or was.

But now the infantilisation has gone further. Lord Blair of Isfahan popped up on CNN the other night, blustering badly when asked if he would compare Mubarak with Saddam Hussein. Absolutely not, he said. Saddam had impoverished a country that once had a higher standard of living than Belgium - while Mubarak had increased Egypt's GDP by 50 per cent in 10 years.

What Blair should have said was that Saddam killed tens of thousands of his own people while Mubarak has killed/hanged/tortured only a few thousand. But Blair's shirt is now almost as blood-spattered as Saddam's; so dictators, it seems, must now be judged only on their economic record. Obama went one further. Mubarak, he told us early yesterday, was "a proud man, but a great patriot".

This was extraordinary. To make such a claim, it was necessary to believe that the massive evidence of savagery by Egypt's state security police over 30 years, the torture and the vicious treatment of demonstrators over the past 13 days, was unknown to the dictator. Mubarak, in his elderly innocence, may have been aware of corruption and perhaps the odd "excess" - a word we are beginning to hear again in Cairo - but not of the systematic abuse of human rights, the falsity of every election.

This is the old Russian fairy tale. The tsar is a great father figure, a revered and perfect leader. It's just that he does not know what his underlings are doing. He doesn't realise how badly the serfs are treated. If only someone would tell him the truth, he would end injustice. The tsar's servants, of course, connived at this.

But Mubarak was not ignorant of the injustice of his regime. He survived by repression and threats and false elections. He always had. Like Sadat. Like Nasser who - according to the testimony of one of his victims who was a friend of mine - permitted his torturers to dangle prisoners over vats of boiling faeces and gently dunk them in it. Over 30 years, successive US ambassadors have informed Mubarak of the cruelties perpetrated in his name. Occasionally, Mubarak would express surprise and once promised to end police brutality, but nothing ever changed. The tsar fully approved of what his secret policemen were doing.

Thus, when David Cameron announced that "if" the authorities were behind the violence in Egypt, it would be "absolutely unacceptable" - a threat that naturally had them shaking in their shoes - the word "if" was a lie. Cameron, unless he doesn't bother to read the Foreign Office briefings on Mubarak, is well aware that the old man was a third-rate dictator who employed violence to stay in power.

The demonstrators in Cairo and Alexandria and Port Said, of course, are nonetheless entering a period of great fear. Their "Day of Departure" on Friday - predicated on the idea that if they really believed Mubarak would leave last week, he would somehow follow the will of the people - turned yesterday into the "Day of Disillusion".

They are now constructing a committee of economists, intellectuals, "honest" politicians to negotiate with Vice-President Omar Suleiman - without apparently realising that Suleiman is the next safe-pair-of-hands general to be approved by the Americans, that Suleiman is a ruthless man who will not hesitate to use the same state security police as Mubarak relied upon to eliminate the state's enemies in Tahrir Square.

Betrayal always follows a successful revolution. And this may yet come to pass. The dark cynicism of the regime remains. Many pro-democracy demonstrators have noticed a strange phenomenon. In the months before the protests broke out on 25 January, a series of attacks on Coptic Christians and their churches spread across Egypt. The Pope called for the protection of Egypt's 10 per cent Christians. The West was appalled. Mubarak blamed it all on the familiar "foreign hand". But then after 25 January, not a hair of a Coptic head has been harmed. Why? Because the perpetrators had other violent missions to perform?

When Mubarak goes, terrible truths will be revealed. The world, as they say, waits. But none wait more attentively, more bravely, more fearfully than the young men and women in Tahrir Square. If they are truly on the edge of victory, they are safe. If they are not, there will come the midnight knock on many a door.

Robert Fisk

Wednesday, 9 February 2011

HANGING ON TO POWER

Blood turns brown with age. Revolutions do not. Vile rags now hang in a corner of the square, the last clothes worn by the martyrs of Tahrir: a doctor, a lawyer among them, a young woman, their pictures strewn above the crowds, the fabric of the T-shirts and trousers stained the colour of mud. But yesterday, the people honoured their dead in their tens of thousands for the largest protest march ever against President Hosni Mubarak's dictatorship, a sweating, pushing, shouting, weeping, joyful people, impatient, fearful that the world may forget their courage and their sacrifice.

It took three hours to force our way into the square, two hours to plunge through a sea of human bodies to leave. High above us, a ghastly photomontage flapped in the wind: Hosni Mubarak's head superimposed upon the terrible picture of Saddam Hussein with a noose round his neck. Uprisings don't follow timetables. And Mubarak will search for some revenge for yesterday's renewed explosion of anger and frustration at his 30-year rule. For two days, his new back-to-work government had tried to portray Egypt as a nation slipping back into its old, autocratic torpor. Gas stations open, a series of obligatory traffic jams, banks handing out money - albeit in suitably small amounts - shops gingerly doing business, ministers sitting to attention on state television as the man who would remain king for another five months lectured them on the need to bring order out of chaos - his only stated reason for hanging grimly to power. But Issam Etman proved him wrong.

Shoved and battered by the thousands around him, he carried his five-year-old daughter Hadiga on his shoulders. "I am here for my daughter," he shouted above the protest. "It is for her freedom that I want Mubarak to go. I am not poor. I run a transport company and a gas station. Everything is shut now and I'm suffering, but I don't care. I am paying my staff from my own pocket. This is about freedom. Anything is worth that."

And all the while, the little girl sat on Issam Etman's shoulders and stared at the epic crowds in wonderment; no Harry Potter extravaganza would match this. Many of the protesters - so many were flocking to the square yesterday evening that the protest site had overflowed onto the Nile river bridges and the other squares of central Cairo - had come for the first time. The soldiers of Egypt's Third Army must have been outnumbered 40,000 to one and they sat meekly on their tanks and armoured personnel carriers, smiling nervously as old men and youths and young women sat around their tank tracks, sleeping on the armour, heads on the great steel wheels; a military force turned to impotence by an army of dissent. Many said they had come because they were frightened; because they feared the world was losing interest in their struggle, because Mubarak had not yet left his palace, because the crowds had grown smaller in recent days, because some of the camera crews had left for other tragedies and other dictatorships, because the smell of betrayal was in the air. If the Republic of Tahrir dries up, then the national awakening is over. But yesterday proved that the revolution is alive.

Its mistake was to underestimate the ability of the regime to live too, to survive, to turn on its tormentors, to switch off the cameras and harass the only voice of these people - the journalists - and to persuade those old enemies of revolution, the "moderates" whom the West loves, to debase their only demand. What is five more months if the old man goes in September? Even Amr Moussa, most respected of the crowds' favourite Egyptians, turns out to want the old boy to carry on to the end. And woeful, in truth, is the political understanding of this innocent but often untutored mass.

Regimes grow iron roots. When the Syrians left Lebanon in 2005, the Lebanese thought that it was enough to lop off the head, to get the soldiers and the intelligence officers out of their country. But I remember the astonishment with which we all discovered the depth of Syria's talons. They lay deep in the earth of Lebanon, to the very bedrock. The assassinations went on. And so, too, it is in Egypt. The Ministry of Interior thugs, the state security police, the dictator who gives them their orders, are still in operation - and if one head should roll, there will be other heads to be pasted onto the familiar portrait to send those cruel men back into the streets.

There are some in Egypt - I met one last night, a friend of mine - who are wealthy and genuinely support the democracy movement and want Mubarak to go but are fearful that if he steps now from his palace, the military will be able to impose their own emergency laws before a single reform has been discussed. "I want to get reforms in place before the man leaves," my friend said. "If he goes now, the new leader will be under no obligation to carry out reforms.

These should be agreed to now and done quickly - it's the legislature, the judiciary, the constitutional changes, the presidential terms that matter. As soon as Mubarak leaves, the men with brass on their shoulders will say: 'It's over - go home!' And then we'll have a five-year military council. So let the old man stay till September."

But it's easy to accuse the hundreds of thousands of democracy protestors of naivety, of simple-mindedness, of over-reliance on the Internet and Facebook.

Indeed, there is growing evidence that "virtual reality" became reality for the young of Egypt, that they came to believe in the screen rather than the street - and that when they took to the streets, they were deeply shocked by the state violence and the regime's continued, brutal, physical strength. Yet for people to taste this new freedom is overwhelming. How can a people who have lived under dictatorship for so long plan their revolution? We in the West forget this. We are so institutionalized that everything in our future is programmed. Egypt is a thunderstorm without direction, an inundation of popular expression which does not fit neatly into our revolutionary history books or our political meteorology.

All revolutions have their "martyrs", and the faces of Ahmed Bassiouni and young Sally Zahrani and Moahmoud Mohamed Hassan float on billboards around the square, along with pictures of dreadfully mutilated heads with the one word "unidentified" printed beside them with appalling finality. If the crowds abandon Tahrir now, these dead will also have been betrayed. And if we really believe the regime-or-chaos theory which still grips Washington and London and Paris, the secular, democratic, civilized nature of this great protest will also be betrayed. The deadly Stalinism of the massive Mugamma government offices, the tattered green flag of the pathetic Arab League headquarters, the military-guarded pile of the Egyptian Museum with the golden death mask of Tutankhamen - a symbol of Egypt's mighty past - buried deep into its halls; these are the stage props of the Republic of Tahrir.

Week three - day sixteen - lacks the romance and the promise of the Day of Rage and the great battles against the Egyptian Ministry of Interior goons and the moment, just over a week ago, when the army refused Mubarak's orders to crush, quite literally, the people in the square. Will there be a week six or a day 32? Will the cameras still be there? Will the people? Will we? Yesterday proved our predictions wrong again. But they will have to remember that the iron fingernails of this regime have long ago grown into the sand, deeper than the pyramids, more powerful than ideology. We have not seen the last of this particular creature. Nor of its vengeance.

Robert Fisk

Friday, 11 February 2011

MOMENT OF HORROR AND FURY

To the horror of Egyptians and the world, President Hosni Mubarak - haggard and apparently disoriented - appeared on state television last night to refuse every demand of his opponents by staying in power for at least another five months. The Egyptian Army, which had already initiated a virtual coup d'état, was nonplussed by the President's speech which had been widely advertised - by both his friends and his enemies - as a farewell address after 30 years of dictatorship. The vast crowds in Tahrir Square were almost insane with anger and resentment.

Mubarak tried - unbelievably - to placate his infuriated people with a promise to investigate the killings of his opponents in what he called "the unfortunate, tragic events", apparently unaware of the mass fury directed at his dictatorship for his three decades of corruption, brutality and repression. The old man had originally appeared ready to give up, faced at last with the fury of millions of Egyptians and the power of history, sealed off from his ministers like a bacillus, only grudgingly permitted by his own army from saying goodbye to the people who hated him.

Yet the very moment that Hosni Mubarak embarked on what was supposed to be his final speech, he made it clear that he intended to cling to power. To the end, the President's information minister insisted he would not leave. There were those who, to the very last moment, feared that Mubarak's departure would be cosmetic - even though his presidency had evaporated in the face of his army's decision to take power earlier in the evening.

History may later decide that the army's lack of faith in Mubarak effectively lost his presidency after three decades of dictatorship, secret police torture and government corruption. Confronted by even greater demonstrations on the streets of Egypt today, even the army could not guarantee the safety of the nation. Yet for Mubarak's opponents, today will not be a day of joy and rejoicing and victory but a potential bloodbath.

But was this a victory for Mubarak or a military coup d'état? Can Egypt ever be free? For the army generals to insist upon his departure was as dramatic as it was dangerous. Are they, a state within a state, now truly the guardians of the nation, defenders of the people - or will they continue to support a man who must be judged now as close to insanity? The chains which bound the military to the corruption of Mubarak's regime were real. Are they to stand by democracy - or cement a new Mubarak regime?

Even as Mubarak was still speaking, the millions in Tahrir Square roared their anger and fury and disbelief. Of course, the millions of courageous Egyptians who fought the whole apparatus of state security run by Mubarak should have been the victors. But as yesterday afternoon's events proved all too clearly, it was the senior generals - who enjoy the luxury of hotel chains, shopping malls, real estate and banking concessions from the same corrupt regime - who permitted Mubarak to survive. At an ominous meeting of the Supreme Council of the Egyptian Armed Forces, Defence Minister Mohamed Tantawi - one of Mubarak''s closest friends agreed to meet the demands of the millions of democracy protestors, without stating that the regime would itself be dissolved. Mubarak himself, commander-in-chief of the army, was not permitted to attend.

But this is a Middle Eastern epic, one of those incremental moments when the Arab people - forgotten, chastised, infantilized, repressed, often beaten, tortured too many times, occasionally hanged - will still strive to give the great wheel of history a shove, and shake off the burden of their lives. Last night, however, dictatorship had still won. Democracy had lost.

All day, the power of the people had grown as the prestige of the president and his hollow party collapsed. The vast crowds in Tahrir Square began yesterday to move out over all of central Cairo, even moving behind the steel gates of the People's Assembly, setting up their tents in front of the pseudo-Greek parliament building in a demand for new and fair elections. Today, they were planning to enter the parliament itself, taking over the symbol of Mubarak's fake "democracy". Fierce arguments among the army hierarchy - and apparently between Vice-President Omar Suleiman and Mubarak himself - continued while strikes and industrial stoppages spread across Egypt. Well over seven million protestors estimated to be on the streets of Egypt yesterday -the largest political demonstration in the country's modern history, greater even than the six million who attended the funeral of Gamal Abdul Nasser, the first Egyptian dictator whose rule continued through Anwar Sada's vain and ultimately fatal presidency and the three dead decades of Mubarak.

It was too early, last night, for the millions in Tahrir Square to understand the legal complexities of Mubarak's speech. But it was patronizing, selfserving and immensely dangerous. The Egyptian constitution insists that presidential power must pass to the speaker of parliament, a colourless Mubarak crony called Fatih Srour, and elections -- fair ones, if this can be imagined - held within 60 days. But many believe that Sulieman may choose to rule by some new emergency law and then push Mubarak out of power, staking out a timetable for new and fraudulent elections and yet another terrible epoch of dictatorship.

The truth, however, is that the millions of Egyptians who have tried to unseat their Great Dictator regard their constitution - and the judiciary and the entire edifice of government institutions - with the same contempt as they do Mubarak. They want a new constitution, new laws to limit the powers and tenure of presidents, new and early elections which will reflect the "will of the people" rather than the will of the president or the transition president, or of generals and brigadiers and state security thugs.

Last night, a military officer guarding the tens of thousands celebrating in Cairo threw down his rifle and joined the demonstrators, yet another sign of the ordinary Egyptian soldier's growing sympathy for the democracy demonstrators. We had witnessed many similar sentiments from the army over the past two weeks. But the critical moment came on the evening of 30 January when, it is now clear, Mubarak ordered the Egyptian Third Army to crush the demonstrators in Tahrir Square with their tanks after flying F-16 fighter bombers at low level over the protestors.

Many of the senior tank commanders could be seen tearing off their headsets - over which they had received the fatal orders - to use their mobile phones. They were, it now transpires, calling their own military families for advice. Fathers who had spent their lives serving the Egyptian army told their sons to disobey, that they must never kill their own people.

Thus when General Hassan al-Rawani told the massive crowds yesterday evening that "everything you want will be realised - all your demands will be met", the people cried back: "The army and the people stand together - the army and the people are united. The army and the people belong to one hand."

But neither the army nor Vice-President Suleiman are likely to be able to face the far greater demonstrations planned for today.

Robert Fisk

Saturday, 12 February 2011

VICTORY OVER MUBARAK

Everyone suddenly burst out singing. And laughing, and crying, and shouting and praying, kneeling on the road and kissing the filthy tarmac right in front of me, and dancing and praising God for ridding them of Hosni Mubarak - a generous moment, for it was their courage rather than divine intervention which rid Egypt of its dictator - and weeping tears which splashed down their clothes. It was as if every man and woman had just got married, as if joy could smother the decades of dictatorship and pain and repression and humiliation and blood. Forever, it will be known as the Egyptian Revolution of 25 January - the day the rising began - and it will be forever the story of a risen people.

The old man had gone at last, handing power not to the Vice-President but - ominously, though the millions of non-violent revolutionaries were in no mood to appreciate this last night - to Egypt's army council, to a field marshal and a lot of brigadier generals, guarantors, for now, of all that the pro-democracy protesters had fought and, in some cases, died for. Yet even the soldiers were happy. At the very moment when the news of Mubarak's demise licked like fire through the demonstrators outside the army-protected state television station on the Nile, the face of one young officer burst into joy.

All day, the demonstrators had been telling the soldiers that they were brothers. Well, we shall see.

Talk of a historic day somehow took the edge off what last night's victory really means for Egyptians. Through sheer willpower, through courage in the face of Mubarak's hateful state security police, through the realisation - yes - that sometimes you have to struggle to over-throw a dictator with more than words and facebooks, through the very act of fighting with fists and stones against cops with stun guns and tear gas and live bullets, they achieved the impossible: the end - they must plead with their God that it is permanent - of almost 60 years of autocracy and repression, 30 of them Mubarak's.

Arabs, maligned, cursed, racially abused in the West, treated as backward by many of the Israelis who wanted to maintain Mubarak's often savage rule, had stood up, abandoned their fear, and tossed away the man whom the West loved as a "moderate" leader who would do their bidding at the price of $1.5bn a year. It's not only East Europeans who can stand up to brutality.

That this man - less than 24 hours earlier - had announced in a moment of lunacy that he still wanted to protect his "children" from "terrorism" and would stay in office, made yesterday's victory all the more precious. On Thursday night, the men and women demanding democracy in Egypt had held their shoes in the air to show their dis-respect for the decrepit leader who treated them as infants, incapable of political and moral dignity. Then yesterday, he simply fled to Sharm el-Sheikh, a Western-style holiday resort on the Red Sea, a place which had about as much in common with Egypt as Marbella or Bali.

So the Egyptian Revolution lay in the hands of the army last night as a series of contradictory statements from the military indicated that Egypt's field marshals, generals and brigadiers were competing for power in the ruins of Mubarak's regime. Israel, according to prom-inent Cairo military families, was trying to persuade Washington to promote their favourite Egyptian - former intelligence capo and Vice-President Omar Suleiman - to the presidency, while Field Marshal Tantawi, the defence minister, wanted his chief of staff, General Sami Anan, to run the country.

When Mubarak and his family were freighted off to Sharm el-Sheikh yesterday afternoon, it only confirmed the impression that his presence was more irrelevant than provocative. The hundreds of thousands of protesters in Tahrir Square sniffed the same decay of power and even Mohamed el-Baradei, the former UN arms inspector and ambitious Nobel Prize-winner, announced that "Egypt will explode" and "must be saved by the army".

Analysts talk about a "network" of generals within the regime, although it is more like a cobweb, a series of competing senior officers whose own personal wealth and jealously guarded privileges were earned by serving the regime whose 83-year old leader now appears as demented as he does senile. The health of the President and the activities of the millions of prodemocracy protesters across Egypt are thus now less important than the vicious infighting within the army.

Yet if they have discarded the rais - the president - the military's high command are men of the old order. Indeed, most of the army's highest ranking officers were long ago sucked into the nexus of regime power. In Mubarak's last government, the vice president was a general, the prime minister was a general, the deputy prime minister was a general, the minister of defence was a general and the minister of interior was a general. Mubarak himself was commander of the air force. The army brought Nasser to power. They supported General Anwar Sadat. They supported General Mubarak. The army introduced dictatorship in 1952 and now the protesters believe it will become the agency of democracy. Some hope.

Thus - sadly - Egypt is the army and the army is Egypt. Or so, alas, it likes to think. It therefore wishes to control - or "protect", as army communiqués constantly reiterate - the protesters demanding the final departure of Mubarak. But Egypt's hundreds of thousands of democratic revolutionaries - enraged by Mubarak's refusal to abandon the presidency - started their own takeover of Cairo yesterday, overflowing from Tahrir Square, not only around the parliament building but the Nile-side state television and radio headquarters and main highways leading to Mubarak's luxurious residency in the wealthy suburb of Heliopolis. Thousands of demonstrators in Alexandria reached the very gates of one of Mubarak's palaces where the presidential guard handed over water and food in a meek gesture of "friendship" for the people. Protesters also took over Talaat Haab Square in the commercial centre of the Cairo as hundreds of academics from the city's three main universities marched to Tahrir at midmorning.

After the fury expressed overnight at Mubarak's paternalistic, deeply insulting speech - in which he spoke about himself and his

1973 war service at great length and referred only vaguely to the duties he would supposedly re-assign to his Vice-President, Omar Suleiman - yesterday's demonstrations began amid humour and extraordinary civility. If Mubarak's henchmen hoped that his near suicidal decision of Thursday would provoke the millions of democracy protesters across Egypt to violence, they were wrong; around Cairo, the young men and women who are the foundation of the Egyptian Revolution behaved with the kind of restraint that President Obama yesterday lamely called for. In many countries, they would have burned government buildings after a presidential speech of such hubris; in Tahrir Square, they staged poetry readings. And then they heard that their wretched antagonist had gone.

But Arab verse does not win revolutions, and every Egyptian knew yesterday that the initiative lay no more with the demonstrators than with the remote figure of the ex-dictator. For the future body politic of Egypt lies with up to a hundred officers, their old fidelity to Mubarak - sorely tested by Thursday's appalling speech, let alone the revolution on the streets - has now been totally abandoned. A military communiqué yesterday morning called for "free and fair elections", adding that Egyptian armed forces were "committed to the demands of the people" who should "resume a normal way of life". Translated into civilian-speak, this means that the revolutionaries should pack up while a coterie of generals divide up the ministries of a new government. In some countries, this is called a "coup d'etat". Around Mubarak's abandoned Cairo palace yesterday morning, the presidential guard, themselves a separate and powerful paramilitary force within the army, unsheathed a mass of barbed wire around the perimeter of the grounds, set up massive sand-bag emplacements and placed soldiers with heavy machineguns behind them. Tanks wire. It was an empty gesture worthy of Mubarak himself. For he had already fled.

But the army's instructions to its soldiers to care for the demonstrators appear to have been followed to the letter in the hours before victory. A 25-year old first lieutenant in the Egyptian Third Army, a highly educated young man with almost fluent English, was helping the demonstrators to check the identities of protesters near the ministry of interior yesterday, cheerfully admitting that he wasn't sure if the protests in Cairo were the best way of achieving democracy. He had not told his parents that he was in central Cairo lest his mother be upset, telling them instead that he was on barrack duties.

But would he shoot the demonstrators in a confrontation, we asked him? "Many people ask me that question," he replied. "I tell them: 'I cannot shoot my father, my family - you are like my father and my own family.' And I have many friends here." And if orders came to shoot the protesters? "I am sure it will not happen," he said. "All the other revolutions [in Egypt] were bloody. I don't want blood here."

The soldier got his history right. Egyptians in Cairo rose against Napoleon's army in 1798, fought the monarchy in 1881 and 1882, staged an insurrection against the British in 1919 and 1952, and re- belled against Sadat in the 1977 food riots and against Mubarak in 1986, when even the police deserted the government. At least four soldiers in Tahrir Square defected to the demonstrators on Thursday. A colonel in the army told me a week ago that "one of our comrades tried to commit suicide" in Tahrir Square. So the generals now fighting like vultures over the wreckage of Mubarak's regime must take care that their own soldiers have not been infected by the revolution.

As for Omar Sulieman, his own post-Mubarak speech on Thurs- day night was almost as childish as the President's. He told the demonstrators to go home - treating them, in the words of one pro- tester, like sheep - and duly blamed "television stations and radios" for violence on the streets, an idea as preposterous as Mubarak's claim - for the umpteenth time - that "foreign hands" were behind the revolution. His ambitions for the presidency may have also ended, an- other old man who thought he could close down the revolution with false promises.

Perhaps the shadow of the army is too dark an image to invoke in the aftermath of so monumental a revolution in Egypt. Siegfried Sassoon's joy on the day of the 1918 Armistice, the end of the First World War - when everyone also suddenly burst out singing - was genuine and deserved. Yet that peace led to further immense suffer- ing. And the Egyptians who have fought for their future in the streets of their nation over the past three weeks will have to preserve their revolution from internal and external enemies if they are to achieve a real democracy. The army has decided to protect the people. But who will curb the power of the army?

Robert Fisk

MUBARAK CHRONOLOGY

14 October 1981

Vice-President Hosni Mubarak is sworn in as President eight days after his predecessor Anwar Sadat was gunned down by Islamist
militants at a parade in Cairo.

26 June 1995

Mubarak survives an assassination attempt in Ethiopia's capital Addis
Ababa.

5 October 1999

Mubarak wins a fourth term, and appoints a new prime minister after
the government resigns.

March 2005

The Kefaya (Enough) Movement stages protests across Egypt against
Mubarak's rule.

11 May 2005

Egypt introduces contested presidential elections, but opposition parties complain that strict rules still prohibit genuine competition.

27 September 2005

Mubarak wins Egypt's first contested general election, a process
which is marred by violence. He is sworn in for his fifth consecutive
term.

19 November 2006

Mubarak declares that he will remain President for the rest of his life.

26 March 2010

Former UN nuclear agency chief Mohamed ElBaradei announces he
would consider running for the presidency if reforms on power were
introduced.

27 March 2010

After gallbladder surgery in Germany, Mubarak returns to Egypt to
reassume his full presidential powers.

25 January 2011

Inspired by the ousting of Tunisia's President Ben Ali on 14 January,
thousands protest across Egypt demanding Mubarak's resignation. It
is called the "Day of Wrath".

29 January 2011

After deploying the army in an attempt to control the widespread protests, Mubarak sacks his cabinet and names intelligence chief Omar Suleiman as vice-president. He refuses to step down.

1 February 2011

One million Egyptians march through Cairo demanding Mubarak's immediate resignation. Mubarak announces he will step down when his term ends in September.

3 February 2011

Mubarak tells reporters he is fed up with being in power, but thinks chaos will ensue if he steps down now. About 300 people have been killed in the unrest, according to UN figures.

5 February 2011

President Obama asks Mubarak to listen to the protesters demanding his resignation. Mubarak removes his son from a senior post and invites opposition groups to negotiate reform. They are dissatisfied with the concessions offered.

10 February 2011

Egypt's army commander addresses Cairo's Tahrir Square, saying "everything you want will be realised". After mounting speculation and reports that resignation is imminent, Mubarak refuses to step down.

11 February 2011

After 18 days of protests, Mubarak finally leaves office.

Saturday, 12 February 2011

GREAT ARE THE CONTRASTS OF HISTORY

Fresh from Northern Ireland and the aftermath of the Portuguese revolution, I arrived in the Middle East in June of 1976, and turned up in Cairo to cover one of Lebanon's interminable civil war ceasefire negotiations. But after a dinner of unwashed vegetables in a local restaurant, I came down with gastroenteritis - "enteric fever" is chiselled on to many a Raj headstone - and lay night after night with rats in my stomach and sweat dripping on to the bed linen, and, on my first walk outside, collapsed on the concrete bench of a bus station amid a canyon of traffic, and a square of broiling iron overhead walkways and fuming, shouting Egyptians.

And there I lay unconscious for five hours. No one came to my help. I woke in pain, determined that the Arab world must be a harsh and cruel place. I even composed my letter of resignation from the post of Middle East correspondent of The Times - after a mere week in the job.

The sheer filth of the Cairo bus station, the smell of urine, the awful, hot concrete Stalinism of the Mugamma building behind me - a Stakhanovite monstrosity wherein I would seek extended visas, day after day - convinced me that I could not work in Sadat's foetid dictatorship. Self-pity was the name of my disease. Tahrir was the name of the square.

Almost 36 years later, I have now prowled this place like a home, its tens of thousands of courageous democrats demanding an Egypt which I - and they - could never have dreamed of. Indeed, most of the young men and women who approached every foreigner and shouted "Welcome to Egypt!" were not even alive when I lay on that concrete bench. The bus station is now a building site for a new hotel - used for lavatories these past three weeks, the smell of urine is still there - the Mugamma, as terrible as ever, stands empty, its legions of civil servants prevented from entering the square by the revolutionaries of the new Egypt.

History has come in great gulps, sometimes bloody, almost always brave, inspiring, terrible. I had come full circle. Thank heavens I never sent that letter of resignation to The Times. I guess reporters, like nations, grow up. Perspective is a rare instinct. What was newspaper reporting three and a half decades ago - the dictatorship of Sadat, soon to be followed by the even more depressing dictatorship of Mubarak - turned this week into a widescreen epic, a cast of millions, an imperishable story of freedom against state repression.

Strange, though, how the world of films gets it right. In The Third Man, there's a wonderful moment when two British officers are waiting beside a night-time wall in post-war Vienna in the hope of capturing the mass murderer Harry Lime. From the shadows comes not Lime but a weird creature holding balloons. Would the British soldiers like to buy a balloon, he asks softly. A couple of weeks ago, I was choking my way through Champillion Street, just off Tahrir Square, with Cecilia Udden of Swedish television, both of us sick with tear gas fumes, the place vibrating with the stun guns of the state security police, when a robed figure emerged from a side street, approaching us through the gloom, dangling something in his hand. "Papyrus?" he asked plaintively. "Want picture of Rameses the Second?"

Great are the contrasts of history, and not always comfortable ones. Talking to fleeing British tourists at Cairo airport, my colleague Don Macintyre (he who looks like Jack Hawkins playing General Allenby in Lawrence of Arabia) interviewed a British couple. But when he asked their names, the woman declined to be identified because she worked for "a government department" in Britain. Yet in Tahrir, Egyptians in danger of instant arrest by Mubarak's thugs proudly gave their full names to us, anxious to demonstrate their belief in freedom and contempt for the police. What does that tell us about ourselves? Anti-Mubarakite Egypt teaches us one thing. Cameronite Britain quite another.

And then there was the man-who-would-be-king, Omar Suleiman, chatting to journalists on Egyptian television, confident, amiable, avuncular. Then he suddenly warned the reporters that "bats out of the night are terrorising the Egyptian people". Was the man cracked?

Back in the 1930s, my dad, Bill, deputy borough treasurer of Birkenhead, discovered that a friend had been incarcerated in what was then called a "lunatic asylum". Fisk to the rescue. Bill turned up at the asylum, listened to his friend's rational explanation that there had been some terrible mistake, and immediately offered to take him to the health authorities and clear up this ghastly mistake. "But I can't leave," Bill's friend suddenly announced, sticking his fingers into a nearby electrical plug. "You see, I'm a light bulb - and if you take me away, all the lights in the asylum will go out!"

So is Omar Suleiman a light bulb? How very Western of me to ask. In Arabic poetry, too, where metaphor is as distinctive as it was in early 17th-century English poetry, the expression "bat out of the night" almost always refers to a frightening creature which emerges only in darkness, blind in its capacity to instil fear and terror. Suleiman was almost certainly talking about the thieves and arsonists who have attacked Egyptian homes by night - many, although not all, of the "bats" have been plain-clothes policemen, a distinction Suleiman naturally did not make - and thus Arabic literary tradition folded into the rhetoric of a dying dictatorship. Was it really dying, we asked ourselves these past three weeks? So did the demonstrators of Tahrir Square, because revolutions, uprisings, "intifadas", political explosions, have neither rules nor timetables. Like every page of history, staring into the looking glass, we have to wait patiently for valour and blood and betrayal. On Thursday night we waited for Mubarak to leave. But this old man turned on his own people with a speech of such narcissism and self-delusion that it took the breath away. Here was the genuine light bulb, the real "bat out of the night".

Last night the bat flew away.

Robert Fisk

Sunday, 13 February 2011

MUBARAK'S SHAMEFUL LEGACY

The cops shot 16-year-old Mariam in the back on 28 January, a live round fired from the roof of the Saida Zeinab police station in the slums of Cairo's old city at the height of the government violence aimed at quelling the revolution, a pot shot of contempt by Mubarak's forces for the homeless street children of Egypt.

She had gone to the police with up to a hundred other beggar boys and girls to demand the release of her friend, 16-year-old Ismail Yassin, who had already been dragged inside the station. Some of the kids outside were only nine years old. Maybe that's why the first policeman on the roof fired warning bullets into the air.

Then he shot Mariam. She was taking pictures of the police on her mobile phone, but fell to the ground with a bullet in her back. The other children carried her to the nearby Mounira hospital - where the staff apparently refused to admit her - and then to the Ahmed Maher hospital, where the bullet was removed. Ismail was freed and made his way to Tahrir Square, where the pro-democracy protesters were under attack by armed men. He was wandering up Khairat Street - drawn towards violence like all the homeless of Cairo - when an unknown gunmen shot him in the head and killed him.

They are everywhere in the capital, the 50,000 street children of Cairo, Mubarak's shameful, unspoken legacy, the detritus of the poor and the defenceless, orphans and outcasts, glue-sniffers, many of them drug-addicted, as young as five, the girls often arrested and - according to the children and charity workers - sexually molested by the police.

Egyptian government statistics claim that only 5,000 beggar children live on the streets, a figure which local non-governmental organisations and Western agencies say is another Mubarak fantasy to cover up a scandal 10 times as big.

Children interviewed by *The Independent* on Sunday, however, have also revealed how Mubarak supporters deliberately brought children to the outskirts of Tahrir Square to throw stones at the pro-democracy supporters, how they persuaded penniless street kids to participate in their pro-Mubarak marches. Swarms of other children forced their way into the square itself because they discovered that the protesters were kind to them, feeding them sandwiches and giving them cigarettes and money.

According to one local Egyptian charity, as many as 12,000 street children were caught up in the opposing street demonstrations of the past three weeks.

"They were told it was their duty - a national patriotic act - to throw stones at the demonstrators, to do violent actions," said an Egyptian doctor in Saida Zeinab. According to the same woman, many children were hit by police rubber bullets when they found themselves on the side of the pro-democracy demonstrators. At least 12 from this district alone were taken to hospital with wounds caused by police weapons.

Ahmed - he is not sure if he is 18 or 19, but is probably much younger - saw Mariam shot. Dressed in an orange T-shirt, faded jeans, plastic sandals and a blue baseball hat, he was shy and frightened, even though the Saida Zeinab police station was burned down by angry crowds later on the same night of 28 January - when the cops fled.

"It was just before Friday prayers and we heard the police were beating people in the street," he said. "I went out and saw lots of people throwing stones - so I started throwing stones at the police.

"Everyone was throwing stones, my family, every family, because everyone hated the police.

"Mariam was taking pictures on her mobile and the police were on the roof. She had her back to the police station, but they shot her anyway. People took her to the hospital and she came out bandaged, but she said the wound still hurt and she thought someone had stolen one of her kidneys.

I saw her on the street afterwards, in the Abu Riche area. Now I don't know where she is."

Children's hostels - operating with British as well as other European donations - have tried to find Mariam, but to no avail.

Ahmed was in Khairat Street when Ismail Yassin was shot. "I was beaten and hit by a 'cartouche' from a police stun gun. A lot of the young people went into the streets to steal - from houses or anywhere. They hit the people in the houses and took whatever they wanted."

Ahmed cleans cars for money - at traffic lights, in traffic jams and at blocked road intersections - and sleeps on the streets, staying awake at night in case thieves assault him, snatching a few hours of sleep after sunrise. Ahmed's parents, like those of many other street children, are alive, but he fell out with them long ago and refuses to go home.

Mohamed is only nine and has confused memories of the revolution that overthrew Mubarak. He and another child were assaulted by three men who threw them into a sewer - apparently in an attempt to take money from them. Then, with his brothers, he went to watch the demonstrations in the Gayar district of Cairo.

"I started throwing stones at people who said 'no' to Hosni Mubarak. I went on my own with people who said they wanted Mubarak.

"They told me to throw stones. The people were older than me." Mohamed is originally from Guena in upper Egypt, from a family of three sisters and three brothers.

"I went back to stay with a friend who was sleeping in a garden," he said. "Then another friend started living in Tahrir and told me to come there. So I went with Karim and Ali and Mohamed and we got food there and we sat with the people. I liked going there. I sometimes begged from the people. And the soldiers always said 'hello' to me and sometimes they gave me food."

These children - often much younger than they claimed - sometimes avoided questions about police behaviour; they were obviously still afraid. Hostel workers spoke of policemen forcing female street children to sleep with them, even stealing money from the girls. Several children said that most of their friends were on drugs. One young man was clearly addicted and spoke almost incoherently of police violence, of carrying knives, of being repeatedly beaten in the Saida Zeinab police station by two cops, whose full names were given to *The Independent* on Sunday.

Many of the children were sucked into the vortex of the revolution, following crowds out of excitement and a sense of adventure.

"People started walking in demonstrations and I just started walking with them," said Goma. He is barefoot and in filthy trousers, and claims to be 16. He is originally from the oasis city of Fayoum and admitted that he didn't know at first whom the people supported.

"Then they started saying they liked Mubarak and they walked to Tahrir," he said. "But when we got into Tahrir, some other people came and threw stones at us. I just threw stones with the Mubarak people. They told me that I should like Mubarak because if he went, some people would come from other countries and become president of Egypt. I got hit by a stone in my back - it still hurts. The enemy threw the stone" - presumably democracy protesters - "so I left because I didn't want a stone in my face or my eye."

The street children of Cairo move in packs, turning up for free lunches with their friends when hostels open their doors, adopting puppy dogs and trying, like well-educated children, to learn how to use computers donated by foreign charities.

But none I met could read - most did not know how to write their own name in Arabic. Some were obviously orphans or semi-abandoned by their parents, but there was a strong theme of fathers forcing their sons and daughters to work the streets for money to buy drugs.

The sick go largely uncared for. The dead don't matter. The body of Ismail Yassin, now a martyr of the Egyptian revolution, remains in a hospital mortuary. Unclaimed.

Robert Fisk

Monday, 14 February 2011

ARMY REMAINS IN CONTROL

Two days after millions of Egyptians won their revolution against the regime of Hosni Mubarak, the country's army - led by Mubarak's lifelong friend, General Mohamed el-Tantawi - further consolidated its power over Egypt yesterday, dissolving parliament and suspending the constitution. As they did so, the prime minister appointed by Mubarak, ex-General Ahmed Shafiq, told Egyptians that his first priorities were "peace and security" to prevent "chaos and disorder" - the very slogan uttered so often by the despised ex-president. Plus ça change?

In their desperation to honour the 'military council's' promise of Cairo-back-to-normal, hundreds of Egyptian troops - many unarmed - appeared in Tahrir Square to urge the remaining protesters to leave the encampment they had occupied for 20 days. At first the crowd

greeted them as friends, offering them food and water. Military policemen in red berets, again without weapons, emerged to control traffic.
But then a young officer began lashing demonstrators with a cane -
old habits die hard in young men wearing uniforms - and for a moment there was a miniature replay of the fury visited upon the state
security police here on 28 January.

It reflected a growing concern among those who overthrew Mubarak that the fruits of their victory may be gobbled up by an army
largely composed of generals who achieved their power and privilege
under Mubarak himself. No-one objects to the dissolution of parliament since Mubarak's assembly elections last year - and all other
years - were so transparently fraudulent. But the 'military council'
gave no indication of the date for the free and fair elections which
Egyptians believed they had been promised.

The suspension of the constitution - a document which the millions of demonstrators anyway regarded as a laissez-passer for
presidential dictatorship - left most Egyptians unmoved. And the
army, having received the fulsome thanks of Israel for promising to
honour the Egyptian-Israeli peace treaty, announced that it would
hold power for only six months; no word, though, on whether they
could renew their military rule after that.

But a clear divergence is emerging between the demands of the
young men and women who brought down the Mubarak regime and
the concessions - if that is what they are - that the army appears willing to grant them. A small rally at the side of Tahrir Square yesterday
held up a series of demands which included the suspension of Mubarak's old emergency law and freedom for political prisoners.

The army has promised to drop the emergency legislation "at the
right opportunity", but as long as it remains in force, it gives the military as much power to ban all protests and demonstrations as
Mubarak possessed; which is one reason why those little battles broke
out between the army and the people in the square yesterday.

As for the freeing of political prisoners, the military has remained
suspiciously silent. Is this because there are prisoners who know too
much about the army's involvement in the previous regime? Or because escaped and newly liberated prisoners are returning to Cairo
and Alexandria from desert camps with terrible stories of torture and
executions by - so they say - military personnel. An Egyptian army officer known to 'The Independent' insisted yesterday that the desert

prisons were run by military intelligence units who worked for the interior ministry - not for the ministry of defence.

As for the top echelons of the state security police who ordered their men - and their faithful "baltagi" plainclothes thugs - to attack peaceful demonstrators during the first week of the revolution, they appear to have taken the usual flight to freedom in the Arab Gulf. According to an officer in the Cairo police criminal investigation department whom I spoke to yesterday, all the officers responsible for the violence which left well over 300 Egyptians dead have fled Egypt with their families for the emirate of Abu Dhabi. The criminals who were paid by the cops to beat the protesters have gone to ground - who knows when their services might next be required? - while the middle-ranking police officers wait for justice to take its course against them. If indeed it does.

All this, of course, depends on the size of the archives left behind by the regime and the degree to which the authorities, currently the army, are prepared to make these papers available to a new and reformed judiciary. As for the city police, who hid in their police stations before they were burned down on 28 January, they turned up at the interior ministry in Cairo yesterday to demand better pay. That the police should now become protesters themselves - they are indeed to receive pay rises - was one of the more imperishable moments of postrevolutionary Egypt.

Now, of course, it is Egypt's turn to watch the effects of its own revolution on its neighbours. Scarcely a family in Egypt was unaware yesterday of the third day of protests against the president in Yemen and the police violence which accompanied them. And it is remarkable that just as Arab protesters mimic their successful counterparts in Egypt, the state security apparatus of each Arab regime faithfully follows the failed tactics of Mubarak's thugs.

Another irony has dawned on Egyptians. Those Arab dictators which claim to represent their people - Algeria comes to mind, and Libya, and Morocco - have singularly failed to represent their people by not congratulating Egypt on its successful democratic revolution. To do so, needless to say, would be to saw off the legs of their own thrones.

Robert Fisk

Tuesday, 15 February 2011

THE EXPLOSION DIDN'T HAPPEN

The old man's voice is scathing, his mind like a razor, that of a veteran fighter, writer, sage, perhaps the most important living witness and historian of modern Egypt, turning on the sins of the regime that tried to shut him up forever. "Mubarak betrayed the republican spirit - and then he wanted to continue through his son Gamal," he says, finger pointed to heaven. "It was a project, not an idea; it was a plan. The last 10 years of the life of this country were wasted because of this question, because of the search for inheritance - as if Egypt was Syria, or Papa Doc and Baby Doc in Haiti."

At 87, Mohamed Heikal is the doyen, the icon - for once the cliché is correct - of Egyptian journalism, friend and adviser and minister to Nasser and to Sadat, the one man who has predicted for 30 years the revolution that he has, amazingly, lived to see.

We didn't believe him. For three decades, I came here to see Heikal and he predicted the implosion of Egypt with absolute conviction, outlining in devastating detail the corruption and violence of the Mubarak regime, and its inevitable collapse. And sometimes I wrote cynically about him, sometimes humorously, occasionally - I fear - patronisingly, rarely as seriously as he deserved. Yesterday, he offered me a cigar and invited me to say if I thought I was still right. No, I said, I was wrong. He was right.

Heikal in old age is a man of such eloquence, such energy, with such a vast memory, that men and women who are younger - a quality he much admires, and which won Egypt's revolution last week - must be silent in his presence. "I lost the most important thing in my life," he says with painful candour. "I lost my youth. I would love to have been out with those young people in the square."

But Heikal is a wily beast. He was here for the Nasser revolution of 1952 and remembers the folly of power displayed by Egypt's dictators." I was completely sure there was going to be an explosion," he says. "What stunned me was the movement of the millions. I was not sure I was going to live to see this day. I was not sure I was going to see the rising of the people.

"My old friend Dr Mohamed Fawzi came to see me a few days ago and said: 'The balloon of lies is getting bigger every day. It will explode with the prick of a pin - and God save us when it explodes.' Then the people came and filled the vacuum.

"I was worried that there would be chaos. But a new generation in Egypt came along, wiser than us a million times over, and they behaved in a moderate, intelligent way. There was no vacuum. The explosion didn't happen.

"What I am worried about is that everything came as a surprise, and nobody is ready for what comes next. Nobody wants to give time for the air to clear. In these circumstances, you can't take the right decisions. These people carry with them huge aspirations.

The Americans and Israel and the Arab world are all pushing. Even the Military Council were not prepared for this. I say: give yourself time to sleep at last.

"Mubarak kept us all in suspense," he goes on. "He was like Alfred Hitchcock, a master of surprise. But this was an Alfred Hitchcock situation without a plot. The man was improvising every day - like an old fox. The millions moved. I watched him - and I was stunned.

"In this grave situation, the regime got into contact with some people in the square, and it asked them if some delegation of powers from Mubarak to the Vice-President would be acceptable, and the people they were talking to said: 'Maybe, yes.' And so Mubarak thought he could make his speech on Thursday night because he was sure he had got an 'OK' from the square. I couldn't believe my ears."

Heikal was pleased that Mubarak delayed the crisis by remaining silent while the crowds built up in Tahrir Square. "In those 18 days, something very important happened. We started with about 50-60,000 people. But as Mubarak delayed and prevaricated like the old fox he is, it gave the chance for the people to come out. This changed the whole equation. Six days into the crisis, Mubarak simply didn't understand what had happened."

Heikal bemoans the wasted years and the deaths of the past three weeks - "our revolution was a great historical tragedy," he says - and does not yet see the nature of post-revolutionary Egypt. "I am happy with the presence of the army - but I want the presence of the people, too. The people are bewildered about what they have achieved."

On Saturday night, Heikal was invited, for the first time in almost three decades, to appear once more on Egyptian state television. His reply was as feisty as it was when Sadat offered him the job of chief of the National Security Council after Nasser's death. "I told Sadat that if we differed as we did when I was a newspaperman on Al-Ahram, how could I lead his National Security Council?" So when the government television asked him to appear this weekend, Heikal replied: "I was prevented by government order from appearing for 30 years and now you tell me that the doors are open again. I was prevented from appearing by government order, and now I am supposed to come by invitation."

A few months ago, after Heikal had visited Lebanon and met Sayyid Hassan Nasrallah, the Hezbollah leader, a furious Egyptian Foreign Minister turned up at Heikal's farm in the Nile Delta. "Do you think you represent the Egyptian people?" the minister shouted at him. Heikal asked the minister: "Do you think you represent the Egyptian people?"

The lines look good on Heikal's face, a wise old bird as well as wily. But he's a bit hard of hearing and feels it necessary to apologise for his 87 years, a young man trapped in an old man's body. And anyone invited to his inner sanctum above the Nile, full of books and beautiful carpets and the smell of fine cigars, can see Heikal's sadness.

"The difference between Mubarak and me is that I never tried to hide my age," he says. "He did. He dyed his hair. So whenever he looked in the mirror, he saw Mubarak as a young man. But all old men have vanity. When I was young and was on television, I used to ask my friends: 'Did I say the right thing?' Now I ask them: 'How did I look?'" For *The Independent's* post-revolutionary portrait of the great man, he whipped off his spectacles. "Vanity!" he cried.

Mubarak, he believes, was terrified that government files would be released if he resigned, that the regime's secrets would come tumbling out. "What I'm afraid of is that the dishonesty of some of the politicians in Egypt will tarnish such a valuable event," Heikal says. "They will use the issue of accountability to settle accounts. I want this country to have a proper investigation, not throw these files away for people to use for their own agenda. It is opportunism by politicians that I am afraid of. All the [regime's] files should be opened. An account should be given to our people for the last 30 years - but it should not be a matter for revenge. If small politicians use this, it will affect the value of what must be done."

Historically, Heikal regards the events of the past three weeks as overwhelming, unstoppable, unprecedented.

"In revolutions, there is no pattern. People want a change from a present to a future. Every revolution is conditioned by where it starts and where it is moving. But this event showed a huge Egyptian mass of people that it is possible to defy the terror of the state. I think this will revolutionise the Arab world."

Locked up by Anwar Sadat shortly before his assassination, Heikal was released from prison by Mubarak, and I recalled that we met within hours of his release, when he - Heikal - was grateful to Mubarak, and sang his praises. "Yes, but as a man of transition," he replied. "I thought he would be President only a short time. He came from the Egyptian military, a national and loved institution. He saw Sadat being killed by his own people - he was present when this happened - and I thought he must have learned a tragic lesson about the Egyptian people when their patience runs out. I thought he could be a good bridge for the future.

"In the last document that Nasser wrote on 30 March 1968, he promised that after the 1967 war, his role must end. 'The people proved to be more powerful than the regime,' he wrote. 'The people have become bigger than the regime.'

"But everyone forgets. Once you enjoy power and the sea of quietness that comes with it, you forget. And day after day, you discover the privileges of power.

"Now we have semi-politicians who want to take advantage of this revolution. Some contenders are already promoting themselves. But the system has to be changed. The people made known what they want. They want something different. All the most modern technology in the world was used in this uprising. The people want something different."

Heikal saw me to the door of the lift, shook hands courteously, eyebrows raised. Yes, I repeated. He was right.

Robert Fisk

Wednesday, 16 February 2011

COPY-CAT COPS

After three weeks of watching the greatest Arab nation hurling a preposterous old man from power, I'm struck by something very odd.

We have been informing the world that the infection of Tunisia's revolution spread to Egypt - and that near-identical democracy protests have broken out in Yemen, Bahrain and in Algeria - but we've all missed the most salient contamination of all: that the state security police who prop up the power of the Arab world's autocrats have used the same hopeless tactics of savagery to crush demonstrators in Sanaa, Bahrain and Algiers as the Tunisian and Egyptian dictators tried so vainly to employ against their own pro-democracy protestors.

Just as the non-violent millions in Cairo learnt from Al-Jazeera and from their opposite numbers in Tunis - even down to the emails from Tunisia urging Egyptians to cut lemons in half and eat them to avoid the effects of teargas - so the state security thugs in Egypt, presumably watching the same programmes, have used precisely the same brutality against the crowds as their colleagues in Tunis. Incredible, when you come to think about it. The cops in Cairo saw the cops in Tunis bludgeoning government opponents to a bloody mess and - totally ignoring the fact that this led to Ben Ali's downfall - went into copy-cat mode.

Having had the pleasure of standing next to these state security warriors in the streets of Cairo, I can attest their tactics from personal experience. First, the uniformed police confronted the demonstrators. Then their ranks parted to allow the baltagi - the former policemen, drug-addicts and ex-prisoners - to run forward and strike the protesters with sticks, police coshes and iron crowbars. Then the criminals retreated to police lines while the cops doused the demonstrators with thousands of tear-gas canisters (again, made in the US). In the end, as I watched with considerable satisfaction, the protesters simply overwhelmed the state security men and their mafiosi.

But what happens when I turn on Al-Jazeera to see where we should travel next? On the streets of Yemen are state security police baton-charging crowds of Sanaa's pro-democracy demonstrators then parting ranks to allow plainclothes thugs to attack the protestors with sticks, police coshes, iron bars and pistols. And the moment the cop-criminals retreat, the Yemeni police douse the crowds with tear-gas rounds. A few minutes later, I am watching Algerian cops batoning the crowds, allowing plainclothes men to race forward with crowbars and coshes, then spraying tear-gas across the streets. Then Bahrain where - I don't need to tell you, do I? - cops baton the demonstrators and slop thousands of tear-gas rounds into the men and women with such promiscuity that the police themselves, overcome by the gas, retch speechless on to the road. Weird, isn't it?

But no, I suspect not. For years, the secret services of these countries have been mimicking their mates for one simple reason: because their intelligence capos have been swapping tips for years. Torture tips, too. The Egyptians learnt how to use electricity in their desert prisons far more forcefully on genitals after a friendly visit from lads based at the Chateauneuf police station in Algiers (who specialise in pumping water into men until they literally burst apart). When I was in Algiers last December, the head of Tunisian state security dropped by for a fraternal visit. Just as Algierians visited Syria back in 1994 to find out how Hafez el-Assad dealt with the 1982 Muslim uprising in Hama: simple - slaughter the people, blow up the city, leave the corpses of innocent and guilty for the survivors to see. Which is what le pouvoir then did to the vicious and armed Islamists as well as their own people.

It was infernal, this open university of torture, a constant round of conferences and first-hand "interrogation" accounts by the sadists of the Arab world, with the constant support of the Pentagon and its scandalous "strategic co-operation" manuals, not to mention the enthusiasm of Israel. But there was a vital flaw in these lectures. If the people once - just once - lost their fear, and rose up to crush their oppressors, the very system of pain and frightfulness would become its own enemy, its ferocity the very reason for its collapse. This is what happened in Tunis. This is what happened in Egypt.

It's an instructive lesson. Bahrain, Algeria and Yemen are all following the identical policies of brutality that failed Messrs Ben Ali and Mubarak. That's not the only strange parallel between the overthrow of these two titans. Mubarak really thought on Thursday night that the people would suffer another five months of his rule. Ben Ali apparently thought much the same.

What all this proves is that the dictators of the Middle East are infinitely more stupid, more vicious, more vain, more arrogant, more ridiculous than even their own people realised. Ghengis Khan and Lord Blair of Isfahan rolled into one.

Robert Fisk

TIDE OF REVOLUTION SLIPPING AWAY

Demonstrators fearful that the tide of revolution is on the ebb in Egypt staged a mass protest in Tahrir Square in Cairo yesterday to demand that a less authoritarian form of government be introduced. The protesters appeared to sense that political power is drifting away from them and the old system is reasserting itself as they gathered after Friday prayers beside the blackened hulk of the old headquarters of the ruling National Democratic Party (NDP).

"I am worried that there are so many forces against the revolution, mainly in the army," said Ahmed Maher, a 30-year-old civil engineer and coordinator of the 6 April Movement, a group that played a crucial role in organising the street protests that ended the rule of President Hosni Mubarak. He added: "By demonstrating, we are showing our anger at what is happening."

Egypt's revolution is uncertain of its identity, or even if it really was a revolution. Mr Maher would prefer radical change but does not expect it. "I realise the revolution will not bring a new Egypt," he says. "We will have better people in charge and perhaps less corruption, but not a different system."

Mr Maher, who was jailed five times and tortured severely under the old regime, does not seem too downcast at present frustrations. The shadowy Supreme Council of the Armed Forces had failed to invite any of the radical groups to a dialogue, but he thought the political situation was fluid and the army would give ground under pressure. He said: "They don't want a clash with us."

There is a tug of war between the army and protesters over the degree to which the old authoritarian state should be dismantled.

The army promises that the old Emergency Law will be abolished but not yet. Thousands of prisoners have been freed but nobody knows how many are still in jail. There are still 10-minute trials by military tribunals handing out long sentences. The media may be more free, but criticism of the military for torturing suspects remains a red line.

After all, it was the army commanders, not protesters, who forced President Mubarak to stand down. "What began as a revolution ended up as a military coup," says one foreign observer. "The generals sacrificed the regime to save the state."

One change that may be irreversible is that Egyptians, certainly in Cairo, are now politicised where they were once apathetic. Officials are no longer entirely above the law, nor are police officers who are accused of killing or injuring protesters.

The self-confidence of the protesters is waning but they recall they forced the army to move against the sclerotic regime of President Mubarak. The chant in Tahrir Square then was: "The army and people are one!" Many are now beginning to doubt this and recall that the army provided the three dictators who have ruled Egypt since 1952.

The groups demonstrating in Tahrir Square lack leaders and a political agenda. At the height of the protests, they received crucial reinforcements from the well-organised militants of the Muslim Brotherhood, Egypt's largest opposition grouping. But the Brotherhood, having got its members out of jail and wanting to maintain good relations with the army, is limiting its cooperation with its former allies. One of its leaders said: "We are not going to be extras in anybody else's movie."

The Brotherhood is itself divided on whether it should remain a secretive and highly ideological movement of militants and how far it should transform itself into a mildly Islamic party like the ruling AKP party in Turkey.

Mr Maher says he expects that the Muslim Brotherhood will get 40 per of the vote in a parliamentary election and the next President will be Amr Moussa, the current head of the Arab League, though he has long played a leading role in the old regime. He recalls that Mr Moussa made contact with him during the protests and advised compromise as the protesters fought to hold Tahrir Square.

"We broke off contact with him," Mr Maher says, "but later he rang us up and said he had been wrong."

Many protesters would prefer Mohammed El-Baradei, the former head of the International Atomic Energy Agency, as candidate to be the next president. But they are irritated by his lack of political experience in Egypt and say he is too used to living in France or Vienna.

The political players in post-Mubarak Egypt are unable, as yet, to measure their own strength or that of their rivals. The groups that organised the mass protests know they lack organisation, money, and support in the countryside where most of the 80 million Egyptians live.

They say that 25 million Egyptians have access to computers and believe, perhaps optimistically, they can quickly organise their sympathisers.

Hundreds of thousands of Yemenis yesterday staged the largest demonstrations yet to demand that the country's long-time ruler Ali Abdullah Saleh step down after 32 years. In an unprecedented move, many mosques in the capital shut down on the Muslim day of prayer as worshippers and clerics streamed outside to protest.

Patrick Cockburn

Wednesday, 25 May 2011

POLICE STATE STILL RULES

The former Egyptian president Hosni Mubarak is to be tried for conspiring to kill demonstrators whose protests brought an end to his 30-year rule.

The move by the military government is seen as an attempt to satisfy growing popular anger in Egypt at its failure to prosecute and purge members of the old regime since taking over from Mr Mubarak, 83, on 11 February.

The former dictator is being charged with the "premeditated murder of some participants in the peaceful protests of the 25 January revolution". He is also accused, along with his two sons Alaa and Gamal and a close business associate, with the abuse of power to make money. Mr Mubarak is currently detained at a hospital in the resort town of Sharm el-Sheikh, while his sons are in Tora prison. His wife Suzanne, 70, was released on bail after handing $4m (£2.5m) and a villa to the state. Charges against Mr Mubarak include accepting as gifts a palace and four villas at Sharm el-Sheikh and being part of a conspiracy to sell gas at a cheap price to Israel.

The prosecution of Mr Mubarak, his family and associates has been a central demand of the protesters who suspect the military government is planning to let them off the hook. Cairo was swept with rumours that Mr Mubarak was to benefit from an immunity deal under which he would give up part of his fortune and apologise to the Egyptian people for the failings of his regime.

A massive rally, called "Egypt's second revolution", is planned for Friday to protest at the lack of change since Mr Mubarak stepped down after at least 846 protesters had been killed. Instead, many of those taking part in subsequent protests have been jailed, beaten and given long sentences after a summary trial by a military tribunal.

"I have not seen such activity in organising a big protest in Cairo since the revolution," one reform activist said.

Protesters are particularly outraged that emergency laws have not been suspended and are demanding that, at the very least, the police and army should stop torturing people. Official brutality and misuse of arbitrary powers goes on as before, if in a somewhat more muted form. For instance, during a Coptic protest last week, one of those arrested was an electrician taking no part in the demonstration. He was detained when returning home with an electric drill which prosecutors claimed was an "offensive weapon".

Egypt is currently ruled by the Supreme Council of the Armed Forces (SCAF), a shadowy body of senior military leaders which has been very slow to dismantle the ruthless police state over which Mr Mubarak presided.

Though SCAF expressed loyalty to the uprising it has failed notably to provide medical aid to thousands injured in the protests and has given no compensation to those who lost breadwinners or businesses. The economy is in bad shape after the revolution at a time when many Egyptians have higher expectations.

Foreign-exchange reserves have been draining away from $36bn to $28bn since the start of the year, tourism earnings are down by $1bn a month, and industry is working at half capacity. Most of the construction sites in Cairo are idle.

The military government is trying to do enough to satisfy popular anger against the Mubaraks and their business cronies without paralysing economic activity or frightening off foreign investment.

Patrick Cockburn

CHAPTER 3

LIBYA SPRING

Anti-Gaddafi protest in front of Libyan embassy, Malta, 22 February 2011.

Tuesday, 22 February 2011

'THERE WILL BE CIVIL WAR'

So even the old, paranoid, crazed fox of Libya - the pallid, infantile, droopcheeked dictator from Sirte, owner of his own female praetorian guard, author of the preposterous Green Book, who once announced he would ride to a Non-Aligned Movement summit in Belgrade on his white charger - is going to ground. Or gone. Last night, the man I first saw more than three decades ago, solemnly saluting a phalanx of black-uniformed frogmen as they flappered their way across the sulphur-hot tarmac of Green Square on a torrid night in Tripoli during a seven hour military parade, appeared to be on the run at last, pursued like the dictators of Tunis and Cairo - by his own furious people.

The YouTube and Facebook pictures told the story with a grainy, fuzzed reality, fantasy turned to fire and burning police stations in Benghazi and Tripoli, to corpses and angry, armed men, of a woman with a pistol leaning from a car door, of a crowd of students - were they readers of his literature? - breaking down a concrete replica of his ghastly book. Gunfire and flames and cellphone screams; quite an epitaph for a regime we all, from time to time, supported.

And here, just to lock our minds on to the brain of truly eccentric desire, is a true story. Only a few days ago, as Colonel Muammar Gaddafi faced the wrath of his own people, he met with an old Arab acquaintance and spent 20 minutes out of four hours asking him if he knew of a good surgeon to lift his face. This is - need I say it about this man? - a true story. The old boy looked bad, sagging face, bloated, simply "magnoon" (mad), a comedy actor who had turned to serious tragedy in his last days, desperate for the last make-up lady, the final knock on the theatre door.

In the event, Saif al-Islam al-Gaddafi, faithful understudy for his father, had to stand in for him on stage as Benghazi and Tripoli burned, threatening "chaos and civil war" if Libyans did not come to heel. "Forget oil, forget gas," this wealthy nincompoop announced. "There will be civil war."

Above the beloved son's head on state television, a green Mediterranean appeared to ooze from his brain. Quite an obituary, when you come to think of it, of nearly 42 years of Gaddafi rule.

Not exactly King Lear, who would "do such things - what they are, yet I know not, but they shall be the terrors of the earth"; more like another dictator in a different bunker, summoning up non-existent armies to save him in his capital, ultimately blaming his own people for his calamity. But forget Hitler. Gaddafi was in a class of his own, Mickey Mouse and Prophet, Batman and Clark Gable and Anthony Quinn playing Omar Mukhtar in Lion of the Desert, Nero and Mussolini (the 1920s version) and, inevitably - the greatest actor of them all - Muammar Gaddafi. He wrote a book - appropriately titled in his present unfortunate circumstances - called Escape to Hell and Other

Stories and demanded a one state solution to the Israeli-Palestinian conflict which would be called "Israeltine".

Shortly thereafter, he threw half the Palestinian residents of Libya out of his country and told them to walk home to their lost land. He stormed out of the Arab League because he deemed it irrelevant - a brief moment of sanity there, one has to admit - and arrived in Cairo for a summit, deliberately confusing a lavatory door with that of the conference chamber until led aside by the Caliph Mubarak who had a thin, suffering smile on his face.

And if what we are witnessing is a true revolution in Libya, then we shall soon be able - unless the Western embassy flunkies get there first for a spot of serious, desperate looting - to rifle through the Tripoli files and read the Libyan version of Lockerbie and the 1989 UTA Flight 722 plane bombing; and of the Berlin disco bombings, for which a host of Arab civilians and Gaddafi's own adopted daughter were killed in America's 1986 revenge raids; and of his IRA arms supplies and of his assassination of opponents at home and abroad, and of the murder of a British policewoman, and of his invasion of Chad and the deals with British oil magnates; and (woe betide us all at this point) of the truth behind the grotesque deportation of the soon-to-expire al-Megrahi, the supposed Lockerbie bomber too ill to die, who may, even now, reveal some secrets which the Fox of Libya - along with Gordon Brown and the Attorney General for Scotland, for all are equal on the Gaddafi world stage - would rather we didn't know about.

And who knows what the Green Book Archives - and please, O insurgents of Libya, do NOT in thy righteous anger burn these priceless documents - will tell us about Lord Blair's supine visit to this hideous old man; an addled figure whose "statesmanlike" gesture (the words, of course, come from that old Marxist fraud Jack Straw, when the author of Escape to Hell promised to hand over the nuclear nicknacks which his scientists had signally failed to turn into a bomb) allowed our own faith-based Leader to claim that, had we not smitten the Saddamites with our justified anger because of their own non-existent weapons of mass destruction, Libya, too, would have joined the Axis of Evil.

Alas, Lord Blair paid no heed to the Gaddafi "whoops" factor, a unique ability to pose as a sane man while secretly believing oneself - like miss-a-heart-beat Omar Suleiman in Cairo - to be a light bulb. Only days after the Blair handshake, the Saudis accused Gaddafi of plotting

- and the details, by the way, were horribly convincing - to murder Britain's ally, King Abdullah of Saudi Arabia. But why be surprised when the man most feared and now most mocked and hated by his own vengeful people wrote, in the aforesaid Escape to Hell that Christ's crucifixion was a historical falsehood and that - as here I say again, a faint ghost of truth does very occasionally adhere to Gaddafi's ravings - a German "Fourth Reich" was lording it over Britain and America? Reflecting on death in this thespian work, he asks if the Grim Reaper is male or female. The leader of the Great Libyan Arab People's Popular Masses, needless to say, seemed to favour the latter.

As with all Middle East stories, a historical narrative precedes the dramatic pageant of Gaddafi's fall. For decades, his opponents tried to kill him; they rose up as nationalists, as prisoners in his torture chambers, as Islamists on the streets of - yes! - Benghazi. And he smote them all down. Indeed, this venerable city had already achieved its martyrdom status in 1979 when Gaddafi publicly hanged dissident students in Benghazi's main square. I am not even mentioning the 1993 disappearance of Libyan human rights defender Mansour al-Kikhiya while attending a Cairo conference after complaining about Gaddafi's execution of political prisoners. And it is important to remember that, 42 years ago, our own Foreign Office welcomed Gaddafi's coup against the effete and corrupt King Idriss because, said our colonial mandarins, it was better to have a spick-and-span colonel in charge of an oil state than a relic of imperialism. Indeed, they showed almost as much enthusiasm as they did for this decaying despot when Lord Blair arrived in Tripoli decades later for the laying on of hands.

As a Libyan opposition group told us years ago - we didn't care about these folks then, of course - "Gaddafi would have us believe he is at the vanguard of every human development that has emerged during his lifetime".

All true, if now reduced to sub-Shakespearean farce. My kingdom for a facelift. At that non-aligned summit in Belgrade, Gaddafi even flew in a planeload of camels to provide him with fresh milk. But he was not allowed to ride his white charger. Tito saw to that. Now there was a real dictator .

Robert Fisk

Wednesday, 23 February 2011

GO DOWN FIGHTING

So he will go down fighting. That's what Muammar Gaddafi told us last night, and most Libyans believe him. This will be no smooth flight to Riyadh or a gentle trip to a Red Sea holiday resort. Raddled, cowled in desert gowns, he raved on.

He had not even begun to use bullets against his enemies - a palpable lie - and "any use of force against the authority of the state shall be punished by death", in itself a palpable truth which Libyans knew all too well without the future tense of Gaddafi's threat. On and on and on he ranted. Like everything Gaddafi, it was very impressive - but went on far too long.

He cursed the people of Benghazi who had already liberated their city - "just wait until the police return to restore order", this desiccated man promised without a smile. His enemies were Islamists, the CIA, the British and the "dogs" of the international press. Yes, we are always dogs, aren't we? I was long ago depicted in a Bahraini newspaper cartoon (Crown Prince, please note) as a rabid dog, worthy of liquidation. But like Gaddafi's speeches, that's par for the course. And then came my favourite bit of the whole Gaddafi exegesis last night: HE HADN'T EVEN BEGUN TO USE VIOLENCE YET!

So let's erase all the YouTubes and Facebooks and the shooting and blood and gouged corpses from Benghazi, and pretend it didn't happen. Let's pretend that the refusal to give visas to foreign correspondents has actually prevented us from hearing the truth. Gaddafi's claim that the protesters in Libya - the millions of demonstrators - "want to turn Libya into an Islamic state" is exactly the same nonsense that Mubarak peddled before the end in Egypt, the very same nonsense that Obama and La Clinton have suggested. Indeed, there were times last night when Gaddafi - in his vengefulness, his contempt for Arabs, for his own people - began to sound very like the speeches of Benjamin Netanyahu. Was there some contact between these two rogues, one wondered, that we didn't know about?

In many ways, Gaddafi's ravings were those of an old man, his fantasies about his enemies - "rats who have taken tablets" who included "agents of Bin Laden" - were as disorganised as the scribbled notes on the piece of paper he held in his right hand, let alone the green-covered volume of laws from which he kept quoting. It was not about love. It was about the threat of execution. "Damn those" trying to stir unrest against Libya. It was a plot, an international conspiracy. "Your children are dying - but for what?" He would fight "until the last drop of my blood with the Libyan people is behind me". America was the enemy (much talk of Fallujah), Israel was the enemy, Sadat was an enemy, colonial fascist Italy was the enemy. Among the heroes and friends was Gaddafi's grandfather, "who fell a martyr in 1911" against the Italian enemy.

Dressed in brown burnous and cap and gown, Gaddafi's appearance last night raised some odd questions. Having kept the international media - the "dogs" in question - out of Libya, he allowed the world to observe a crazed nation: YouTube and blogs of terrible violence versus state television pictures of an entirely unhinged dictator justifying what he had either not seen on YouTube or hadn't been shown. And there's an interesting question here: dictators and princes who let the international press into their countries - Messrs Ben Ali/Mubarak/Saleh/Prince Salman - are permitting it to film their own humiliation. Their reward is painful indeed. But sultans like Gaddafi who keep the journos out fare little different.

The hand-held immediacy of the mobile phone, the intimacy of sound and the crack of gunfire are in some ways more compelling than the edited, digital film of the networks. Exactly the same happened in Gaza when the Israelis decided, Gaddafi-like, to keep foreign journalists out of their 2009 bloodletting: the bloggers and YouTubers (and Al Jazeera) simply gave us a reality we didn't normally experience from the "professional" satellite boys. Perhaps, in the end, it takes a dictator with his own monopoly on cameras to tell the truth. "I will die as a martyr," Gaddafi said last night. Almost certainly true.

Robert Fisk

Thursday, 24 February 2011

FLEEING TRIPOLI

Up to 15,000 men, women and children besieged Tripoli's international airport last night, shouting and screaming for seats on the few airliners still prepared to fly to Muammar Gaddafi's rump state, paying Libyan police bribe after bribe to reach the ticket desks in a rain-soaked mob of hungry, desperate families. Many were trampled as Libyan security men savagely beat those who pushed their way to the front.

Among them were Gaddafi's fellow Arabs, thousands of them Egyptians, some of whom had been living at the airport for two days without food or sanitation. The place stank of faeces and urine and fear. Yet a 45-minute visit into the city for a new airline ticket to another destination is the only chance to see Gaddafi's capital if you are a "dog" of the international press.

There was little sign of opposition to the Great Leader. Squads of young men with Kalashnikov rifles stood on the side roads next to barricades of upturned chairs and wooden doors. But these were pro-Gaddafi vigilantes - a faint echo of the armed Egyptian "neighbourhood guard" I saw in Cairo a month ago - and had pinned photographs of their leader's infamous Green Book to their checkpoint signs.

There is little food in Tripoli, and over the city there fell a blanket of drab, sullen rain. It guttered onto an empty Green Square and down the Italianate streets of the old capital of Tripolitania. But there were no tanks, no armoured personnel carriers, no soldiers, not a fighter plane in the air; just a few police and elderly men and women walking the pavements - a numbed populous. Sadly for the West and for the people of the free city of Benghazi, Libya's capital appeared as quiet as any dictator would wish.

But this is an illusion. Petrol and food prices have trebled; entire towns outside Tripoli have been torn apart by fighting between pro- and anti-Gaddafi forces. In the suburbs of the city, especially in the Noufreen district, militias fought for 24 hours on Sunday with machine guns and pistols, a battle the Gadaffi forces won. In the end, the exodus of expatriates will do far more than street warfare to bring down the regime.

I was told that at least 30,000 Turks, who make up the bulk of the Libyan construction and engineering industry, have now fled the capital, along with tens of thousands of other foreign workers.

On my own aircraft out of Tripoli, an evacuation flight to Europe, there were Polish, German, Japanese and Italian businessmen, all of whom told me they had closed down major companies in the past week. Worse still for Gaddafi, the oil, chemical and uranium fields of Libya lie to the south of "liberated" Benghazi.

Gaddafi's hungry capital controls only water resources, so a temporary division of Libya, which may have entered Gaddafi's mind, would not be sustainable.

Libyans and expatriates I spoke to yesterday said they thought he was clinically insane, but they expressed more anger at his son, Saif al-Islam. "We thought Saif was the new light, the 'liberal'", a Libyan businessman sad to me. "Now we realise he is crazier and more cruel than his father."

The panic that has now taken hold in what is left of Gaddafi's Libya was all too evident at the airport. In the crush of people fighting for tickets, one man, witnessed by an evacuated Tokyo car dealer, was beaten so viciously on the head that "his face fell apart".

Talking to Libyans in Tripoli and expatriates at the airport, it is clear that neither tanks nor armour were used in the streets of Tripoli. Air attacks targeted Benghazi and other towns, but not the capital. Yet all spoke of a wave of looting and arson by Libyans who believed that with the fall of Benghazi, Gaddafi was finished and the country open to anarchy.

The centre of the city was largely closed up. All foreign offices have been shut including overseas airlines, and every bakery I saw was shuttered. If Rumours abound that members of Gaddafi's family are trying to flee abroad. Although William Hague's ramblings about Gaddafi's flight to Venezuela have been disproved, I spoke to a number of Libyans who believed that Burkina Faso might be his only viable retreat. Two nights ago, a Libyan private jet approached Beirut airport with a request to land but was refused permission when the crew declined to identify their eight passengers. And last night, a Libyan Arab Airlines flight reported by Al-Jazeera to be carrying Gaddafi's daughter was refused permission to land in Malta.

Gaddafi is blamed by Shia Muslims in Lebanon, Iraq and Iran for the murder of Imam Moussa Sadr, a supposedly charismatic divine who unwisely accepted an invitation to visit Gaddafi in 1978 and, after an apparent argument about money, was never seen again. Nor was a Lebanese journalist accompanying him on the trip.

While dark humour has never been a strong quality in Libyans, there was one moment at Tripoli airport yesterday which proved it does exist. An incoming passenger from a Libyan Arab Airlines flight at the front of an immigration queue bellowed out: "And long life to our great leader Muammar Gaddafi." Then he burst into laughter - and the immigration officers did the same.

Robert Fisk

Sunday, 3 April 2011

RAG-TAG MILITIAMEN

In the restaurant of the Amal Africa hotel in Ajdabiya south of Benghazi, waiters have started to ask journalists to pay their bills before they eat. This urgency on the part of the hotel management reflects their bitter experience seeing journalists - their only customers - abandon meals half-eaten and leave, bills unpaid, because of a sudden and unexpected advance by the pro-Gaddafi forces. It is a bizarre little war. For several weeks, the world has watched a motley force of rebel militiamen and a so-far-unseen, but probably quite small, government force, race to-and-fro on the main road south of Benghazi. The frontline reporting is brave but gives the impression that this is a regular military campaign. In television studios and in newspapers, arrows on maps show the advance and retreat of pocket-sized forces over vast distances (the Libyan coastline is 2,000km long) as if the Afrika Corps and the 8th Army were battling it out. They capture and recapture "strategic oil ports" and places that are just a scattering of houses.

Since yesterday, rebel fighters without training or weapons, together with the foreign media, are being sternly forbidden from driving to the frontline. It must have become obvious to the rebel leaders in Benghazi that television pictures of their forces - essentially untrained gunmen in their pickups looking like extras from a Mad Max film - were damaging the credibility of the rebel cause in Europe and the US.

The new propaganda line of the rebels' Transitional National Council is that professional soldiers, who have turned against Gaddafi over the last 40 years, will now take command and, in the words of one television reporter, "lick into shape the rag-tag militiamen".

But the new military leadership, which Britain, France and to a decreasing extent the US, will be supporting, inspires even less confidence than their men. The careers of several make them sound like characters out of the more sinister Graham Greene novels. They include men such as Colonel Khalifa Haftar, former commander of the Libyan army in Chad who was captured and changed sides in 1988, setting up the anti-Gaddafi Libyan National Army reportedly with CIA and Saudi backing. For the last 20 years, he has been living quietly in Virginia before returning to Benghazi to lead the fight against Gaddafi.

Even shadier is the background of Abdul Hakeen al-Hassadi, a Libyan who fought against the US in Afghanistan, was arrested in Pakistan, imprisoned probably at Bagram, Afghanistan, and then mysteriously released. The US Deputy Secretary of State, James Steinberg, told Congressmen he would speak of Mr Hassadi's career only in a closed session. It is these characters, and others like them, whom Britain is now fighting to install in Tripoli to replace Colonel Gaddafi. The accusation of Peter Galbraith, the deputy head of the UN mission in Afghanistan, later sacked, was that the crippling weakness of the US was that it had "no credible local partner in Afghanistan." This is true in trumps in Libya.

The Libyan militiamen look like a rabble even by the lowly standards of militias in Lebanon, Iraq and Afghanistan. They could only be effective if they were given enough training to act with foreign special forces calling in tactical air strikes every time they face an obstacle. This is what happened in Afghanistan in 2001 and northern Iraq in 2003.

Even well-organised militias are dangerous to do business with because they are prone to paranoia, believing they have been sniped at or spied on by some innocent civilian. I remember, during a war between Druze and Christians south of Beirut in 1983, trying to persuade a Druze fighter that a toasting fork he had found in a house was not specially designed to out the eyes of Druze prisoners. So strong were his suspicions that he had been planning to shoot the Christian householders.

There is still something extraordinary about the alacrity with which Britain has plunged into the dangerous but also comic opera world of Libyan politics. And it has done so despite the recent examples in Iraq and Afghanistan of what can go wrong when you join somebody else's civil war - for that is what we have done, despite all the demonising of Gaddafi and glorification of his opponents.

Life in Libya always seems to have a farcical but dangerous element to it. The first time I went in the early 1980s was to see the

Libyan army withdraw from Chad. Somewhere in the southern desert, the vehicle I was in ran out of petrol in the middle of a minefield where we were stuck for hours. Later I was taken to see a model farm in an oasis which turned out to be abandoned. The only inhabitants were little green frogs hopping happily about amid the broken pipes and water-logged palm trees.

For many years, Gaddafi's aides, responding to the latest whim of the leader, would invite the foreign press over to interview him. These interviews seldom took place, and journalists would sit discontentedly in hotels waiting for their editors to let them go home. I found the best antidote to boredom was thick 19th century novels. To this day, Tripoli makes me think of Jane Austen, most of whose books I read lying on a bed in the Libya Palace Hotel.

The mistake in Libya was ever to become involved in trying to impose a no-fly zone. This was only going to have an effect if it turned into a nodrive zone, and this works best when the enemy is unwary enough to drive around in tanks and armoured vehicles and rely on heavy artillery that can be destroyed from the air.

If foreign military force was to be used to save the people of Benghazi from massacre, it would have been better to impose a ceasefire from the beginning. This would have to be policed by foreign forces, but it was and is an achievable aim. It is politically more neutral and avoids charges of reborn imperialism. It has not happened because the not-so-covert aim from the start was to get rid of Gaddafi.

One advantage of Libya is that the failings became obvious quickly. Never has "mission creep" crept so fast. The failings of local allies are more obvious more quickly in Libya than they were in Baghdad or Kabul. The difficulty in breaking the military stalemate opens the door to a ceasefire agreement and a resort to political and economic pressure to displace Gaddafi rather than the present illconsidered war.

Patrick Cockburn

Friday, 8 April 2011

NATO MISTAKES

The difficult relationship between Nato forces and the Libyan rebels came under further strain yesterday after Western aircraft killed

13 fighters and injured many more in a mistaken attack on rebel tanks.

The incident, the third in recent days in which Nato have hit the wrong side, caused widespread anger in Ajdabiya among rebels, many of whom also believe that the western air strikes should have begun sooner and gone further. And it led to further recriminations between the Benghazi rebel leadership and the coalition authorities.

The hospital in Ajdabiya has accepted a stream of the dead and the maimed from this savage civil war, civilian and military, most of them victims of regime forces. But the bodies which arrived yesterday were the result of "friendly fire". They were revolutionaries who had been hit in the air strikes, 30km from Brega, on the main road which has become a battleground in the eastern front.

Rebel fighters wept as they hugged each other kneeling on the floor of a corridor with bloodstained uniforms piled up in the corner. Along with the grief there was deep anger, directed not this time at Muammar Gaddafi, but the west, for the massacre of their comrades. A militiaman in a coma with severe burns all over his body, his face half-hidden by a thick layer of white anti-septic cream, was carried into Ajdabiya by other fighters shouting in anger and in grief. In another area, Yasin Ibadullah had just seen what remained of another victim, his friend Saleh Mohammed Ali and he was in no mood to hear about the problems pilots may have in finding targets in a fluctuating frontline. "They have all the equipment, all the technology, we haven't got them," he shouted. "They must have seen we were going forward, we were attacking, we were going forward. Why did they do this? Do they want Gaddafi to win?" The soldiers were not the only ones to express their anger at the botched attack. Dr Suleiman Rifadi, studying an X-ray of one the wounded, asked: "Instead of attacking us, why don't they bomb the Gaddafi troops?" Earlier yesterday, the rebels had brought up flat-bed trucks carrying tanks and vehicles with multiple rocket launchers on the back. This seems to have been part of a general move to steady the front line between Ajdabiya and the oil town of Brega. Guards at the last checkpoint out of Ajdabiya on the road to Brega were turning back fighters who had not been authorised. Some refugees were still coming from the south with cheap possessions including blankets and white plastic chairs piled in the back of pick-ups.

The arrival of the reinforcements immediately led to a disaster. Nato pilots presumably thought that all tanks and armoured vehicles in this highly contested area two hours drive south of Benghazi must be fighting for the Libyan government.

The first sign that something was wrong came when militiamen hurriedly cleared the road at the southern entrance to Ajdabiya, which is marked by an arch looking like a MacDonald's sign. Ambulances coming from the direction of Brega raced through with gunmen in pick-ups shouting that they had been bombed.

As has often been the case in this conflict, there was confusion about what led up to the pulverising bombing.

Some of the rebels, known as the Shabaab, said they were going towards the city, under regime control after changing hands several times. There was also a sudden retreat, a recurring feature of this campaign, and some of the vehicles incinerated in the attack were facing east towards opposition held-Ajdabiya.

It is not the first such incident. Last Saturday 13 Shabaab fighters were killed 10 miles along the same road after Nato jets, believed to be A-10 Warthog tankbusters, responded to "celebratory firing" from an anti-aircraft gun into the air with missile launches. Three vehicles, including an ambulance, were destroyed. It is to precisely prevent such "collateral damage", that a British military team is currently in Benghazi putting in a secure communications system between Benghazi and Nato headquarters at Mons in Belgium.

The revolutionaries have reached an agreement with Nato to paint the top of their vehicle yellow to be identified as "friendly forces". A Shabaab commander, Mustafa Gadr, claimed this has been adhered to by his fighters. But while some cars have giant red, black and green flags tied to their roofs, there is little evidence of the yellow markings in the field among the dozens of cars and trucks, most of them privately owned, which pour forward every day.

But the rebels had little time for such explanations. "This time there was no one firing at anything in the sky, so they could not have thought that they were under attack," said Ahmed Misani, a 33-year-old engineer fighting for the revolution. "They could not have thought that we were Gaddafi men. We would like to know what they [the pilots] were thinking when they dropped those bombs. They would not see the children of the men who died. We would like to know what we should tell them."

One series of attacks for which Nato was absolved of blame by the rebel government were at oilfields at Sarir and Messala, south of

Ajdabiya. The Tripoli regime had claimed RAF planes had targeted the field causing extensive damage. The head of the Nato mission, Lieu-tenant-General Charles Bouchard said: "We are aware that pro-Gaddafi forces have attacked this area in recent days. To try to blame it on Nato shows how desperate the regime is."

The rebel government has just exported a million barrels of oil with a tanker leaving Tobruk on Wednesday evening. Abdel Hafidh Ghoga, spokesman for the opposition's provisional government, said: "These are attempts by Gaddafi's regime to strangle our economy."

Patrick Cockburn

Sunday, 10 April 2011

THE ROAD BETWEEN AJDABIYA AND BENGHAZI

People in Benghazi are becoming increasingly frightened of a sec-ond attempt by pro-Gaddafi forces to take the city. For all the propaganda slogans about overthrowing the dictator, it is beginning to occur to many that Nato airpower is not quite the recipe for survival and victory they thought it was a few weeks back.

A good place to judge the balance of forces between Gaddafi and the rebels last week was the western entrance to the deserted town of Ajdabiya, south of Benghazi. The place is marked by a high archway and a wrecked cement sentry box containing scraps of rotting food. On its broken walls are pasted sad pictures of young men who have gone missing, with the phone numbers of their families underneath. We arrived mid-morning, having been warned that it was a mistake to get there too early: rebel fighters could still be asleep and it was possible to drive straight through the rebel lines, without knowing they were there, and into the frontline of the pro-Gaddafi troops.

This was an exaggeration. Some rebel soldiers in uniform were turning back militiamen and journalists, to the irritation of both. The soldiers cleared the road for giant flatbed trucks going up to the front with vehicle-mounted Katyusha rocket launchers and a lethal-looking contraption welded to the back of a truck which is, in fact, a rocket firing pod that is normally fitted to the underside of aircraft. In the other direction a couple of dozen flat-bed trucks were coming back from the front to which they had delivered some 20 tanks earlier in the morning.

There was an atmosphere of friendly confusion, like the meeting of a local fox hunt, because we imagined that the frontline was far down the road towards the oil town of Brega. It turned out to be a lot closer than that. Suddenly white civilian ambulances raced past us. A soldier in one of them shouted they had been bombed. He did not say by whom, but we assumed it was another Nato "friendly fire" mistake.

Soon there were plumes of smoke in the distance as four or five shells or rockets landed. Militiamen started streaming back towards Ajdabiya.

We stopped at a small hospital there where doctors have become used to examining patients while giving media interviews. They were full of self-righteous and not entirely reasonable rage about Nato bombing the rebels and not Gaddafi's men. Any event in eastern Libya at the moment can become the occasion for a political rally. In this case the reception of the wounded as they were carried from the ambulances into the hospital was delayed by political speeches and chants of "God is great". Nor did the ordeal of the wounded end there. In hospitals throughout the Middle East, families and friends consider they have a divine right to visit patients.

In Ajdabiya hospital, sobbing soldiers crowded into a ward so that stretcher-bearers could hardly get in.

Angry doctors manhandled the grieving fighters out of the room for a few minutes before they burst in again.

The Nato attack on the rebel tanks turned out to be much as the first survivors had described it. The rebels had moved up tanks, ageing Libyan army T-54s that had been in storage for 30 years and half a dozen more modern T-72 tanks. They claim they had told Nato but it seems likely, given the general chaos in Benghazi, that they did not. Not surprisingly, the Nato pilots assumed that the tanks must belong to the government.

The incident on the Ajdabiya-Brega road is important because it shows that the rebels are not going to be a serious fighting force for months and possibly not even then. David Cameron and Nicolas Sarkozy have entered a war into which they will inevitably be sucked deeper because the rebel enclave around Benghazi is completely dependent on outside military support.

The Gaddafi forces show ominous signs of adapting faster than their enemies.

They fire accurate artillery barrages and attack out of the desert in the same sort of pick-up vehicles as the rebels. What holds them back is that they are at the end of long supply lines and they do not have enough men to hold the ground they take.

The same is true of the anti-Gaddafi fighters. Though there are plenty of people willing to demonstrate in Benghazi there are surprisingly few militiamen at the front. These are often derided by the foreign press for their military ineptitude or lack of experience, but what is most striking is that there are not enough of them.

The roadside from Benghazi is littered with the burned-out remains of tanks and trucks dating from the last time Gaddafi came close to capturing the city. He may not try to do so again and, if he does, it will probably be in vehicles that are the same as those used by the rebels. If the Gaddafi forces do advance, there is nothing much to stop them.

On the road between Ajdabiya and Benghazi, there are no fallback positions.

If the front does cave in, Nato aircraft will have to try to tell a dirty white Gaddafi pick-up with machine gun in the back from a dirty white prodemocracy pick-up similarly armed.

Back in Benghazi away from the chaos of the front, this is not the picture the rebel military commanders want to give. At a press conference, the joint Chief of Staff General Abdul Fattah Younis, former head of Gaddafi's special forces, seeks to give the impression that all is under control. Asked about the Nato bombing of the tanks, he says that "accidents happen in war". He describes the panicked flight of militiamen as a military manoeuvre to throw back a temporary advance by Gaddafi's troops.

General Younis's air of calm is very soothing, and many in Benghazi who have not been near the frontline wish to believe that what he says is true. Libyan reporters clapped and cheered when he said that the rebels had not and would not accept foreign advisers. But this bravado may not last very long. Iman Bugaighis, a Newcastletrained lecturer in orthodontics at Benghazi University turned rebel spokeswoman, said "we ask them to use attack helicopters" at least in the besieged city of Misrata.

There is an undercurrent of fear in Benghazi, and it would not take much to start a panic. Libyans are beginning to learn the ways of survival well known in countries such as Iraq and Lebanon, where war frequently turns part of the population into refugees. The Kurds, with grim experience of taking flight, have a saying: "If you are going to run, then run early." Wait too long and you cannot get out.

Patrick Cockburn

Thursday, 14 April 2011

FRANCE AND BRITAIN COMMITTED TO REMOVING GADDAFI

Britain and France are asking other members of Nato to step up air strikes on Libyan government forces at a meeting of foreign ministers in Qatar that has underlined the radically different policies of the countries involved in the Libyan crisis.

Divisions between the foreign ministers were also evident over issues such as using frozen Libyan state assets to fund the opposition in eastern Libya and the feasibility of arming the rebels. Germany expressed doubts about the legality of using money belonging to the Libyan government. The divisions spring primarily from the differing objectives of the Nato, Arab and African foreign ministers. Though military intervention by France and Britain was first justified as being for the defence of civilians, in practice they are committed to overthrowing Muammar Gaddafi and his regime.

The opposition Transitional National Government based in Benghazi is insisting that it will not negotiate without the departure of Colonel Gaddafi and his family, but it has scanty military resources. It is only Nato air strikes that are preventing the rebels from being overrun.

French foreign minister, Alain Juppé, criticised Nato for not carrying out enough air strikes to stop the shelling of the besieged city of Misrata. William Hague, the Foreign Secretary, said aircraft from other states must join attacks: "There are many other nations around Europe and indeed Arab nations who are part of this coalition. There is scope for some of them to move some of their aircraft from air defence into ground-strike capability."

The eagerness of Britain and France to increase the pressure on Colonel Gaddafi was underscored by the announcement yesterday that David Cameron was traveling to Paris last night to discuss the Libyan conflict with President Sarkozy. The meeting is a day before Nato members are scheduled to meet in Berlin. Rebel leaders at the meeting in Doha say they want more air attacks and claim Nato is using "minimum" power and should escalate attacks on heavy weapons used by regime forces. Last night Nato confirmed that its planes had attacked a munitions dump, 13km from the Libyan capital Tripoli.

The rebels can only put a few thousand barely trained militiamen into the field, and even an escalation of the air war would not tip the military balance towards them. "Getting armed is not our priority," said Ali El-Essawi, the foreign minister of the National Council, acknowledging that the coalition is not going to supply arms in large quantities.

Mr Hague called for a temporary financial mechanism to support the rebel administration in eastern Libya. The rebels say they need $1.5bn and Italy suggested using frozen Libyan state assets.

But the German foreign minister Guido Westerwelle criticised this move, asking: "The question is, is it legal? The answer is we don't know."

The rebels have in the past insisted that one of their problems is that they do not have heavy weapons, but they do not have anybody trained to use them. After his unsuccessful war in Chad in the 1980s, Colonel Gaddafi largely dissolved the Libyan army so there is no cadre of military specialists to go to the front or train new recruits. At the 17th February Camp in Benghazi some 3,000 men are receiving instruction, but most of this is "theoretical" according to officers and includes only a few days of weapons' practice.

The presence of Moussa Koussa, the former Libyan foreign minister who defected to Britain, on the margins of the Doha conference has so far had little impact. The rebels refuse to speak to him and it is unclear how far he represents any constituency among senior Libyan officials around Colonel Gaddafi who might want to get rid of their leader.

Libyan opposition spokesman Mahmud Awad Shammam said the national council approved of a Turkish plan for a peaceful transition in Libya, but "they have to say the magic word - that Gaddafi must go".

In Tripoli, government spokesman Mussa Ibrahim attacked the West's "imperialist way of thinking", which he claimed was trying to determine the future of Libya.

Patrick Cockburn

OLDSTYLE IMPERIAL VENTURE

Flames billow up from the hulks of eight Libyan navy vessels destroyed by Nato air attacks as they lay in ports along the Libyan coast. Their destruction shows how Colonel Muammar Gaddafi is being squeezed militarily, but also the degree to which the US, France and Britain, and not the Libyan rebels, are now the main players in the struggle for power in Libya.

Probably Gaddafi will ultimately go down because he is too weak to withstand the forces arrayed against him. Failure to end his regime would be too humiliating and politically damaging for Nato after 2,700 air strikes. But, as with the capture of Baghdad in 2003, the fall of the regime may usher in a new round of a long-running Libyan crisis that continues for years to come.

It has all developed rather differently from what the French and British appear to have imagined when they first intervened in March to save the citizens of Benghazi from Gaddafi's advancing tanks. If this was their sole aim, the air strikes were successful. The roadside from Benghazi to Ajdabiya is still littered with the carcasses of burned-out armoured vehicles. But months after William Hague was suggesting that Gaddafi was already en route for Venezuela he is still in Tripoli.

Three months after the start of the Libyan uprising Gaddafi's troops have failed to capture Misrata, but the rebels do not look capable of advancing towards Tripoli. They have broken the siege of Misrata partly because their militiamen now clutch hand radios and can call in Nato air strikes. This close air support is effective and is along the lines of the tactical air support given by the US to the Northern Alliance soldiers in Afghanistan in 2001 and the Kurdish peshmerga fighters in northern Iraq two years later. The Libyan government and opposition forces are both weak. The fighting forces that have been clashing on the desert road between Brega and Ajdabiya, south of Benghazi, often number no more than a few hundred half-trained fighters. Gaddafi's troops, with which he tries to control this vast country, number only 10,000 to 15,000. This is not always obvious to anybody who is not an eyewitness because the foreign media on the spot is bashful about mentioning that there are sometimes more journalists than fighters at the front.

One dispiriting outcome of the Libyan uprising is that the future of Libya is decreasingly likely to be determined by Libyans. Foreign intervention is turning into an oldstyle imperial venture. Much the same thing happened in Iraq in 2003 and in Afghanistan in the past few years. In Iraq, the US invasion to overthrow Saddam Hussein, a ruler detested by most Iraqis, soon turned into what many Iraqis saw as a foreign occupation.

As in Iraq and Afghanistan, the weakness of France and Britain is their lack of a local partner who is as powerful and representative as they pretend. In the rebel capital Benghazi there is little sign of the leaders of the transitional national council, which is scarcely surprising, because so much of their time is spent in Paris and London. In Washington, the White House was a little more cautious last week when Mahmoud Jibril, the interim Libyan prime minister, and other council members came to bolster their credibility and hopefully get some financial support. More circumspectly, the Libyan rebel leaders were there to allay American suspicions that the Libyan opposition is not quite as cuddly as it claims and includes al-Qa'ida sympathisers waiting their chance to seize power.

The Libyan opposition may be weak but is not quite so naive or inexperienced as it sometimes appears. Its leaders are quick to play down eastern Libya's tradition of militant Islam. In the town of Al Bayda, on the long road from the Egyptian frontier to Benghazi, I saw a large notice in French addressed to any passing foreigners, denying any link with al-Qa'ida. This is largely but not entirely true. One Libyan observer in Benghazi explained: "The only people in this part of the country who have any recent military experience are those who were fighting the Americans in Afghanistan, so of course we send them to the front."

Wars often widen and deepen existing fissures in a society. The rebel transitional national council likes to play down suggestions that it is primarily a movement from Cyrenaica, the great bulge of eastern Libya where Gaddafi has always been unpopular. But he has held on to most of western Libya. Today these two halves of Libya, separated by hundreds of miles of desert, increasingly feel like separate countries.

Libyans on the ground have fewer inhibitions about discussing these differences.

Outside some beach huts in Benghazi used to house refugees, I spoke to oil workers from the oil port of Brega, a town of about 4,000, who had fled when Gaddafi's forces captured it. A manager from the gas fields said: "Gaddafi's people got hold of a book with all our names because they wanted to see who came from east Libya and in their eyes would naturally be a rebel."

Of course, Gaddafi's opponents don't just come from the east. It is fair to assume that most Libyans from all parts of the country want him to go.

He clings on because he rules through his family, clan, tribe and allied tribes, combined with his ebbing control of the ramshackle Libyan government and military machine. Everything within the part of Libya he still controls depends on Gaddafi personally. Once he goes there will be a political vacuum that the opposition will scarcely be able to fill.

Could the war be ended earlier by negotiation? Here, again, the problem is the weakness of the organised opposition. If they have the backing of enhanced Nato military involvement they can take power. Without it, they can't. They therefore have every incentive to demand that Gaddafi goes as a precondition for a ceasefire and negotiations. Since only Gaddafi can deliver a ceasefire and meaningful talks, this means the war will be fought to a finish. The departure of Gaddafi should be the aim of negotiations not their starting point.

One surprising aspect of the conflict so far is that there has not been a greater effort to involve Algeria and Egypt, the two most powerful states in North Africa. This would make the departure of Gaddafi easier to negotiate and would make the whole Libyan adventure look less like West European imperialism reborn. The aim of Nato intervention was supposedly to limit civilian casualties, but its leaders have blundered into a political strategy that makes a prolonged conflict and heavy civilian loss of life inevitable.

Patrick Cockburn

THE PRESS IN LIBYA

In the first months of the Arab Spring, foreign journalists got well-merited credit for helping to foment and publicise popular uprisings against the region's despots. Satellite TV stations such as Al Jazeera Arabic, in particular, struck at the roots of power in Arab police states, by making official censorship irrelevant and by competing successfully against government propaganda.

Regimes threatened by change have, since those early days, paid backhanded compliments to the foreign media by throwing correspondents out of countries where they would like to report and by denying them visas to come back in. Trying to visit Yemen earlier this year, I was told that not only was there no chance of my being granted a journalist's visa, but that real tourists - amazingly there is a trickle of such people wanting to see the wonders of Yemen - were being turned back at Sanaa airport on the grounds that they must secretly be journalists. The Bahrain government has an even meaner trick: give a visa to a journalist at a Bahraini embassy abroad and deny him entry when his plane lands.

It has taken time for this policy of near total exclusion to take hold, but it means that, today, foreign journalistic coverage of Syria, Yemen and, to a lesser extent, Bahrain is usually long-distance, reliant on cellphone film of demonstrations and riots which cannot be verified.

I was in Tehran earlier this year and failed to see any demonstrations in the centre of the city, though there were plenty of riot police standing about. I was therefore amazed to find a dramatic video on YouTube dated, so far as I recall, 27 February, showing a violent demonstration.

Then I noticed the protesters in the video were wearing only shirts though it was wet and freezing in Tehran and the men I could see in the streets were in jackets. Presumably somebody had redated a video shot in the summer of 2009 when there were prolonged riots.

With so many countries out of bounds, journalists have flocked to Benghazi, in Libya, which can be reached from Egypt without a visa. Alternatively they go to Tripoli, where the government allows a carefully monitored press corps to operate under strict supervision. Having arrived in these two cities, the ways in which the journalists report diverge sharply. Everybody reporting out of Tripoli expresses understandable scepticism about what government minders seek to show them as regards civilian casualties caused by Nato air strikes or demonstrations of support for Gaddafi. By way of contrast, the foreign press corps in Benghazi, capital of the rebel-held territory, shows surprising credulity towards more subtle but equally selfserving stories from the rebel government or its sympathisers. Ever since the Libyan uprising started on 15 February, the foreign media have regurgitated stories of atrocities carried out by Gaddafi's forces.

It is now becoming clear that reputable human rights organisations such as Amnesty International and Human Rights Watch have been unable to find evidence for the worst of these. For instance, they could find no credible witnesses to the mass rapes said to have been ordered by Gaddafi. Foreign mercenaries supposedly recruited by Gaddafi and shown off to the press were later quietly released when they turned out to be undocumented labourers from central and west Africa.

The crimes for which there is proof against Gaddafi are more prosaic, such as the bombardment of civilians in Misrata who have no way to escape.

There is also proof of the shooting of unarmed protesters and people at funerals early on in the uprising. Amnesty estimates that some 100-110 people were killed in Benghazi and 59-64 in Baida, though it warns that some of the dead may have been government supporters.

The Libyan insurgents were adept at dealing with the press from an early stage and this included skilful propaganda to put the blame for unexplained killings on the other side. One story, to which credence was given by the foreign media early on in Benghazi, was that eight to 10 government troops who refused to shoot protesters were executed by their own side. Their bodies were shown on TV. But Donatella Rovera, senior crisis response adviser for Amnesty International, says there is strong evidence for a different explanation. She says amateur video shows them alive after they had been captured, suggesting it was the rebels who killed them.

It is a weakness of journalists that they give wide publicity to atrocities, evidence for which may be shaky when first revealed. But when the stories turn out to be untrue or exaggerated, they rate scarcely a mention. But atrocity stories develop a life of their own and have real, and sometimes fatal, consequences long after the basis for them is deflated. Earlier in the year in Benghazi I spoke to refugees, mostly oil workers from Brega, an oil port in the Gulf of Sirte which had been captured by Gaddafi forces. One of the reasons they had fled was that they believed their wives and daughters were in danger of being raped by foreign mercenaries. They knew about this threat from watching satellite TV.

It is all credit to Amnesty International and Human Rights Watch that they have taken a sceptical attitude to atrocities until proven. Contrast this responsible attitude with that of Hillary Clinton or the prosecutor of the International Criminal Court, Luis Moreno-Ocampo, who blithely suggested that Gaddafi was using rape as a weapon of war to punish the rebels. Equally irresponsible would be a decision by the ICC to prosecute Gaddafi and his lieutenants, thus making it far less likely that Gaddafi can be eased out of power without a fight to the finish. This systematic demonisation of Gaddafi - a brutal despot he may be, but not a monster on the scale of Saddam Hussein - also makes it difficult to negotiate a ceasefire with him, though he is the only man who can deliver one.

There is nothing particularly surprising about the rebels in Benghazi making things up or producing dubious witnesses to Gaddafi's crimes. They are fighting a war against a despot whom they fear and hate and they will understandably use black propaganda as a weapon of war. But it does show naivety on the part of the foreign media, who almost universally sympathise with the rebels, that they swallow whole so many atrocity stories fed to them by the rebel authorities and their sympathisers.

Patrick Cockburn

Saturday, 22 October 2011

'GADDAFI CANNOT HURT HIS PEOPLE ANY LONGER'

The blood had been washed off and the faces, eyes shut, were in repose. But the terrible wounds of the last violent moments were left uncovered by the shrouds of white cloth that had been hastily thrown over them. The bodies were on stretchers, Muammar Gaddafi in a temporary military barracks, Mutassim Gaddafi in a container.

These were temporary resting places for the former dictator and his son. After being brought back to Misrata from Sirte, the scene of the killings, the corpses had been moved from place to place - at one point to the home of a former rebel official and then to a meat warehouse. Officials of the new government said this was to prevent the residents of this city, who had suffered a long and bloody siege at the hands of the regime, from venting their anger on their dead enemies.

But it was as if no one wanted responsibility for disposing of these grisly symbols of the revolution's triumph after such a bitter civil war. Some of the country's rulers talked about handing them over to Gaddafi's tribe for burial. Others were adamant that a shrine should not be created and the best course of action would be a burial at sea.

Looking down at the body of Colonel Gaddafi, Firuz al-Maghri, a 55-year-old schoolteacher who had been allowed into the barracks by a friend in the opposition militia, shook his head as he recalled a brother and a cousin who had died in Tripoli's Abu Salim prison, a place of fear and despair. "Twelve hundred prisoners were murdered there," he said. "It is difficult for outsiders to understand, but he was responsible for so many lives lost, families who never found out what happened to those who disappeared. We feared him, I was afraid. But seeing him like this...."

Captain Rahim Abu-Bakr, an engineer who became a fighter, patted Mr Maghri's shoulder. "It does not matter," he said. "He cannot hurt people any longer. What happened at the end to him and his son was bound to happen. But this was a bad death. I do not like being here."

Colonel Gaddafi appeared to have been shot in the head, the bullet wound clearly visible under his previously curly hair for which he was famous- it now lay lank. Mutassim had injuries to his chest and stomach. But exactly what happened when the final reckoning came at Sirte remains unclear.

Libya's new government, the National Transitional Council, has declared that tomorrow will be National Liberation Day to commemorate the departure of Colonel Gaddafi. But no one really believes the account given by Mahmoud Jibril, the Prime Minister, that Colonel Gaddafi was killed when loyalist forces made a lastditch attempt to rescue him. "He was already under arrest and he was hit in the crossfire," Mr Jibril said.

For many of the rebels at Sirte, it had been another day of frustration in the long and grinding battle for Gaddafi's birthplace, with the last pockets of loyalist fighters offering obdurate resistance. What was somewhat unusual were prolonged and fierce Nato air strikes, something that had become less frequent with the opposition's victory. They were French warplanes hitting a convoy of vehicles leaving Sirte at high speed. It had become the policy of Nato not to attack retreating regime soldiers because they did not pose any obvious danger to civilians and to avoid unnecessary bloodletting - and facilitate reconciliation.

But the attacks had taken place after the interception of messages by Western intelligence, suggesting high levels of remnants of the regime were on the move. Eleven vehicles were destroyed and the rest split into groups. But these, too, were hunted down from the air and a few, including the one carrying Colonel Gaddafi, returned to the outskirts of Sirte.

Colonel Gaddafi and a handful of his men then abandoned their vehicles and crawled into two drainage pipes. The rebels chased the fugitives, but say they were still unaware of who they were. Then, a little later, a man ran out waving a piece of white rag. "My master is here, he has been injured, it is Muammar Gaddafi, Muammar Gaddafi," the man apparently said. The soldier, a member of the Leader Guard, was dragged away.

Those there at the time describe a sense of astonishment among the rebel fighters when they discovered that the figure emerging from a ditch with a pistol in hand, but looking cowed, was indeed Colonel Gaddafi. This turned to elation, mocking of the former master of Libya - then vicious rage. "I don't think anyone thought he would be there, we all thought that he would be in the south, or maybe across in Niger or Algeria. We were as shocked as he was at first," said Abdullah Hakim Husseini, who had taken part in the brutal investing of Sirte from the start. "We were so happy when we knew it was him. I thought, 'at last, it's all over'."

Because there had been little expectation of catching the main prize, there was no procedure in place for what to do with him. Mr Husseini said some of the officers tried to call headquarters in Tripoli and Misrata. But the rebels, an egalitarian bunch with little respect for rank, pushed them aside. Mr Husseini said: "OK for sure, he was being beaten, kicked, with rifle butts, boots. He looked confused and afraid, he was saying 'help me, help me', but his voice was really strained, he was croaking. A few of us were around him, we thought we should get him somewhere we could question him about the others. But he was then taken away in a wave of people and then there were shots."

Other reports described him being told as he was hit: "This is for Misrata, you dog." Colonel Gaddafi replied: "Do you know right from wrong?"

Kim Sengupta

CHAPTER 4

BAHRAIN SPRING

Pearl Monument, 23 August 2008. Erected in 1982, demolished 18 March 2011.

Saturday, 19 February 2011

ARABS SHOOTING AT ARABS

"Massacre - it's a massacre," the doctors were shouting. Three dead. Four dead. One man was carried past me on a stretcher in the emergency room, blood spurting on to the floor from a massive bullet wound in his thigh. A few feet away, six nurses were fighting for the life of a pale-faced, bearded man with blood oozing out of his chest. "I have to take him to theatre now," a doctor screamed. "There is no time - he's dying!"

Others were closer to death. One poor youth - 18, 19 years old, perhaps - had a terrible head wound, a bullet hole in the leg and a bloody mess on his chest. The doctor beside him turned to me weeping, tears splashing on to his blood-stained gown. "He has a fragmented bullet in his brain and I can't get the bits out, and the bones on the left side of his head are completely smashed. His arteries are all broken. I just can't help him." Blood was cascading on to the floor. It was pitiful, outrageous, shameful. These were not armed men but mourners returning from a funeral, Shia Muslims of course, shot down by their own Bahraini army yesterday afternoon.

A medical orderly was returning with thousands of other men and women from the funeral at Daih of one of the demonstrators killed at Pearl Square in the early hours of Thursday.

"We decided to walk to the hospital because we knew there was a demonstration. Some of us were carrying tree branches as a token of peace which we wanted to give to the soldiers near the square, and we were shouting 'peace, peace. There was no provocation - nothing against the government. Then suddenly the soldiers started shooting. One was firing a machine gun from the top of a personnel carrier. There were police but they just left as the soldiers shot at us. But you know, the people in Bahrain have changed. They didn't want to run away. They faced the bullets with their bodies."

The demonstration at the hospital had already drawn thousands of Shia protesters - including hundreds of doctors and nurses from all over Manama, still in their white gowns - to demand the resignation of the Bahraini Minister of Health, Faisal Mohamed al-Homor, for refusing to allow ambulances to fetch the dead and injured from Thursday morning's police attack on the Pearl Square demonstrators.

But their fury turned to near-hysteria when the first wounded were brought in yesterday. Up to 100 doctors crowded into the emergency rooms, shouting and cursing their King and their government as paramedics fought to push trolleys loaded with the latest victims through screaming crowds. One man had a thick wad of bandages stuffed into his chest but blood was already staining his torso, dripping off the trolley. "He has a live round in his chest - and now there is air and blood in his lungs," the nurse beside him told me. "I think he is going." Thus did the anger of Bahrain's army - and, I suppose, the anger of the al-Khalifa family, the King included - reach the Sulmaniya medical centre.

The staff felt that they too were victims. And they were right. Five ambulances sent to the street - yesterday's victims were shot down opposite a fire station close to Pearl Square - were stopped by the army. Moments later, the hospital discovered that all their mobile phones had been switched off. Inside the hospital was a doctor, Sadeq al-Aberi, who was himself badly hurt by the police when he went to help the wounded on Thursday morning.

Rumours burned like petrol in Bahrain yesterday and many medical staff were insisting that up to 60 corpses had been taken from Pearl Square on Thursday morning and that police were seen by crowds loading bodies into three refrigerated trucks. One man showed me a mobile phone snapshot in which the three trucks could be seen clearly, parked behind several army armoured personnel carriers. According to other demonstrators, the vehicles, which bore Saudi registration plates, were later seen on the highway to dismiss such ghoulish stories, but I found one man - another male nurse at the hospital who works under the umbrella of the United Nations - who told me that an American colleague, he gave his name as "Jarrod", had videotaped the bodies being put into the trucks but was then arrested by the police and had not been seen since.

Why has the royal family of Bahrain allowed its soldiers to open fire at peaceful demonstrators? To turn on Bahraini civilians with live fire within 24 hours of the earlier killings seems like an act of lunacy.

But the heavy hand of Saudi Arabia may not be far away. The Saudis are fearful that the demonstrations in Manama and the towns of Bahrain will light equally provocative fires in the east of their kingdom, where a substantial Shia minority lives around Dhahran and other towns close to the Kuwaiti border. Their desire to see the Shia of Bahrain crushed as quickly as possible was made very clear at Thursday's Gulf summit here, with all the sheikhs and princes agreeing that there would be no Egyptian-style revolution in a kingdom which has a Shia majority of perhaps 70 per cent and a small Sunni minority which includes the royal family.

Yet Egypt's revolution is on everyone's lips in Bahrain. Outside the hospital, they were shouting: "The people want to topple the minister," a slight variation of the chant of the Egyptians who got rid of Mubarak, "The people want to topple the government."

And many in the crowd said - as the Egyptians said - that they had lost their fear of the authorities, of the police and army.

The policemen and soldiers for whom they now express such disgust were all too evident on the streets of Manama yesterday, watching sullenly from midnight-blue armoured vehicles or perched on American-made tanks. There appeared to be no British weaponry in evidence - although these are early days and there was Russianmade armour alongside the M-60 tanks. In the past, small Shia uprisings were ruthlessly crushed in Bahrain with the help of a Jordanian torturer and a senior intelligence factotum who just happened to be a former British Special Branch officer.

And the stakes here are high. This is the first serious insurrection in the wealthy Gulf states - more dangerous to the Saudis than the Islamists who took over the centre of Mecca more than 30 years ago - and Bahrain's al-Khalifa family realise just how fraught the coming days will be for them. A source which has always proved reliable over many years told me that late on Wednesday night, a member of the al-Khalifa family - said to be the Crown Prince - held a series of telephone conversations with a prominent Shia cleric, the Wifaq Shia party leader, Ali Salman, who was camping in Pearl Square. The Prince apparently offered a series of reforms and government changes which he thought the cleric had approved. But the demonstrators stayed in the square. They demanded the dissolution of parliament. Then came the police.

In the early afternoon yesterday, around 3,000 people held a rally in support of the al-Khalifas and there was much waving of the national flag from the windows of cars. This may make the front pages of the Bahraini press today - but it won't end the Shia uprising. And last night's chaos at Manama's greatest hospital - the blood slopping off the wounded, the shouts for help from those on the stretchers, the doctors who had never before seen such gunshot wounds; one of them simply shook his head in disbelief when a woman went into a fit next to a man who was sheathed in blood - has only further embittered the Shia of this nation.

A doctor who gave his name as Hussein stopped me leaving the emergency room because he wanted to explain his anger. "The Israelis do this sort of thing to the Palestinians - but these are Arabs shooting at Arabs," he bellowed above the din of screams and shouts of fury. "This is the Bahraini government doing this to their own people. I was in Egypt two weeks ago, working at the Qasr el-Aini hospital - but things are much more fucked up here."

Robert Fisk

PEARL SQUARE

Chanting, singing and waving roses, Bahrain's Shia Muslims ran in their tens of thousands back into Pearl Square in the centre of Manama yesterday after two days of bloodshed as police and soldiers battled to keep them from the streets of the capital. The army's tanks withdrew from the area - Bahrain's version of Cairo's Tahrir Square - in the morning, and then more than a thousand riot police, standing in ranks before the democracy protesters, suddenly retreated. Several of them ran away in front of us, pursued by women in chadors waving flowers.

Just why the Bahraini military, after firing live bullets into the crowds 24 hours earlier, allowed the protesters to take back the square yesterday was a mystery to many of them. Perhaps Crown Prince Salman ben Hamad al-Khalifa, who appealed to both the protesters and his own soldiers and police to show restraint on Friday night, believed that a return to the mini-insurrection in the square earlier this week would persuade the Shia opposition to open negotiations with the royal family. Indeed, Prince Salman appeared on television last night to say that talks with the opposition had begun and that "a new era" had started in the history of Bahrain.

Perhaps the Crown Prince was forced to end the brutality of the security forces after more calls from the White House. "This nation is not for only one section - it is not for Sunnis or Shias," he said in a state television broadcast. "It is for Bahrain and for Bahrainis." Opposition MPs had demanded a withdrawal of army tanks from the square, along with police units, as a condition of opening talks with the royal family. But yesterday afternoon, many of those who stormed joyously towards the giant concrete pearl monument had gone much further in their aspirations, wanting the abolition of the monarchy itself.

Many held posters bearing the faces of Saddam Hussein, ex-Egyptian president Mubarak and former Tunisian dictator Bin Ali, all of the portraits crossed out alongside a picture of King Hamad and the words "Down, Down Hamad." Crowds sang "go away Khalifas" and said that only a new constitution and the trial of police and soldiers who had fired at them with live rounds, rubber-coated steel bullets and tear-gas grenades would satisfy them. There was also a distinct note of anger with America when Shia men and women found - amid the debris of the protesters' camp destroyed by the police early on Thursday - dozens of tear-gas and baton rounds imported from the United States. One rubber-bullet cartridge - and Bahrainis have died from these weapons - carried its manufacturer's identity and military codes: "Non-Lethal Technologies, Homer City, PA 15748 USA, www.nonlethaltechnologies.com, Solid Rubber Baton, MP-4-R3." Cartridges from a stun gun carried the coding "DISPO PROP 200M 02-SAE-08 2 BANG Delay 1,5S NIC - 07/07-03 2 KNALL VZ 1,5". It was unclear if this weapon was made in the US, Britain or France - all major arms suppliers to Bahrain.

Many of the protesters who "retook" the central square yesterday were still asking how Bahraini troops could have shot at their own citizens on Friday. However, it is now clear that many soldiers in the "Bahraini" army are not Bahrainis at all but Pakistanis, many of whom had trained in their own country's army - and who had no hesitation at all in shooting at their own fellow Pakistanis as well as at the Taliban in the massive offensives against the Taliban over the past three years. Speaking Urdu, Pushtu - even Baluch - these men also make up a core unit of the Emirates army. In any event, these soldiers had disappeared from Pearl Square. But are they to return?

Saudi Arabia is only one of the Gulf states fearful that gains by the Shia majority in Bahrain will provoke the Shia minority in Saudi Arabia to demand reforms identical to their co-religionists in the tiny nation that borders the Saudi kingdom. And if President Obama was insisting that there should be no more violence by the Bahraini security forces, you can be sure that the Saudis would have been advising the opposite. Last night, the Shias appeared to have won the right to occupy the square again; but whether the police will allow them to keep their encampment, which was already being resupplied with tents yesterday evening, is quite another matter.

Robert Fisk

Sunday, 20 February 2011

CALL TO END KHALIFA FAMILY RULE

Bahrain is not Egypt. Bahrain is not Tunisia. And Bahrain is not Libya or Algeria or Yemen. True, the tens of thousands gathering again yesterday at the Pearl roundabout - most of them Shia but some of them Sunni Muslims - dressed themselves in Bahraini flags, just as the Cairo millions wore Egyptian flags in Tahrir Square.

But this miniature sultanist kingdom is not yet experiencing a revolution. The uprising of the country's 70 per cent - or is it 80 per cent? - Shia population is more a civil rights movement than a mass of republican rebels, but Crown Prince Salman bin Hamad al-Khalifa had better meet their demands quickly if he doesn't want an insurrection.

Indeed, the calls for an end to the entire 200-year-old Khalifa family rule in Bahrain are growing way ahead of the original aims of this explosion of anger: an elected prime minister, a constitutional monarchy, an end to discrimination. The cries of disgust at the Khalifas are much louder, the slogans more incendiary; and the vast array of supposedly opposition personalities talking to the Crown Prince is far behind the mood of the crowds who were yesterday erecting makeshift homes - tented, fully carpeted, complete with tea stalls and portable lavatories - in the very centre of Manama. The royal family would like them to leave but they have no intention of doing so. Yesterday, thousands of employees of the huge Alba aluminum plant marched to the roundabout to remind King Hamad and the Crown Prince that a powerful industrial and trade union movement now lies behind this sea of largely Shia protesters.

Yet Crown Prince Salman talks more about stability, calm, security and "national cohesion" than serious electoral and constitutional reform. Is he trying to "do a Mubarak" and make promises - genuine ones for the moment, perhaps, but kingly pledges do tend to fade with "stability" and time - which will not be met?

In an interview with CNN, he acknowledged the Belfast parallels, exclaiming that "what we don't want to do, like in Northern Ireland, is to descend into militia warfare or sectarianism". But the crazed shooting of the Bahraini army on Thursday evening - 50 wounded, three critically, one already pronounced brain dead - was a small-size Bloody Sunday and it didn't take long for the original civil rights movement in Northern Ireland to be outrun by a new IRA. Clearly, the royal family has been shocked at the events of the last week. Sultan al-Khalifa's admission that "this is not the Bahrain I know, I never thought I would see the day that something like this would happen" proves as much. But his words suggest that this huge manifestation of public fury was merely provoked by television pictures of the Tunisian and Egyptian revolutions. For the record, the Shia rebellion against the country's Sunni rulers has been going on for years, with hundreds of political prisoners tortured in four prisons in and around Manama, their tormentors often from the Jordanian army - just as many Bahraini soldiers come from the Punjab and Baluchistan in Pakistan. Yesterday, there were repeated demands for the release of political prisoners, banners carrying photographs of young men who are still in jail years after their original sentencing: they run into the hundreds.

Then there are the disturbing stories of the refrigerated trucks which reportedly took dozens of corpses for secret burial, perhaps in Saudi Arabia.

These could be part of the carapace of rumour that has settled over the events of the past few days, but now some of the names of the disappeared - men who were present at the shootings near the Pearl roundabout last week - are known.

Twelve of their names have just been released. So where is 14-year old Ahmed Salah Issa, Hossein Hassan Ali, aged 18, Ahmed Ali Mohsen, 25 and Badria Abda Ali, a woman of unknown age? And where is Hani Mohamed Ali, 27, Mahdi al-Mahousi, 24, Mohamed Abdullah, 18, Hamed Abdullah al-Faraj, 21, Fadel Jassem, 45, and Hossein Salman, 48? English residents of a nearby apartment block were warned before the shooting that if they took photographs of the soldiers, they would be shot.

Hassan Ali Radhi, the youngest of the 18 Bahrain Shia MPs, agrees that there is an increasing gap now between demonstrators and the official political opposition that is being sought out by Crown Prince Salman.

"We are waiting for an initiative from the Crown Prince," he told me. "He has not mentioned reform or constitutional monarchy and a fully elected parliament. If people have a properly elected government, including the prime minister, they will blame their representatives if things go wrong. Now, they blame the King.

"What we are suggesting is a removal of the barriers between the people and the ruling family. When Hillary Clinton came to Bahrain, I told her that we don't want to see the US 5th Fleet in Bahrain [its military headquarters] as an obstacle to change, but currently, Bahrain is the worst strategic ally for the US."

The head of the Alba factory trade union, Ali Bin Ali - who is a Sunni - warned that his members could go on strike if they wanted to.

"Now that people have been shot down on the roads, we will be political," he said.

Which, of course, is not what the Crown Prince wants to hear.

Robert Fisk

Tuesday, 15 March 2011

SAUDI ARMED INTERVENTION

Saudi Arabia sent troops into Bahrain yesterday to quell protests by the Shia Muslim majority against the Sunni monarchy, in a move that the opposition denounced as an act of war.

Saudi armoured vehicles rolled along the 16-mile causeway linking Saudi Arabia and Bahrain in an unprecedented armed intervention likely to provoke a new crisis in the Gulf.

About 1,000 Saudi soldiers entered the island, a Saudi official said. Witnesses said about 150 armoured vehicles and 50 other vehicles - including jeeps, buses, ambulances and water tankers - took up positions in the district of Riffa, where the royal family lives and where there is a military hospital.

The Saudi intervention is the first time that any Arab state has acted to quell protests in another since the wave of uprisings began in the region. The Bahraini government had earlier called for support from its neighbours after fighting in the streets of the capital, Manama, on Sunday, in which demonstrators routed riot police.

On Sunday morning the police attacked a small camp of pro-democracy protesters with tear gas and rubber bullets, but the raid provoked fighting in which the protesters seized control of much of Manama's financial district. This led the ruling al-Khalifa family to request a task force from the other five members of the Gulf Co-operation Council (GCC), which also includes Saudi Arabia, Oman, the United Arab Emirates, Qatar and Kuwait.

The Saudi rulers are worried that unrest among the Shias of Bahrain will spread to their own Shia population in the neighbouring Eastern Province. Saudi security forces have been trying to prevent protests in the kingdom from gaining momentum.

The opposition in Bahrain, including the Shia Wefaq party, issued a statement saying: "We consider the entry of Saudi Arabia or other

Gulf forces into the Kingdom of Bahrain's air, sea or land territories a blatant occupation."

It added that Saudi intervention threatened Bahrainis "with an undeclared war by armed troops". So far the Saudi troops, presumed to be accompanied by smaller forces from other GCC states, have not appeared on the streets, where security remains in the hands of the police. Demonstrators have erected barricades blocking the main road leading to the financial district. Police checkpoints have sealed the road to the airport.

The protesters appear to have moved into the business district in order to raise pressure on the government.

Businessmen working in Bahrain's offshore banking hub were forced to walk miles to their offices in high-rise buildings in the centre of Manama. Protesters had gathered earlier outside the Bahrain Financial Harbour, which is owned by the Prime Minister, Khalifa bin Salman al-Khalifa, who has been accused of corruption. They also moved to the campus of the main university and against the royal palace in Riffa, where they were opposed by police and Sunni civilians wielding swords.

Bahrain has hitherto been an absolute monarchy, with the King appointing 40 members of the Senate who can overrule the 40-member lower house of parliament. Gerrymandering prevents the Shia from winning a majority of the seats in the lower house. The sudden escalation of the crisis in Bahrain comes just after the United States Defence Secretary, Robert Gates, visited the island to urge leaders to move on reform. He said he had told King Hamad bin Isa al-Khalifa and the Crown Prince that "change could be led or could be imposed". Mr Gates said there was no evidence of Iranian involvement, but that Iran might exploit the protests for its own ends. He added: "Time is not our friend."

Bahrain is the base for the US Navy's Fifth Fleet, making what happens there significant to the US position in the Gulf and its ability to confront Iran.

Bahraini leaders have long claimed their opponents are agents of Iran, but US diplomatic cables released by Wiki-Leaks say there is little evidence of this. The six senior Shia clerics in Bahrain are not considered militant, although they have backed the protests.

The protesters at first sought to downplay sectarian differences on the island, saying they were inspired by the demand for democracy, rule of law and civil rights in Tunisia and Egypt. The initial demand was for a constitutional monarchy, but after police killed seven protesters last month attitudes among the opposition hardened and many now want an end to the monarchy.

Robert Fisk

Wednesday, 16 March 2011

MARTIAL LAW

The king of Bahrain has declared martial law, giving the military authority to end pro-democracy protests with the backing of 2,000 troops from Saudi Arabia and the United Arab Emirates.

Some 10,000 Bahraini demonstrators marched on the Saudi embassy in the capital, Manama, yesterday to protest against the Saudi intervention, which an opposition statement said amounted to an occupation.

Significant parts of the island kingdom, which has a population of 600,000, remain in the hands of protesters, one of whom was reported to have been killed yesterday by the security services.

Iran has denounced the entry of foreign troops into Bahrain as unacceptable and says that the United States is responsible for Saudi actions, which will have "dangerous consequences".

As the main Shia power of the Gulf, Iran is sympathetic to the Shia of Bahrain, who make up 70 per cent of the kingdom's population and have been traditionally discriminated against by the Sunni ruling class. "The presence of foreign forces and interference in Bahrain's internal affairs is unacceptable and will further complicate the issue," Ramin Mehmanparast, the Iranian Foreign Ministry spokesman, said. Iran denies any involvement in the month-long protests and US embassy cables released by WikiLeaks say that there is no evidence for long-standing Bahraini government claims that the Shia opposition receives support and weapons from Iran. Bahrain has withdrawn its ambassador to Iran for consultations.

Iran claims that the US dragged Saudi Arabia into invading while the Pentagon denies that it had any advance warning of Saudi military intervention.

But Bahrain is a vital US ally because it is home to the US Navy's Fifth Fleet and the US has been far more supportive of the ruling al-Khalifa family than it was of President Hosni Mubarak of Egypt or President Zine El Abidine Ben Ali of Tunisia. The White House has publicly called on the government of Bahrain to enter a dialogue with the opposition.

The three-month state of emergency hands significant powers to the Bahraini security forces, which are dominated by the Sunni minority. One of the protesters' complaints is that important jobs go to Sunnis, and that Sunnis from Middle East and South Asian countries are brought in as security men and given citizenship to keep the Shia as second-class citizens. The actual imposition of martial law may not make much difference to the security forces' powers since Bahrain is an absolute monarchy. But it is probably a sign of action to come, such as driving protesters from the streets by imposing a curfew, banning public meetings and clamping down on the press.

Despite some reports that the protesters planned to reopen a main road to Bahrain's financial district, metal barricades and piles of sand and rocks still blocked it. At checkpoints near the roundabout, activists, some wearing yellow vests, checked identities and waved cars through. Otherwise the streets were largely empty and shops closed. "We are staying peacefully. Even if they attack," Ali Mansoor, an activist at the Pearl roundabout, told Reuters. "Saudi Arabia has no right to come to Bahrain. Our problem is with the government not Saudi Arabia."

In the first sign of resistance to the Saudi force a security official in Saudi Arabia said a Saudi sergeant was shot and killed by a protester yesterday in Manama. No other details were immediately provided about the soldier, identified as Sergeant Ahmed al-Raddadi. There are growing signs of division between Shia and Sunni. People were placing rocks, skips, bins and pieces of metal on the road to prevent strangers from entering their neighbourhoods. Sectarian clashes between young men hurling rocks and using knives and clubs have become common. Such fighting broke out in different parts of Bahrain overnight Monday, with Sunnis and Shias trading accusations in the media.

Bahrain University and many schools have closed. An armed gang stormed the printing press of Bahrain's only opposition newspaper Al Wasat and tried to smash its presses and stop its publication.

It was later published using machinery from other papers.

The opposition had begun by demanding civil, legal and political rights, but the rejection of compromise by the royal family and the violence of the security forces has led to an escalation of their demands. On 17 February the police attacked sleeping protesters at the Pearl roundabout and killed at least four of them. Opposition demands became more radical, seeking a constitutional monarchy or even the removal of the King. A further miscalculation by the authorities on Sunday resulted in riot police attacking protesters near the financial district, provoking a counterattack by thousands of protesters who drove the police from the streets. That led the royal family to ask Saudi Arabia for help as a member of the Gulf Cooperation Council to which Kuwait, Bahrain, Qatar, United Arab Emirates and Oman also belong. Bahrain's crisis now involves all of the Gulf countries.

Robert Fisk

Thursday, 17 March 2011

BAHRAIN ARMY ASSAULT

Thousands of soldiers and police, backed by tanks and helicopters, advanced behind clouds of tear gas to crush pro-democracy protesters in Bahrain yesterday.

The assault, which came immediately after the arrival of a thousand Saudi troops in British-made armoured vehicles in the island kingdom, swiftly drove demonstrators from their camp at Pearl Square, the symbolic heart of the protest. Three protesters and three policemen were reported to have been killed.

Clouds of black smoke rose over the centre of the capital Manama, as the Sunni al-Khalifa monarchy made a risky bid to continue its 200-year long rule over the majority Shia population.

The white tents of protesters were set on fire and there was the sound of what appeared to be live rounds being fired as well as rubber bullets and tear gas grenades. Two policemen were reported to have been killed by people fleeing the square in their cars.

"The military has taken over and are shooting from helicopters at people in Pearl Square," said Ali Salman, the president of the al-Wefaq, the largest opposition party in Bahrain, in a telephone interview. "The army has seized all the roads and they are stopping people going to Salmaniya hospital or doctors leaving there. They have to go to a smaller hospital that is less well-equipped."

Mr Salman said that Saudi troops were not taking part in the government action against the protesters but while Saudis "are in Bahrain it is a green light to our army to kill people. The Saudis don't want any of the GCC [Gulf Cooperation Council] countries to be democratic."

Of the 560,000 Bahraini citizens some 370,000, about two thirds, are Shia. All the army and almost all the police are Sunni. The total population of the island is about 1.2 million of whom half are foreign workers.

The riot police and soldiers began their all-out assault at 7am, but met only limited resistance at Pearl Square that ended after two hours. At Budaya health centre a witness, who had gone to give blood, told a news agency that he had seen about 50 casualties but the facilities were too small for the injured even to find anywhere to sit down.

"I've seen some terrific wounds, lots of people hurt by bird shot," he said. "One had half his head injured with that. One had his hand blown up by some kind of bullet. He was using his other hand to show the victory sign."

The Bahraini government story of events in Pearl Square is that its forces were attacked by 250 "saboteurs" throwing petrol bombs and they were forced to retaliate.

In Shia areas of the country people went to mosques to pray as a sign of protest as the army assault began. Soldiers were reported to be entering Shia villages outside Manama where they were met with stones and petrol bombs in some places. A 4am to 4pm curfew has been imposed in most of the country and security forces have banned journalists from moving around. Mobile phones appear to have been jammed as government forces attacked and internet services were very slow.

Mr Salman said his party was not calling for immediate demonstrations and told protesters not to confront the army, but "after two or three days people will find a way of expressing their feelings." He did not believe there was any chance of a dialogue between the reformers and the government "so long as the killing goes on".

The all-out attack by a Sunni regime notorious for its sectarianism on its own mainly Shia population, with the backing of Saudi

Arabia and other Sunni monarchies, is likely to provoke a long term crisis in the Gulf and deepen divisions between Shia and Sunni.

Iraq and Iran are both majority Shia states and both reacted angrily to news of the crack-down. In southern Iraq 4,000 people marched chanting "Bahrain is the Gaza of the Gulf", equating Bahraini government action against their own people with Israeli attacks on the Palestinians in the Gaza Strip.

In Iran, the largest Shia country in terms of population, President Mahmoud Ahmedinejad compared the Saudi action to that of Saddam Hussein in invading Kuwait in 1990 and how it had ultimately led to his downfall. He said on state television: "What has happened is bad, unjustifiable and irreparable."

In the past, however, Iran has been cautious about going beyond rhetorical attacks on Saudi Arabia or the small Sunni states on the western side of the Gulf. "The people's demands for change must be respected," said Mr Ahmedinejad.

"How is it possible to stop waves of humanity with military force?" The US is in a difficult position and is very publicly distancing itself from the Saudi action and that of the Bahraini government. US Secretary of State Hillary Clinton expressed alarm at the "provocative acts and sectarian violence."

The contradictions in the American position were underlined when she phoned the Saudi Foreign Minister Prince Saudi to stress that Saudi soldiers in their armoured vehicles should be used to promote dialogue.

But while the US is asking for moderation it probably draws the line at the overthrow of the monarchy in Bahrain by a Shia protest movement, however peaceful and democratic.

Robert Fisk

Sunday, 15 May 2011

SHIA REPRESSION

'Let us drown the revolution in Jewish blood" was the slogan of the tsars when they orchestrated pogroms against Jews across Russia in the years before the First World War. The battle-cry of the al-Khalifa monarchy in Bahrain ever since they started to crush the pro-democracy protests in the island kingdom two months ago might well be "to drown the revolution in Shia blood". Just as the tsars once used Cossacks to kill and torture Jews and burn their synagogues, so Bahrain's minority Sunni regime sends out its black-masked security forces night after night to terrorise the majority Shia population for demanding equal political and civil rights.

Usually troops and police make their raids on Shia districts between 1am and 4am, dragging people from their beds and beating them in front of their families. Those detained face mistreatment and torture in prison. One pro-democracy activist, Abdulhadi al-Khawaja, brought before a military court last week with severe facial injuries, said he had suffered four fractures to the left side of his face, including a broken jaw that needed four hours' surgery.

The suppression of the protests came after Saudi Arabia and the Gulf Co-operation Council - also known as the "kings' club" of six Gulf monarchs - sent 1,500 troops to Bahrain to aid the crackdown, which began on 15 March. It soon became clear that the government is engaged in a savage onslaught on the entire Shia community - some 70 per cent of the population - in Bahrain.

First came a wave of arrests with about 1,000 people detained, of whom the government claims some 300 have been released, though it will not give figures for those still under arrest. Many say they were tortured and, where photographs of those who died under interrogation are available, they show clear marks of beating and whipping. There is no sign yet that King Hamad bin Isa al-Khalifa's declaration that martial law will end on 1 June is anything more than a propaganda exercise to convince the outside world, and foreign business in particular, that Bahrain is returning to normal.

The repression is across the board.

Sometimes the masked security men who raid Shia villages at night also bulldoze Shia mosques and religious meeting places. At least 27 of these have so far been wrecked or destroyed, while anti-Shia and pro-government graffiti is often sprayed on any walls that survive.

The government is scarcely seeking to conceal the sectarian nature of its repression. Defending the destruction of Shia mosques and husseiniyahs (religious meeting houses), it claims that they were constructed without building permission. Critics point out that one of them was 400 years old. Nor is it likely that the government has been seized with a sudden enthusiasm for enforcing building regulations since the middle of March.

The government is determined to destroy all physical rallying points for the protesters. One of the first such places to be destroyed was the Pearl Square monument, an elegant structure commemorating the pearl fishers of the Gulf, which was bulldozed soon after the square had been cleared of demonstrators. A measure of the government's paranoia is that it has now withdrawn its own half-dinar coins showing the iconic Pearl Square monument.

Facing little criticism from the United States, so concerned about human rights abuses in Libya, the al-Khalifa family is ruthlessly crushing opposition at every level. Nurses and doctors in a health system largely run by Shias have been beaten and arrested for treating protesters. Teachers and students are being detained. Some 1,000 professional people have been sacked and have lost their pensions. The one opposition newspaper has been closed. Bahraini students who joined protests abroad have had their funding withdrawn.

The original 14 February protest movement was moderate, contained Sunni as well as Shia activists, and went out of its way to be non-sectarian.

Its slogans included demands that Bahrain's powerful prime minister for the past 40 years, Sheikh Khalifa bin Salman al-Khalifa, step down and for fair elections. It also wanted equal rights for all, including an end to anti-Shia discrimination under which the majority were excluded from joining the 60,000-strong army, police and security forces. Security jobs went instead to Sunni recruits from Pakistan, Jordan, Syria and other Sunni states who were immediately given Bahraini citizenship. Sometimes the anti-Shia bias is explicit.

One pro-government newspaper prominently published a letter that compared the protesters to "termites", which are intelligent but multiply at alarming speed, and "are very similar to the 14 February group that tried to destroy our beautiful, precious country." The writer recommends exterminating the "white ants so they don't come back".

The purpose of the systematic torture and mistreatment inflicted on the detainees is first to create a feeling of terror in the civilian population. It is not only protesters or pro-democracy activists that are being targeted. Al-Jazeera satellite television, based in and funded by neighbouring Qatar, which played such a role in publicising protests and their attempted repression in Tunisia, Egypt, Syria, Yemen and Libya, was initially much more reticent about reporting events in Bahrain. But al-Jazeera revealed this week that the Bahraini police have been raiding girls' schools, detaining and beating schoolgirls, and are accused of threatening to rape them.

One 16-year-old called "Heba" was taken with three of her schoolfriends and held for three days, during which they were beaten. She said an officer "hit me on the head and I started to bleed" and she was thrown against a wall. Although the girls were beaten severely, she said, they scarcely felt the pain because they were so frightened of being raped. The Bahraini opposition party Al Wefaq says that 15 girls' schools have been raided by the police and girls as young as 12 threatened with rape.

Aside from intimidation there is a further motive for the beatings and torture: namely, to extract evidence that, against all appearances, the opposition is planning armed revolt and is manipulated by foreign powers, notably Iran. The aim, in the case of Abdulhadi al-Khawaja, was evidently to beat out of him a confession that he was attempting to "topple the regime forcibly in collaboration with a terrorist organisation working for a foreign country".

The al-Khalifas are aware that their strongest card in trying to discredit the opposition is to claim it has Iranian links. US embassy cables revealed by Wikileaks show that the Bahrain government was continually making this claim to a sceptical US embassy over the years, but has never provided any evidence. This propaganda claiming Iranian plots is crude, but plays successfully in Sunni Gulf states that see an Iranian hand behind every Shia demand for equal rights and an end to discrimination. It also gets an audience in Washington, conscious that its Fifth Fleet is based in Bahrain and fearful of anything that could strengthen Iran.

The Bahraini monarchy, having effectively declared war on the majority of its own people, is likely to win in the short term because its opponents are not armed. The cost will be that Bahrain, once deemed more liberal than its neighbours, is turning into the Gulf's version of Belfast or Beirut when they were convulsed by sectarian hatred.

Patrick Cockburn

Sunday, 20 May 2011

SAUDI PROTECTORATE

Shia leaders have accused the Bahraini government of using violence, intimidation and mass sackings to drive their community out.

Bahrain's Crown Prince Salman bin Hamad al-Khalifa met David Cameron in London yesterday in an attempt to restore the island's tarnished reputation, but there is no sign of government repression easing. Critics of the regime say that Prince Salman - once an advocate of dialogue with the majority Shia community - has lost influence to Saudi-backed hardliners within the al-Khalifa royal family.

A former minister in the Gulf state, who did not want to be named, said: "The government assault on the Shia only makes sense if the government intends to alter the demographic balance in Bahrain against the Shia and in favour of the Sunni." By alienating the majority community the al-Khalifas were making themselves wholly dependent on Saudi Arabia, he said.

Shia politicians in Bahrain say that demographic change is already under way. Ali al-Aswad, a Shia MP, said that about 2,000 employees, mostly Shia, had been dismissed or suspended. "The government is trying to force them and their families to leave Bahrain. Some have already gone to Kuwait and the United Arab Emirates and others are applying for visas to get work elsewhere."

This figure is confirmed by the International Labour Organisation.

Mohammed Sadiq, of the Justice for Bahrain group, said that about 850 Bahraini students in Britain are having their grants withdrawn for attending pro-democracy rallies. Many are likely to apply for asylum. He says: "A further 1,500 Bahraini students in UK are funded privately but their future is often in doubt because their relatives at home who pay their fees have been arrested or sacked."

The bulldozing of at least 27 Shia mosques, along with many other religious meeting houses, since the start of the crackdown in mid-March has sent a message to the community as a whole that its future on the island is in doubt. Youssif al-Khoei of the al-Khoei Foundation, a UK-based charity, said: "One of the mosques demolished was 400 years old and its destruction, along with so many others, is deeply frightening to the Shia community in Bahrain which is one of the oldest in the world."

The population of Bahrain is 1.2 million, of which half are native Bahrainis and of these some 70 per cent are estimated to be Shia. The al-Khalifa monarchy is Sunni, as are almost all the 60,000-strong security forces. A long-standing Shia demand is that the government stops fast-tracking the naturalisation of foreign Sunni and refusing to grant citizenship to Shia. Mr Sadiq says that at least 10,000 and possibly 20,000 foreigners have "been granted Bahrain citizenship since the crackdown". In Pakistan a report that 1,000 security men were being recruited by Bahrain led to Shia-Sunni riots and may have led to the killing of a Saudi diplomat.

The excuse for the mass sackings in both the state and private sectors is their participation in a general strike in favour of democracy and reform on 13 March. Trade unions in Bahrain say that private employers have come under intense government pressure to dismiss workers who supported the protests. Mass firings have taken place at companies such as the Bahrain Petroleum Company and Gulf Air.

The severity of the crackdown in Bahrain is mystifying, say local politicians in the Gulf. "I expected the King to try to stay above the conflict rather than wholly join the Sunni side," said one political leader.

The pro-democracy protests were milder in Bahrain than in Tunisia, Egypt, Syria, Libya or Yemen and demonstrators made only limited demands for a change of regime. But the Saudi and al-Khalifa royal families appear to have panicked after the fall of Hosni Mubarak of Egypt. "The explanation for what happened is that the Saudis flipped," said one observer.

The Sunni kings of the Gulf rule in the only place on earth where absolute monarchies are still the norm and are paranoid about any threat to their status.

Though there is no evidence of Iran's interference in Bahrain, they believe much of their own propaganda about it manipulating the pro-democracy protests. In reality the Bahraini Shia look to Najaf in Iraq for religious leadership. They have so far insisted that the Bahraini Shia response should be non-violent, but warn that this restraint cannot go on forever.

Patrick Cockburn

Thursday, 2 June 2011

TARGETING WOMEN

Bahrain's security forces are increasingly targeting women in their campaign against prodemocracy protesters despite yesterday lifting martial law in the island kingdom.

Ayat al-Gormezi, 20, a poet and student arrested two months ago after reading out a poem at a pro-democracy rally, is due to go on trial today before a military tribunal, her mother said. Ayat was forced to turn herself in when masked policemen threatened to kill her brothers unless she did so.

She has not been seen since her arrest, though her mother did talk to her once by phone and Ayat said that she had been forced to sign a false confession.

Her mother has since been told that her daughter has been in a military hospital after being tortured.

"We are the people who will kill humiliation and assassinate misery," a film captures Ayat telling a cheering crowd of protesters in Pearl Square in February. "We are the people who will destroy the foundation of injustice." She addresses King Hamad bin Isa al-Khalifa directly and says to him: "Don't you hear their cries, don't you hear their screams?" As she finishes, the crowd shouts: "Down with Hamad."

Ayat's call for change was no more radical than that heard in the streets of Tunis, Cairo and Benghazi at about the same time. But her reference to the king might explain the fury shown by the Bahraini security forces who, going by photographs of the scene, smashed up her bedroom when they raided her house and could not find her.

There are signs that Bahraini police, riot police and special security are detaining and mistreating more and more women. Many are held incommunicado, forced to sign confessions or threatened with rape, according to Bahraini human rights groups.

Bahrain is the first country affected by the Arab Spring where women have been singled out as targets for repression. Human rights groups say that hundreds have been arrested. Many women complain of being severely beaten while in custody. One woman journalist was beaten so badly that she could not walk.

A woman doctor, who was later released but may be charged, says she was threatened with rape. She told Reuters news agency that the police said: "We are 14 guys in this room, do you know what we can do to you? It's the emergency law [martial law] and we are free to do what we want."

The ending of martial law and a call for dialogue from King Hamad appear to be part of a campaign to show that normal life is returning to Bahrain. The Bahraini government is eager to host the Formula One motor race, which was postponed from earlier in the year, but may be rescheduled to take place in Bahrain by the sports governing body meeting in Barcelona tomorrow.

Despite the lifting of martial law, imposed on 15 March, there is no sign of repression easing. Some 600 people are still detained, at least 2,000 have been sacked, and some 27 mosques of the Shia, who make up 70 per cent of the population, have been bulldozed.

The protests started on 14 February in emulation of events in Egypt and Tunisia with a campaign for political reform, a central demand being civil and political equality for the majority Shia. The al-Khalifa royal family and the ruling class in Bahrain are Sunni.

The targeting of women by the security forces may, like the destruction of mosques, have the broader aim of demonstrating to the Shia community that the Sunni elite will show no restraint in preventing the Shia winning political power. Shia leaders complain that the state-controlled media is continuing to pump out sectarian anti-Shia propaganda.

The government is eager to show that Bahrain can return to being an untroubled business and tourist hub for the Gulf. Having the Formula One race rescheduled to take place on the island later this year would be an important success in this direction.

The New York based Human Rights Watch has written to the Federation Internationale de l'Automobile (FIA), saying that the race would take place in an environment of unrelenting "punitive retribution" against prodemocracy protesters.

If the race does go ahead it will be without a quarter of the staff of the Bahrain International Circuit, the host organisation, who have been arrested, including two senior staff. Most have been sacked or suspended, accused of approving of the postponement of the Formula One event earlier in the year.

The government has been detaining and beating local reporters. The one international journalist based permanently in Bahrain was ordered out this month. Even foreign correspondents with entry visas have been denied entry when they arrive in Bahrain.

Patrick Cockburn

Friday, 6 June 2011

DEMENTED SAVAGERY

How to explain the ferocity of the Bahraini al-Khalifa royal family's assault on the majority of its own people? Despite an end to martial law, the security forces show no signs of ceasing to beat detainees to the point of death, threaten schoolgirls with rape and force women to drink bottles of urine.

The systematic use of torture in Bahrain has all the demented savagery of the European witch trials in the 16th and 17th centuries. In both cases, interrogators wanted to give substance to imagined conspiracies by extracting forced confessions. In Europe, innocent women were forced to confess to witchcraft, while in Bahrain the aim of the torturers is to get their victims to admit to seeking to overthrow the government. Often they are accused of having treasonous links with Iran, something for which the New York-based Human Rights Watch says there is "zero evidence".

A simpler motive for the across-the-board repression of the Shia, who make up 70 per cent of the Arab population of Bahrain, is that it is a crude assertion of power by the Sunni ruling class backed by Saudi Arabia. The aim is simply to terrorise the Shia into never again demanding civil and political rights as they did during peaceful demonstrations which started on 14 February in emulation of protests in Egypt and Tunisia.

The tragedy of Bahrain is that none of the present toxic developments were necessary even from the egocentric point of view of the al-Khalifas. Of all the uprisings which have taken place during the Arab Spring, Bahrain had the most ingredients for compromise between protesters and the powers-that-be. The demand of the main opposition was not an end to the monarchy, but greater democracy, less discrimination and an end to the policy of naturalising Sunni immigrants in a bid to change the demographic balance against the Shia.

In practical political terms a deal between government and opposition would have required the king to dismiss his prime minister,

Khalifa bin Salman al-Khalifa, who has held his job for 40 years and is famous for his vast wealth and extensive ownership of property in Bahrain.

It never happened. Instead the al-Khalifas panicked, probably thinking they would be the next regime to go down after Tunisia and Egypt. The US, despite having its Fifth Fleet based in Bahrain, suddenly appeared to be a shaky supporter. Saudi Arabia and the monarchs of the Gulf wanted what they saw as a Shia uprising crushed.

The government played the sectarian card, portraying the Bahraini Shia as pawns of Iran and frightening the Sunni minority on the island. It bulldozed Shia mosques and prayer houses. Attending the most peaceful prodemocracy rally before the crack down started on 15 March was portrayed as treason and those that had not demonstrated have been forced to confess that they did.

In the short term, the al-Khalifa's strategy has worked and the opposition is cowed, but the price may be permanent hatred of the majority of Bahrainis for the monarchy. The regime may try to change the demographic balance by driving thousands of Shia from the island by intimidation and sacking. Inevitably it will have to rely on Saudi Arabia to an even greater degree than in the past, making the island little more than a Saudi protectorate.

Patrick Cockburn

Saturday, 11 June 2011

TORTURING A POET

Bahraini security forces beat the detained poet Ayat al-Gormezi across the face with electric cable and forced her to clean with her bare hands lavatories just used by police, members of her family said yesterday in a graphic account of the torture and humiliation suffered by those rounded up in the Gulf nation's crackdown on dissent.

The 20-year-old trainee teacher, who spent nine days in a tiny cell with the air conditioning turned to freezing, is due back in court this weekend on charges of inciting hatred, insulting the king and illegal assembly, and her family fear she may suffer further mistreatment in custody amid threats of another round of interrogation.

Masked police arrested Ayat at her home on 30 March for reciting a poem criticising the monarchy during a prodemocracy rally in the capital Manama in February. Her family were able to talk to her by phone from prison, but they only learned about her mistreatment, amounting to torture, when she spoke to them at her arraignment earlier this month.

In a phone interview with *The Independent* from Bahrain yesterday, her mother, Sa'ada Hassan Ahmed, related Ayat's account of what happened after her arrest. The details of her interrogation and imprisonment are similar to the experiences of other women detained by Bahraini security forces since they launched a full scale repression on 15 March against all those demanding democratic reform in the island kingdom.

Ayat gave herself up to police after they threatened to kill her brothers. She was taken away in a car with two security officials - a man and a woman - both of whom were masked and dressed in civilian clothes. They immediately started to beat her and threaten her, saying she would be raped and sexually assaulted with degrading photographs of her put on the internet.

"When she reached the interrogation centre in Manama she was put in the very small cell and kept there for nine days," her mother said. "The beatings with electric cable made her lips swell up." At times, Ayat thought the air conditioning in the cell was emitting some form of gas, which made her feel she was suffocating. Throughout this period the police made no real attempt to interrogate her.

Her family say the days after Ayat was taken away was a period of intense psychological torture. "We knew nothing about what had happened to her though we heard rumours that she had been raped or killed," her brother Yousif Mohammed said.

Her mother went from police station to police station asking for news of Ayat, but learned nothing. Sa'ada was finally told by the police that she should file a missing persons report, though she complained that this was absurd since it was the police who had detained her daughter.

And in a sinister development, pictures of Ayat began to turn up on dating and pornographic websites. This may relate to the threats made by police when she was first arrested that shameful photographs of her would be posted online.

After nine days, Ayat was moved to Isa prison and, 15 days after she was first taken away, she was allowed to make a phone call to her parents telling them that she was alive. The physical torture stopped, but she was kept under psychological pressure.

"At some point," her mother says, "she was forced to sign a document but she was blindfolded and did not know what it said."

She was told to clean up other cells and the corridor of the bloc she was in but was allowed no contact with other prisoners. On several occasions she was taken back to the interrogation centre where she had first been held and a video was taken of her giving her name and saying that she was a Shia and she hated Sunnis.

Asked for further details of Ayat's interrogation in Isa prison, her mother said she did not know because they did not have long enough to talk when they met during the arraignment. They were told the previous day to bring a lawyer, though it is unclear how freely he was able to talk to his client.

While Ayat was meeting her family during the arraignment, a policeman overheard her giving details of her mistreatment. He said that if she continued to do so, she would be returned to the interrogation centre and tortured again.

Patrick Cockburn

Thursday, 26 June 2011

ANSWERING PROTEST WITH LIFE IN PRISON

Bahrain has sentenced eight leading political activists to life in prison on charges of conspiring to overthrow the Government in a move likely to intensify unrest and discredit a proposal by the king for a national dialogue.

One of the 21 defendants - dressed in grey prison uniforms as they faced a military court - shouted: "We will continue our peaceful struggle," while others shook their fists and cried: "Peaceful, peaceful." They were forced out of the courtroom by police.

Crowds blocked roads with heaps of sand and urged marches as news spread of the convictions of the group, which includes some of the island kingdom's most popular leaders.

All but one belong to Bahrain's majority Shia community, which accuses the Government of persecution and discrimination.

Anybody in Bahrain who supported the pro-democracy movement, which began at the height of the Arab Spring on 14 February, is vulnerable to being accused of plotting against the Government at the behest of Iran. The sentenced activists were accused of having links to "a terrorist organisation abroad". Fourteen were tried in court and the other seven in absentia. In addition to the eight life sentences, 10 activists were given 15-year terms, two others received five years and one was sentenced to two years.

The decision is likely to undermine a US and UK-backed attempt to persuade the Sunni al-Khalifa monarchy to start a dialogue with the opposition.

America and Britain have been embarrassed by accusations of hypocrisy for denouncing human rights violations in Libya while ignoring compelling evidence of systematic torture by the state security forces in Bahrain.

King Hamad bin Isa al-Khalifa had called for a dialogue to start on 1 July, but this is likely to be a dead letter - either because a serious initiative was never intended or he does not have the power within the royal family to moderate the security forces' actions. Among those sentenced to life were Abdulhadi al-Khawaja, a human rights activist; Abdel Wahab Hussain, the head of the Wafa party; and Hassan Mushaima, leader of the opposition Haq group.

Ibrahim Sharif, a Sunni leader who is head of the secular party Waad, was one of those who received five years in prison.

Wefaq, the main Shia opposition party, said after the verdicts that it was doubtful about attending the national dialogue talks.

The trial of 47 doctors and nurses resumes next week, during which senior consultants will be accused of supporting revolution, concealing weapons and distributing bags of blood for protesters to smear on themselves.

The defendants say they were abused, tortured and forced to sign false confessions and that they were only giving medical aid to protesters injured by the security forces.

At a session of the military court trying the medical staff this week, the defendants' lawyers were only allowed to meet with them for 15 minutes before the trial.

They could put questions to the seven prosecution witnesses only through the judge, who disallowed many of them. Families of those on trial allege one of the witnesses was the main interrogator who had tortured defendants.

The Government has been largely successful in persuading the ruling Sunni minority that pro-democracy protests were an Iranian-orchestrated conspiracy to take over the island. The arrival of a Saudi-led military force in mid-March ushered in a brutal crackdown in which Shia mosques were targeted for destruction. The Government claimed bulldozing the mosques had no sectarian implications but was simply to apply unenforced building regulations.

Patrick Cockburn

CHAPTER 5

YEMEN SPRING

Yemen protesters for freedom and democracy, London, 2 April 2011.

Wednesday, 4 May 2011

AL-QA'IDA IN YEMEN

These days there are far more "terrorist experts" earning their living because of their supposed knowledge of al-Qa'ida than there are real members of al-Qa'ida. This is an important reason why the organisation will not fade from the headlines or from the list of threats that governments see as facing their countries despite the death of Osama bin Laden.

None of these "experts", whether they work for governments, intelligence services, the armed forces, the media or in academia, will ever have an interest in declaring al-Qa'ida or groups like it as defunct or irrelevant. Their continued employment, budgets and influence has to be justified by continuous threat inflation.

It is not that Al-Qa'ida poses no threat, but it differs markedly from public perception. The group was never a well-coordinated worldwide network of terrorists answering to a central headquarters in Afghanistan or Pakistan.

But after 9/11 it had such a fearsome reputation, and occupied such a pre-eminent place in US demonology, that any hint of its presence was highly publicised and had an immediate international political impact. No government could afford to allow the US to endure another 9/11.

Obsession with al-Qa'ida leads to political tunnel vision. For example Yemen, the mountainous republic tucked away in the southwest corner of the Arabian Peninsula, has a population of 24 million mostly impoverished people, but US policy towards the Yemeni government is largely determined by the activities of an estimated 300 members of Al-Qa'ida in the Arabian Peninsula (AQAP).

This handful of AQAP members do not have to do very much to cause turmoil at airports across the world. Two abortive bomb attempts organised from Yemen last year, both foiled, proved almost as successful in terms of generating disruption and fear as if the bombs had gone off as planned, as AQAP itself boasted.

The way in which the presence of al-Qa'ida has political repercussions out of all proportions to its size is demonstrated above all by Afghanistan. The US military has said that there may be little more than 100 al-Qa'ida members in Afghanistan compared to a Nato estimate of 25,000 Taliban. Yet President Obama's justification for sending 30,000 more troops to Afghanistan to fight in an unpopular conflict was the need to combat al-Qa'ida, which the US public does care about, rather than the Taliban, which it largely does not.

If Afghanistan is not a refuge for al-Qa'ida, how about across the border in north-west Pakistan? The semi-autonomous Federally Administered Tribal Areas (Fata) used to be a place of refuge for al-Qa'ida and was frequently referred to as "the most dangerous place the world", but much of it is now occupied by the Pakistani army and there are continual US drone strikes seeking out Taliban and al-Qa'ida leaders seeking sanctuary in its rugged terrain. There was a good reason why bin Laden preferred to live far away from here in his villa in Abbottabad just north of Islamabad.

Many of the remaining al-Qa'ida havens are a series of franchises and several of these are absorbed in local disputes. In Iraq, al-Qa'ida became powerful for several years after 2003 as the Sunni community fought the US occupation and the Shia-and Kurdish-dominated Iraqi government. It drew strength from these struggles, but grossly overplayed its hand by trying to dominate the Sunni and wage war against the majority Shia. These days it seldom attacks US troops, though it continues to wage bloody sectarian warfare against the Shia.

In the Arabian Peninsula, al-Qa'ida retreated from Saudi Arabia to set up AQAP in Yemen in 2009. Its best-known member here is Anwar al-Awlaki, an American citizen speaking fluent English who is one of the few al-Qa'ida leaders who can articulate the group's ideology in convincing terms. He was also linked to the shooting of 13 people by a US army major in Fort Hood in Texas. The street protests in Yemen may make it easy for al-Qa'ida to move around, but also means that opponents of the political status quo now have alternative means of opposing it.

Somalia and the Horn of Africa are probably the best places for al-Qa'ida to gain in strength. Since last year it is allied to al-Shabaab, the Somali group that controls much of the south of the country. It says it was behind suicide attacks in Uganda last year that killed 76 people. From the point of view of a secret movement planning to attack US targets, Somalia - much of which has descended into anarchy - has the advantage that militants can cross its land borders without being checked.

Further west, Al-Qa'ida in the Islamic Maghreb - many of its fighters survivors of the Algerian civil war in the 1990s - has a shadowy existence in the Sahara, kidnapping tourists and making occasional forays into the cities. It may have been behind a bomb that killed 16 people in Marrakech last week, but as a movement it does not seem to be going anywhere.

Patrick Cockburn

PRESIDENT SALEH FALLS

The uprisings sweeping the Arab world appeared to have won their third victory over authoritarian rule by overthrowing President Ali Abdullah Saleh of Yemen after 33 years in power. He left for Saudi Arabia on Saturday to be treated for injuries received in an explosion in his presidential palace and is unlikely to return.

Thousands of people danced and sang and slaughtered cows in the streets of the capital Sanaa yesterday as news spread that Yemen had joined Tunisia and Egypt in ousting a widely detested leader who had controlled the state for decades. Anti-Saleh demonstrators held up signs saying "Yemen is more beautiful without you" and "Name: A Free Yemen. Date of birth: June 4, 2011".

Women in black joined swelling numbers of jubilant demonstrators. One placard carried by them read: "The oppressor is gone, but the people stay." Soldiers joined in the dancing and singing and were hoisted on to the shoulders of the crowds. President Saleh, in power since 1978, has not formally ceded power, but it is unlikely that the forces he commanded will hold together without his presence or that Saudi Arabia will let him return. There are unconfirmed reports that senior government ministers and top officials close to him were trying to board flights out of the country from Sanaa airport.

A senior official from the ruling party said Mr Saleh would be back within "days" amid reports he had awoken from successful surgery to remove shrapnel from his chest, but the roaring crowds were disinclined to believe him. "If Saleh comes back, we'll be ready for him," shouted Abdul Muein Asbahi, as he fired confetti into the air.

The uprising in Yemen started on 27 January inspired by pro-democracy anti-government demonstrations in Tunisia and Egypt and took over a square in the capital. The government organised counter-demonstrations and repression became increasingly violent. On 18 March, government snipers shot dead 52 protesters leading to the defection of senior army officers and important tribal leaders, who pledged to defend the protesters.

Saudi Arabia and the US have been trying to arrange a smooth transition and prevent a vacuum of power which Washington fears might be used by AQAP to expand its influence. President Saleh had been deft in publicising the presence of AQAP fighters to extract financial aid and weapons, though his critics said he exaggerated and manipulated the Islamic fundamentalist threat. He agreed three times to a US-backed Gulf Arab mediation under which he would step down but reneged on the deals.

There has been growing violence in Sanaa, the second city Taiz and other Yemeni cities in recent weeks between pro and anti-Saleh forces that threatened to develop into a civil war. But last night, the acting president Abdel Rabbo Mansour Hadi, who took over after President Saleh left the country, agreed a day-long truce with the so-called Ahmar group, which is part of the powerful Hashid tribal federation. Government troops are to withdraw from Sanaa, where the Ahmars have their headquarters.

A civil war may be avoided because, although a power vacuum may develop, the state has been traditionally feeble in Yemen and leaders are used to coping with the lack of government authority. The 24 million people are said to own about 60 million weapons, which means small-scale fighting is common, but so too are truces.

The success of the pro-democracy protests in Yemen would not have happened if the political elite was not itself split. Until the end, President Saleh had the loyalty of military units commanded by his close relatives. These are now negotiating to see how far they will have a role in any new regime.

The departure of President Saleh, who is in his late 60s, came after a devastating explosion in a mosque in the presidential compound where he was attending Friday prayers. He is reported to have been hit in the chest by pieces of wood, but the exact nature of his wounds is still unclear. The blast killed 11 of his bodyguards and wounded five senior officials. The government said his wounds were light, but his failure to appear on television led to speculation that they were severe. When he did finally speak it was on radio when he claimed, in a weak voice, that tribal rivals were behind the attack.

It was first announced that a rocket had struck the mosque but there is speculation in Sanaa that it is more likely that such a precisely targeted explosion was the result of a bomb planted by insiders within the regime.

Though President Saleh's presence in hospital in Riyadh decapitates the regime politically, his son Ahmed, commander of the presidential guard, remains in Sanaa, as do two nephews and two half-brothers, also commanders of elite units. They are strong enough to defend themselves, but without President Saleh's presence are unlikely to be able to maintain their grip on government.

Patrick Cockburn

Friday, 10 June 2011

DESCENDING INTO CIVIL WAR

The US has stepped up its covert air war against al-Qa'ida in Yemen as the country appears to be descending into civil war and government authority disintegrates. US aircraft are reported to have killed militant suspects in south Yemen last week, and pilotless drones have been used in attacks against other al-Qa'ida targets.

Army units loyal to President Ali Abdullah Saleh fired shots into the air in the capital, Sanaa, yesterday, claiming that he is about to return from Saudi Arabia where he is in hospital being treated for wounds sustained in an explosion in a mosque in the presidential compound last Friday. US and Arab officials say a bomb was planted in the mosque, and the President was not hit by a rocket or shell fired by the opposition as they said originally. Amid signs that government control, never strong in Yemen, is weakening, armed tribesmen have seized large parts of the second-biggest city Taiz, 150 miles south of Sanaa. Government forces are still holding a presidential palace and hospital in the centre of the city of one million people; tribesmen hold the rest.

A shaky truce is holding in Sanaa since the bomb attack that killed 11 presidential guards and wounded several senior officials as well as the President. US officials in the Saudi capital, Riyadh, had said he was burnt over 40 per cent of his body and it would be weeks, if not months, before he could exercise power.

But the government website claimed yesterday that "he has overcome health difficulties after successful surgery to remove shrapnel". A Saudi official was quoted as saying that he is undergoing cosmetic surgery to treat "light burns on the scalp". If President Saleh does return, fighting is likely to erupt immediately, but, even if he does not, military units commanded by members of his family and their allies will not give up power easily. The US and Saudi Arabia have been trying to arrange an orderly transition of power through the Vice-

President, Abed Rabbo Mansour Hadi. The US says it is worried that al-Qa'ida will use the chaos to expand its influence, though the numbers of al-Qa'ida in Yemen have been put at about 300 to 400 in a nation of 24 million.

The defence ministry says that 12 suspected al-Qa'ida members were killed as government troops fought towards Zinjibar, a town in the south taken by militants last week. But critics in Sanaa say that President Saleh encouraged Islamic fundamentalist fighters to take over the town to frighten the US into again backing his government. Zinjibar, where 50,000 people once lived, is now said to be a ghost town.

The US has declared Yemen to be the most important stronghold of al-Qa'ida, but recent bomb attacks directed against the US from the country over the past year have been abortive. And even failed al-Qa'ida plots have a political impact on the US out of all proportion to their significance or likelihood of success. A drone strike on 5 May was directed at US-born al-Qa'ida cleric, Anwar al-Awlaki, influential because of his intelligence, eloquence and command of English, and failed to kill him only because of a malfunctioning motor.

The al-Qa'ida leader Ayman al-Zawahri, believed to be in Pakistan, has declared solidarity with the uprising, saying on a video that Yemenis should not be tricked by the US and its Gulf allies "who want to replace one American agent with another".

Parts of Yemen are cut off from each other because of the collapse of security, so people are beginning to go hungry because basic foodstuffs cannot be delivered and there is a shortage of fuel, water, gas and electricity.

In Sanaa, shops have closed because of fear of fighting or looting and many government ministries are not functioning. The World Food Programme says that the prices of wheat-flour, sugar and vegetables have doubled since last year.

The street protests which first began to erode President Saleh's rule after he had held power for 32 years have been marginalised by other opponents of the old regime. These include important tribes and part of the armed forces. The protesters say they reject any deal with the pro-Saleh forces chanting "No to Saleh's return."

Patrick Cockburn

CHAPTER 6

SYRIA SPRING

Syrian refugees at the Turkish-Syrian border, 11 June 2011.

Thursday, 31 March 2011

NOT GIVING IN TO ARAB SPRING

He was not a humble President. He did not give way. There were hints, of course - an end to emergency legislation, "reforms" - but when he spoke yesterday, trying to calm a crisis that has seen more than 60 people killed in a fortnight and threatens his very office, President Bashar al-Assad of Syria did not give the impression of a man on the run.

Was it Libya that gave him the "oomph" to go on, the encouragement to stand up and say that "reform is not a seasonable issue" - an accurate translation of his belief that Syria does not have to conform to the Middle East revolution? Either way, the Baath party is going to fight on. Assad remains the President of Syria. No change. Well, of course, we shall see. Muammar Gaddafi of Libya is not a wise example to follow in time of need. Friday is another day, the traditional day of memorial and trial and questioning. If he can get through tomorrow without further killing in Deraa and Latakia, Assad may make it. He is young, his wife - wrongly derided by those who hate Syria - is a great asset to him, and his rule has banished the worst excesses of his father, Hafez. But - and it is a big "but" - torture does continue, the iniquities of the mukhabarat security services continue, freedom in Syria is as hard to find as an oasis in the desert, and the Syrian parliament remains, in the words of Al Jazeera's analyst Marwan Beshara, "a circus of support".

Yet there are more "buts" in Syria. It is a hard, tough country, without the avenues to free speech which were available in Egypt, to be sure, but a centre of Arab nationalism. Not for nothing do Syrians shout Um al Arabiya Wahida ("mother of one Arab nation"). Not for nothing do Syrians remember that they and they alone opposed the Sykes-Picot agreement that divided the region between France and Britain in 1916 with force of arms, their horse-riding army mowed down by French tanks at the battle of Maysaloon, their king given the monarchy of Iraq as a consolation prize by Winston Churchill.

This does not justify Bashar's autocratic rule. But it says something about it. Syrians do not obey the rules. Syrians do not follow the other Arabs like sheep. They fought harder than any others for a Palestinian-Israeli peace - which Assad described as "stagnant" yesterday, the unrest a "test for the nation" rather than a test for the President. In truth, the Hauran region - Deraa is in the Hauran, the scene of a fearsome series of government killings last week - has always been rebellious, even under French rule. But can Bashar al-Assad hold his country together?

He has managed, with a minority Alawite power (for which read Shia), to bring the Sunni Muslim majority of Syria into the economic establishment. Indeed, the Sunnis are the economy of Syria, a powerful elite who have no interest in unrest, disunity or foreign plots. It was odd that Assad talked about foreign "conspiracies" yesterday. It's an old adage that does him no credit; foreign "conspiracies" have always been discovered when dictators feel unsafe. Yet Damascus has been attacked by Israeli agents and Saddamist agents and Turkish right-wing agents over the past 40 years. It has a resonance, this talk of the moamarer - the "plot" - which makes Syrians into patriots rather than freedom fighters.

Of course, there is a lot wrong with Syria - and Bashar al-Assad may have pushed his luck yesterday, failing to announce the "reforms" and freedoms that Syrians expected of him. Instead of "God, Syria and Bashar", it was "God, Syria and my People" - but was that enough? He would not make reforms under pressure - "reforms", by the way, means democracy - but he surely is under pressure when government snipers have shot down the innocent in the streets of Syria's cities. He may not be in a mood for concessions. But is Syria not in need of these?

Its economy floats near bankruptcy - it was judged by the Swedish diplomatic corps to be unaffected by the West's economic catastrophe on the grounds that it did not really exist - and its Kurdish minority in the north are in a state of semi-revolt. But Assad has two friends who give him power: the Hizbollah in Lebanon and the Islamic Republic of Iran. If the Israelis need peace in Lebanon, they need Assad, and if Assad wants to maintain his regional power, he needs Iran. Syria is the Arab gate through which Iran can walk. Iran is the Muslim gate through which Assad - and remember, he is an Alawite and therefore a Shia - can walk. It is all too easy for Madame Clinton to berate Syria for killing its own people - a phrase she does not, of course, use for Bahrain - but the Americans need Syria to extract their last troops from Iraq.

It is also easy to turn Syria's problems into sectarianism. Nikolaos Van Dam, a brilliant Dutch diplomat, wrote a fine book emphasising that the struggle for power in Syria lay with the Alawites and that this minority effectively governed the country.

Yet Syria has always remained a unitary state, and it has complied with the West's demands for security cooperation - until the Americans came across the border into Syria and shot up a Syrian security agent's house. So compliant has it been that the US actually sent a poor Canadian to Damascus - "renditioned", in the popular phrase - to be atrociously tortured and kept in a sewer until the Americans realised he was innocent and sheepishly allowed him to return to Toronto.

These, needless, to say, are not issues which are going to be discussed on the television news shows or by the US Secretary of State - who is so concerned about the innocents of Libya that her air force is bombing Gaddafi but is so little concerned about the innocents of Syria that her air force will definitely not be bombing Syria.

Syria needs to be renewed. It does need an end to emergency laws, a free media and a fair judiciary and the release of political prisoners and - herewith let it be said - an end to meddling in Lebanon. That figure of 60 dead, a Human Rights Watch estimate, may in fact be much higher. Tomorrow, President Bashar al-Assad will supposedly tell us his future for Syria. It better be good.

Robert Fisk

Wednesday, 20 April 2011

CAN THIS CORRUPT REGIME BE CLEANSED?

"People are looking for security forces who will not treat the people like animals." So said Daeiri el-Eiti last night, a Syrian activist, summing up the thoughts of his country. He was right. In Banias, in Latakia, in Homs, in Aleppo, in Deraa, even in Damascus itself, it is the same thing. As a friend of Bashar al-Assad, the President, said last night, "Bashar is like Fukushima. He is irradiated."

Is this true? Can this be the end for the Ba'ath party of Syria, the very end of the "Renaissance Party" of the country which Bashar's father Hafez supported? Is this the end of the Syrian security forces? It seems incredible, but it looks as if all Bashar's dutiful offers of generosity - an end to the state of emergency, for example - have failed. There are those in Syria who say it is over, that there is nothing Bashar al-Assad can do to save his regime. We shall see.

The security forces - and we shall use the word "security" in quotation marks from here on - are fearful. There are long histories of torture and executions behind them and there are many within the military security apparatus inside Syria who are fearful of a riposte. For many years, the torture regime has imposed the most terrible revenge upon opponents of both the President and his father. There was the "German chair" which broke the back of opponents and there was the "Syrian chair" which broke their backs more slowly.

The current President knows all this and has tried to bring it to a halt. Largely, he has been successful.

His regime has largely proved to be humanitarian. But he has not been a successful leader. In his desperate attempts to persuade

Syrians that he can control his country, he has accused America, France and Lebanon of being responsible for the violence of demonstrators in his country.

Nobody in Syria believes this. The idea that Lebanon - let alone America and France - can cause demonstrations is ridiculous.

The problem lies, as Mr Eiti says, in that Syria remains a dictatorship and that Assad remains a dictator. His failure to rid his own family of the corrupt men within it (I am speaking of his uncle in particular) is the main problem for the regime. This is not a Gaddafi-corrupted government.

This is not a Mubarak government.

This is an Alawi regime - and essentially a Shia regime - which has been corrupted by its own family. The Assad family knows what it must do to cleanse the family name. Can Bashar do it? Does he have the power to do it? This is all that matters now if he is going to save his regime.

Robert Fisk

Saturday, 23 April 2011

THE PEOPLE WANT CHANGE

Every dictator knows that, when he starts making concessions, he is at his most vulnerable. It is an exquisite torture for the regime in power. Each gesture, each freeing of political prisoners, each concession - and the crowds demand more. Yesterday, it was President Bashar al-Assad who was under torture.

Had he not lifted the state of emergency for Syrians? Had he not allowed them permission to protest peacefully - albeit with permission to be obtained 24 hours in advance - and released a token number of prisoners? Had he not scrapped the hated state security court? But no such luck.

In Damascus, in Hama - that ancient city that tried to destroy Bashar's father Hafez with an Islamic uprising in the February of 1982 - and in Banias and Latakia and Deraa, they came out in their tens of thousands yesterday. They wanted 6,000 more political prisoners freed, they wanted an end to torture, an end to the security police. And they wanted Bashar al-Assad to go.

Syria is a proud country, but Tunisia and Egypt were studied by the Syrians (if not by Bashar himself - a big mistake). If the Arabs of north Africa could have their dignity, why couldn't the Syrians? And an end to the monopoly of the Ba'ath Party, while they were at it. And free newspapers; all the demands that they thought would be met 11 years ago, when Bashar walked behind his father's coffin and friends of the President told us that things were going to change. This was a confident new state under Bashar, they insisted.

But they didn't change. Bashar found that family and party and the massive security apparatus were too strong for him, too necessary for him. He failed. And now that failure is self-evident: in the tear gas fired at the crowds in Damascus; in the live rounds reportedly fired into the crowds in Hama, that dangerous, frightening city wherein there is not a man or woman over 30 who did not lose a relative or friend 29 years ago.

Bashar al-Assad is a tough guy. He stood up to Israel and American pressure. He supported Hezbollah and Iran and Hamas. But Syrians had other demands. They cared more about their domestic freedom than battles in Lebanon, more about torture in Tadmor prison than fighting for the Palestinians. And now they have marched with that ultimate demand: the end of the regime.

I'm not sure they'll get it yet. The Syrian Ministry of the Interior was playing the sectarian card again yesterday; the protesters were sectarian, they claimed. There may be some truth in this; but it is a small truth. The people on the streets of Syria want change. They were not, to be sure, in the vast numbers that Egypt produced to rid themselves of Mubarak; nor even the numbers of Tunisians. But it has begun.

Robert Fisk

Monday, 25 April 2011

GUNNING DOWN PROTESTERS

President Bashar al-Assad's war with his own Syrian people is moving perilously close to Lebanon. Indeed, over the past few days, Lebanese opposition leaders have been voicing their suspicions that the Baathist regime in Damascus - in an attempt to distract attention away from the Syrian popular uprising - is deliberately stirring sectarian tensions in a country which has only just commemorated the 36th anniversary of its own terrifying 15-year civil war, which cost 150,000 lives.

In the northern Lebanese city of Tripoli on Friday, rival pro- and anti-Assad demonstrations were held and the Lebanese Government flooded the streets with troops and internal security force members. Tripoli contains a sizeable community of Alawites, the Shia offshoot to which the Assad family belongs, most of them with close family ties to Syria.

Rather more disturbing was that the Shia Hezbollah in Lebanon - the only serious militia in the country and Israel's principal enemy here - accepted Syria's claim that the opposition Lebanese Future Movement MP Jamal Jarrah was involved in what the Assad regime calls the "armed insurgency" in the Syrian cities of Deraa, Latakia, Banias and Aleppo. Syrian television has shown interviews with two extremely frightened men it said had been caught with weapons and one of whom had, it said, confessed to bringing money and guns into Syria on the instructions of Jarrah. The MP and his party have indignantly denied the claim, but a Hezbollah official now says that Jarrah should be brought before Lebanese justice.

So, too, has the Syrian ambassador to Lebanon, Ali Abdul Karim Ali, who visited the Lebanese foreign ministry - obviously on orders from Damascus - to demand that Jarrah be brought to justice. The Future Movement, whose leader, Saad Hariri, remains the caretaker Lebanese Prime Minister in the continued absence of a government in the country, indignantly protested that Ali's move was Syrian interference in the internal affairs of Lebanon. Hezbollah has been busily praising - like its Iranian sponsors - the Egyptian revolution while condemning the demonstrations inside Syria.

So far, most Lebanese have been very careful to distance themselves from the Syrian imbroglio. The Druze leader, Walid Jumblatt, wrote in his weekly editorial in Al-Anba last week that because of his "attachment to Syria and its people and its stability", he believed that the authorities in Damascus should "undertake an internal restructuring of their security forces" as other Arab states have already done.

He has a point, of course. For it is now all too clear that the enormous hatred of the brutal mukhabarat secret police in Syria lies at the heart of the protests. On Friday, the security police opened live fire at protesters in 14 separate towns and cities across Syria - clearly a decision taken at the highest level of the regime.

Among those suppressing the protests were soldiers from the infamous Fourth Unit of the Syrian army, which answers directly not to the chief of staff but to President Assad's younger brother Maher, whose name appears on the banners of many of the protesters.

Human Rights Watch, which talks from Beirut directly to eyewitnesses of the massacres all over Syria, now has the names of exactly 76 protesters killed - or murdered - by the security forces over Friday and Saturday. Based on online collaboration, Syrian human rights activists have 112 names. Clearly about 100, including young children, died in a 48-hour period, but some bodies were not taken to hospitals where the state security police were noting their names and insisting that their burials should be private.

It is an odd phenomenon of all the Middle East revolutions that security police gun down protesters - and then gun down mourners at the funerals, and then shoot dead mourners at the funerals of those mourners shot dead the previous day.

According to Human Rights Watch's senior researcher on Syria, Nadim Houry, the death toll since the demonstrations began now totals 300. "It's clear that the Syrian security forces are ready to go very far to quell this," he says. "As far as this goes - and the other revolutions - it's a blast from the past. These regimes don't learn from each other - the protesters do. It would be funny if it wasn't so tragic. The language of the regimes - of foreign plots - is falling apart; people don't buy it any more."

Ironically, President Obama was the only international leader to suggest a "foreign hand" in Syria's crisis. He said that Iran was supporting the "outrageous" behaviour of the Syrian authorities.

Many Arabs were appalled that Mr Obama would apparently try to make cheap propaganda over the tragedy - there is, in fact, not the slightest evidence that Iran has been actively involved with the events in Syria - when he might have been dignified enough to have sent his sympathy to the mourners and told the protesters that America was with them.

But as Nadim Houry says, many regimes in the region - the Saudis, the Iranians, the Israelis and Turkey, for example - will be happy if Bashar Assad survives. "The real problem is, where do you go from here? he says. "The regime has drawn its 'line in the sand'. But it did learn from other Arab revolutions to keep crowds from the centre of cities.

"In Homs, protesters pitched tents in the central square but the security forces arrived en masse and broke them up, tore down the tents and washed the streets overnight. A man living next to the Homs square told me that 'When the sun rose, it was almost as if no one had been there the night before'.

"Then on Friday, when people began to walk into Damascus, they were simply shot down in the suburbs.

Only in Banias on Friday did the Syrian mukhabarat leave the city - and the protests there passed off peacefully."

Robert Fisk

Wednesday, 27 April 2011

TELEVISION HORROR SHOW

Every night, Syrian state television is a horror show.

Naked corpses with multiple bullet wounds, backs of heads sliced off. All Syrian soldiers, the television insists, murdered by "the treacherous armed criminal gangs" near Deraa.

One of the bodies - of a young officer in his twenties - has had his eyes gouged out. "Knives and sharp tools" appear to have been used on the soldiers, the commentary tells us.

There seems no doubt that the bodies are real and little doubt that they are indeed members of the Syrian "security" forces - the word security needs to be placed in inverted commas these days - nor that the weeping, distraught parents in the background are indeed their families. Pictures show the bodies, newly washed for burial, taken from the Tishrin Military Hospital in Damascus.

Their names are known. Mohamed Ali, Ibrahim Hoss, Ahmed Abdullah, Nida al-Hoshi, Basil Ali, Hazem Mohamed Ali, Mohamed Alla are all carried in flag-draped coffins from the army's mortuary by military police. They are from Tartous, Banias, Aleppo, Damascus. When al-Hoshi's funeral cortege was passing up the Mediterranean coast road to the north, they were ambushed by "an armed gang".

It's easy to be cynical about these dreadful pictures and the gloss put on their deaths. Shooting at funerals, after all, has hitherto been the prerogative of the government's armed cops rather than "armed gangs". And Syrian television has shown not a single dead civilian or civilian funeral after the death of perhaps 320 demonstrators in more than a month. Another 20 were reported killed around Deraa yesterday.

But these reports are important.

For if the dead soldiers are victims of revenge killings by outraged families who have lost their loved ones at the hands of the secret police, it means that the opposition is prepared to use force against their aggressors. But if there really are armed groups roaming Syria, then President Bashar al-Assad's Baathist regime is on the road to civil war.

Hitherto, the demonstrators - prodemocracy or anti-Bashar or both - have been giving us the story line; their YouTube footage, internet descriptions, the stunning pictures of Syrian T-72 tanks powering through the streets of Deraa - not to mention the pathetic attempt to attack one with an empty glass bottle - have dominated our perception of the all powerful dictatorship crushing its people in blood. And truth lies behind what they say. After the 1982 slaughter in Hama, no one is in any doubt that Syrian Baathists play by Hama rules. But their explanation for the daily series of macabre pictures on state television also lacks conviction. According to those bravely trying to telephone news out of Syria - although not from Deraa, where the telephones and internet have been completely shut down - the mutilated bodies are those of troops who refused to shoot at their own people and who were immediately punished by execution and mutilation by the shabiha, the "hoodlums" of Alawi fighters, and then cynically displayed on television to back up false government claims it is fighting an armed insurgency and that the people of Deraa themselves had invited the army into their city to save them from "terrorists".

Which sounds a little like the flipside of the government's own propaganda.

Of course, the Syrian authorities have only themselves to blame for their lack of credibility. Having cited "foreign plots" - the explanation of all the region's potentates when their backs are to the wall - the authorities have studiously banned all foreign journalists from entering Syria to prove or disprove these claims. The ministry of tourism has even been sent a list of Middle East correspondents by the ministry of interior to ensure that no reporters slip into Syria with a sudden desire to study the Roman ruins of Palmyra.

Thus history is written in rumours which begin, I suppose, with the last words displayed on Syrian television's evening news: "Martyrs Never Die." Clearly they do expire, but which martyrs are we talking about? A good tale from Deraa - one without a shred of evidence so far - is that after tanks of the Fourth Army Brigade of Maher Assad (little brother of the President) stormed into the city, elements of the regular army's Fifth Brigade near Deraa - supposedly commanded by an officer called Rifai, although even this is in dispute - turned their guns on Maher's invaders.

But the Fifth, so the story goes, has no tanks and includes air force personnel who are not allowed to fly their jets.

So are there now armed civilians - an oxymoron that seems lost on the regime - now fighting back in a systematic fashion? In Lebanon, whose capital is closer to Damascus that Deraa, there is growing fear that this bloodshed is only two hours away by road. Syria's friends in Lebanon are now claiming that the Saudis - allies of the outgoing government in Beirut - have been subventing the revolution in Syria.

One former minister produced on television copies of cheques for $300,000 (£180,000) supposedly carrying the signature of Prince Turki bin Abdul Aziz, the former Saudi intelligence head - and in that capacity once on good terms with a certain Osama bin Laden - and brother of King Abdullah, and given to Lebanese political figures to instil unrest in Syria. One of those accused of involvement by Syria is the former Lebanese minister Mohamed Beydoun. The latter has said that his accusers are guilty of "incitement to murder" and Prince Turki has indignantly called the cheques "false". But the Syrian-supported Hezbollah has now endorsed the claim and at least one Lebanese MP, Ahmed Fatfat, has at last uttered the fateful words. By these accusations against the "Future Movement" - the largest grouping in the outgoing government - he said, "the Hezbollah and its crew are preparing the way for civil war in Lebanon".

Now the Syrian media have pointed the finger at Lebanese MP Okab Sadr, stating that he had been arrested - along with "Israeli officers" - in the Syrian city of Banias. In fact, Mr Sadr is safe in Lebanon where he has emerged to say that the only reason he would go to Banias would be to give blood at the hospital to its inhabitants.

In the northern Lebanese city of Tripoli this Friday, pro and anti-Assad supporters plan to hold further and larger demonstrations after morning prayers. Many Lebanese in the north fear that in the event of a civil conflict inside Syria, Tripoli will become a "capital" of northern Syria, though whether it would be a rebel or an Assad stronghold is open to question.

Somewhat more disturbing right now - and much nearer the truth - is that Ali Aid, a rather tough character from the Jebel Mohsen area of the Alawi mountains of Syria, has left his son Rifaat in charge of his proto-militia movement. He has instead built himself a fine villa next to the Syrian-Lebanese border. The problem is that Major Ali Aid is living in his new home - which lies on the Lebanese side of the frontier.

Robert Fisk

Friday, 29 April 2011

IT'S THE KILLINGS THAT TERRIFY THE PEOPLE

In Damascus, the posters - in their tens of thousands around the streets - read: "Anxious or calm, you must obey the law." But pictures of President Bashar al-Assad and his father Hafez have been taken down, by the security police no less, in case they inflame Syrians.

There are thieves with steel-tipped rubber coshes on the Damascus airport road at night, and in the terminal the cops ask arriving passengers to declare iPods and laptops. In the village of Hala outside Deraa, Muslim inhabitants told their Christian neighbours to join the demonstrations against the regime - or leave. Out of the darkness of Syria come such tales.

And they are true. Syrians arriving in Lebanon are bringing the most specific details of what is going on inside their country, of Fifth Brigade soldiers fighting the armed units of Maher Assad's Fourth Brigade outside Deraa, of random killings around Damascus by the ever-growing armed bands of Shabiha ("the mafia") from the Alawite mountains, of massive stocking up of food. One woman has just left her mother in the capital with 10 kilos of pasta, 10 kilos of rice, five kilos of sugar, box after box of drinking water.

In Deraa - surrounded, without electricity or water or supplies - the price of bread has risen 500 per cent and men are smuggling food into the city over the fields at night.

But it is the killings which terrify the people. Are they committed by the Shabiha from the port city of Latakia - created by the Assad family in the 70s to control smuggling and protection rackets - or by the secret police to sow a fear that might break the uprising against Assad? Or by the murderers who thrive amid anarchy and lawlessness? Three men carrying sacks of vegetables outside Damascus at night were confronted by armed men last week. They refused to stop. So they were executed.

The Syrian government is appealing to the minorities - to the Christians and the Kurds - to stay loyal to the authorities; minorities have always been safe in Syria, and many have stayed away from protests against the regime. But in the village of Hala, Christian shops are shut as their owners contemplate what are clearly sectarian demands to join in the uprising against Assad. In an attempt to rid Syria of "foreign" influence, the ministry of education has ordered a number of schools to end all English teaching - even banning the names of schools in French and English from school uniforms. Even the kindergarten where the President's two young children are educated has been subject to the prohibitions.

There are bright lights, of course, not least among the brave men and women who are using the internet and Facebook to keep open the flow of information from Syria. *The Independent* can reveal that a system of committees has been set up across the cities of Syria, usually comprising only 10 or 12 friends who have known and trusted each other for years. Each of them enlists 10 of their own friends - and they persuade 10 more each - to furnish information and pictures.

Many were put in touch with each other via the cyber kings of Beirut - many of them also Syrian - and thus "circles of trust" have spread at the cost of the secret police snooping that has been part of Syrian life for four decades.

Thus there now exist - in Damascus alone - "The Co-ordination of Douma", "The Co-ordination of al-Maydan" (in the centre of the city), "The Co-ordination of Daraya", "The Co-ordination of Harasta" and others.

Some of them are trying to penetrate the mukhabarat secret police, to get the brutal cops to work for them on the grounds that - come the end of the Assad regime, if that end ever comes - they will be spared the trials and revenge punishments to come. One Beirut blogger says that several of the cops have already declared themselves for the uprising - but are unwilling to trust them in case it is a trap to discover the identity of those behind the committees. Yet Syrians in

Lebanon say that the Syrian security police - often appointed through graft rather than any technical or detective abilities - simply do not understand the technology that is being used against them. One Syrian security official sent three Facebook posts. The first said: "God, Syria and Bashar al-Assad or nothing." The second read: "It's the time to declare war for Allah." The third announced: "The legacy of God on earth is an Islamic Republic."

"The fool was obviously supporting Bashar - but then wanted to frighten people by suggesting Islamists would take over a post-Assad Syria," one of the Syrian bloggers in Beirut says. "But he didn't realise that we could tell at once that they all came from the same Facebook page!" The same man in Beirut found himself under interrogation by Syrian state security police several weeks ago. "He was a senior officer - but he didn't even know what Google was." Many of the Syrians sending information out of their country are anxious that exaggerations and rumours will damage the credibility of their reports. For this reason, they are trying to avoid dispatches which cannot be verified; that two Iranian snipers, for example, have arrived to help the security police; that one man was actually interrogated by two Iranians - a friend suspects that the cops were from the north and spoke in the Kurdish language, which the detainee misidentified as Iranian.

More serious - and true - is the report that Khaled Sid Mohand, an Algerian journalist working for France Culture and Le Monde, was arrested in Damascus on 9 April and has disappeared into a security prison. A released detainee says that he saw Mohand in Security Section 255 in Baghdad Street in the capital some days later. But this story may not be correct. Diplomats have been unable to see the missing journalist.

There are also reports that two young European women working for a Western embassy were arrested and gagged when they left a party at 3am several days ago, and only released several hours later after interrogation. "It means that there is no longer any immunity for foreigners," a Syrian citizen said yesterday. "We heard that a North American had also been taken from his home and questioned by armed men."

Especially intriguing - because there are many apparent witnesses of this episode - is a report that Syrian Fourth Brigade troops in Deraa dumped dozens of weapons in the main square of the city in front of the Omari mosque, telling civilians that they could take them to defend themselves.

Suspecting that they were supposed to carry them in demonstrations and then be shot as "terrorists", the people took the weapons to the nearest military base and gave them back to the soldiers.

The rumours of army defections continue, however, including splits in the Fifth Brigade at Deraa, whose commander's name can now be confirmed as General Mohamed Saleh al-Rifai. According to Syrians arriving in Lebanon, the highways are used by hundreds of packed military trucks although the streets of most cities - including Damascus - are virtually empty at night. Shops are closing early, gunfire is often heard, checkpoints at night are often manned by armed men in civilian clothes. Darkness indeed.

Robert Fisk

Saturday, 11 June 2011

INCREASING VIOLENCE

In a calculated show of defiance to the international community, Syrian army tanks yesterday shelled civilian homes driving hundreds of people out of the country in brutal retaliation for protests against the rule of President Bashar al-Assad.

Troops from the regime's notorious 4th Division - headed by the president's brother Maher - burnt crops and slaughtered livestock in an overpowering show of military might in the north of the country after the regime blamed "armed gangs" for the deaths of 120 of its security forces last week in the rebellious town of Jisr al-Shughour. Some witnesses claimed that the security forces were killed during fighting between loyalist troops and defectors who refused to fire on unarmed civilians. Snipers fired on demonstrators in protests elsewhere in the country yesterday with 28 people killed, according to rights groups.

But the focus of the military assault was in the hills and villages of northwest Syria near the border with Turkey. One witness who fled his village yesterday told *The Independent* that the military was "shelling everything".

"They entered my town with tanks and started shooting everywhere," said the man, who arrived at the Turkish border yesterday.

"They were breaking down doors and shooting the houses with machine guns. I just thank God that I left and that my life was saved."

Witnesses told Reuters that at least 15,000 troops along with some 40 tanks and troop carriers had surrounded Jisr al-Shughour, but that the town was now largely deserted. "People were not going to sit and be slaughtered like lambs," said one refugee.

As the army massed on the city's outskirts, refugees continued to pour towards the Turkish border. Bloodsoaked civilians who had been injured during the army's advance were treated on the ground, while others chanted anti-government slogans in defiance of the regime.

Around 3,000 refugees are now sheltering in Turkey after fleeing through the mountainous woodlands of northwest Syria. One woman who arrived yesterday after fleeing from the town of Sarmaniya, about six miles south of Jisr al-Shughour, said: "They destroyed everything. They killed the animals, they burnt the crops. The tanks were shelling buildings and I heard machine-gun fire. They destroyed my town."

The continuing crackdown comes despite growing diplomatic pressure led by Britain and France calling for an end to violence and to allow international monitors into the country.

Syria's position in the Middle East, its alliance with Iran and a border with Israel make it a key player in the region's politics. Yet some worry that the deteriorating situation could lead to civil war in a country riven by religious sects.

The regime of President Bashar al-Assad, who became leader after the death of his father in 2000, has kept up the relentless battering of the protest movement, which shows no signs of dying down, despite estimates that 1,300 civilians have been killed since mid-March. Yet in spite of the weekly toll of death and bloodshed protesters continue to take to the streets in growing numbers every Friday.

Thousands again defied the Baathist regime and protested following yesterday's midday prayers. Snipers fired at them from the rooftops in Damascus and the security services also fired on large crowds in Deraa, the southern city which was subjected to a relentless army siege after widespread unrest broke out in March.

The international action follows growing outrage over atrocities in Syria, including attacks on children. the death of a 15-year-old boy,

Thamer al-Sahri, whose bullet-ridden body was released by Syrian authorities and returned to the family home near Deraa. The teenager, who was missing an eye and several teeth, was arrested after attending a demonstration near his home. He was close friends with Hamza al-Khatib, another young schoolboy who went to the same protest and died after being tortured in custody. Amnesty said last night that 32 children remained in custody between the ages of 12 and 17.

"The more the regime cracks down the more the people protest," said Andrew Tabler, an expert on Syria from the Washington Institute of Near East Policy. He added that high reports of child torture had been instrumental in keeping the momentum of the protests going.

Wissam Tarif, executive director of Syrian human rights organisation Insan, said: "When more defections start happening we can talk about the regime collapsing," he said. "This cannot become more violent than it is. It will be limited."

The Independent

CHAPTER 7

FADE TO AUTUMN

Thursday, 19 May 2011

WEST CAN NO LONGER RELY ON COMPLIANT DICTATORS

Ok, so here's what President Barack Obama should say today about the Middle East. We will leave Afghanistan tomorrow. We will leave Iraq tomorrow. We will stop giving unconditional, craven support to Israel. Americans will force the Israelis - and the European Union - to end their siege of Gaza. We will withhold all future funding for Israel unless it ends, totally and unconditionally, its building of colonies on Arab land that does not belong to it. We will cease all cooperation and business deals with the vicious dictators of the Arab world - whether they be Saudi or Syrian or Libyan - and we will support democracy even in those countries where we have massive business interests. Oh yes, and we will talk to Hamas.

Of course, President Barack Obama will not say this. A vain and cowardly man, he will talk about the West's "friends" in the Middle East, about the security of Israel - security not being a word he has ever devoted to Palestinians - and he will waffle on and on about the Arab Spring as if he ever supported it (until, of course, the dictators were on the run), as if - when they desperately needed his support - he had given his moral authority to the people of Egypt; and, no doubt, we will hear him say what a great religion Islam is (but not too great, or Republicans will start recalling the Barack Hussein Obama birth certificate again) and we will be asked - oh, I fear we will - to turn our backs on the Bin Laden past, to seek "closure" and "move on" (which I'm afraid the Taliban don't quite agree with).

Mr Obama and his equally gutless Secretary of State have no idea what they are facing in the Middle East. The Arabs are no longer afraid. They are tired of our "friends" and sick of our enemies. Very soon, the Palestinians of Gaza will march to the border of Israel and demand to "go home".

We got a signal of this on the Syrian and Lebanese borders on Sunday. What will the Israelis do? Kill the Palestinians in their thousands? And what will Mr Obama say then? (He will, of course, "call for restraint on both sides", a phrase he inherited from his torturing predecessor).

I rather think that the Americans suffer from what the Israelis suffer from: self-delusional arguments. The Americans keep referring to the goodness of Islam, the Israelis to how they understand the "Arab mind". But they do not. Islam as a religion has nothing to do with it, any more than Christianity (a word I don't hear much of these days) or Judaism. It's about dignity, honour, courage, human rights - qualities which, in other circumstances, the United States always praises - which Arabs believe they are owed. And they are right. It is time for Americans to free themselves from their fear of Israel's lobbyists - in fact the Likud Party's lobbyists - and their repulsive slurs of anti-Semitism against anyone who dares to criticise Israel. It is time for them to take heart from the immensely brave members of the American-Jewish community who speak out about the injustices that Israel as well as the Arab leaders commit.

But will our favourite President say anything like this today? Forget it. This is a mealy-mouthed President who should - why have we forgotten this? - have turned down his Nobel Peace Prize because he can't even close Guantanamo, let alone bring us peace. And what did he say in his Nobel speech? That he, Barack Obama, had to live in the real world, that he was not Gandhi, as if - and all praise to The Irish Times for spotting this - Gandhi didn't have to fight the British empire. So we will be treated to all the usual analysts in the States, saying how fine the President's words are, praising this wretched man's speechifying.

And then comes the weekend when Mr Obama has to address the American Israel Public Affairs Committee, the biggest, most powerful lobbyist "friend" of Israel in America. Then it will be all back to the start, security, security, security, little - if any mention - of the Israeli colonies in the West Bank and, I feel sure of this, much mention of terrorism, terrorism, terrorism, terrorism, terrorism, terrorism,

terrorism. And no doubt a mention of the killing (let us not use the word execution) of Osama bin Laden.

What Mr Obama doesn't understand however - and, of course, Mrs Clinton has not the slightest idea - is that, in the new Arab world, there can be no more reliance on dictator-toadies, no more flattery. The CIA may have its cash funds to hand but I suspect few Arabs will want to touch them. The Egyptians will not tolerate the siege of Gaza. Nor, I think, will the Palestinians. Nor the Lebanese, for that matter; and nor the Syrians when they have got rid of the clansmen who rule them. The Europeans will work that out quicker than the Americans - we are, after all, rather closer to the Arab world - and we will not forever let our lives be guided by America's fawning indifference to Israeli theft of property.

It is, of course, going to be a huge shift of tectonic plates for Israelis - who should be congratulating their Arab neighbours, and the Palestinians for unifying their cause, and who should be showing friendship rather than fear. My own crystal ball long ago broke. But I am reminded of what Winston Churchill said in 1940, that "what General Weygand called the battle for France is over. The battle of Britain is about to begin."

Well, the old Middle East is over. The new Middle East is about to begin. And we better wake up.

Robert Fisk

Sunday, 12 June 2011

HOPES FOR DEMOCRACY FADE

The Arab awakening is turning into the Arab nightmare. Instead of ushering in democracy, the uprisings in at least three Arab states are fast becoming vicious civil wars. In the past 10 days, crucial developments in Syria, Libya and Yemen have set these countries spiralling into violent and intractable struggles for power.

In Syria, thousands of troops are assaulting the northern town of Jisr al-Shughour where the government claims 120 of its soldiers and police were killed last week. Leaving aside exactly how they died, the government in Damascus is making it lethally clear that in future its opponents, peaceful opponents or not, will be treated as if they were armed gunmen. An extraordinary aspect of the Syrian uprisings is that people go on demonstrating in their tens of thousands despite so many being shot down. But some are evidently coming to believe that their only alternative is to fight back.

A week ago in Yemen, the 'Failure to evict the Saleh clan opens the way for a collapse in state authority' demonstrators, who have been marching and rallying in the streets of Sanaa since the start of the year, celebrated jubilantly on hearing the news that President Ali Abdullah Saleh had left the country for hospital in Saudi Arabia after being injured in a bomb attack. "The people, at last, have defeated the regime," the protesters chanted. But it is ludicrous to portray this as a triumph for peaceful protest, since the reason Saleh went to Riyadh was injuries inflicted by a bomb planted in the presidential compound. It is becoming depressingly clear that the Saleh regime is not as dependent on the presence of the president himself as many imagined. Other members of the Saleh clan are in command of well-armed and well trained military units that remain in control of most of Yemen.

Even before what was clearly a well-planned assassination attempt against Saleh, the street protesters were looking marginalised. They were able to stay in "Change Square" only because traditional players, including powerful tribal and military leaders, had switched sides and were defending them.

Is Yemen on the way to permanent confrontation of the type that reduced Somalia to ruinous anarchy? In the past, Yemenis often argued that, while Yemeni politics was very divisive and violent, the ruling elite had a remarkable capacity to reach last-minute compromises. Maybe this was true, but the failure to evict the Saleh clan, even when its leader is out of the country, bodes ill and opens the way for a collapse of state authority.

Libya has also moved a long way from the democratic hopes of February.

An important signal since the start of June has been the intervention of Nato attack helicopters, making the rebels more an auxiliary force in a foreign-run campaign. The deployment of the rebels is now largely decided by Nato, without whose air power the local anti-Gaddafi forces would long ago have been defeated. Most Libyans probably want Gaddafi to go, but the Transitional National Council in Benghazi may not have the legitimacy or the support to replace him. He is very likely to be displaced before the end of the year, but this will be a victory primarily won by Nato and not popular revolution.

A fourth country where the Arab awakening seemed to be on the verge of success is Bahrain. But since the Saudi-led intervention, and the assault on pro-democracy protesters and the Shia population as a whole since 15 March, this tiny kingdom has been convulsed by a civil war that rages just beneath the surface. The decision by Bahraini al-Khalifa royals to play the sectarian card and pretend the demand for democratic reform was a revolutionary plot orchestrated by Iran has won many believers among the Sunni. Quite why the family should have decided to declare war on most of the Arab population of Bahrain remains something of a mystery since this will make it permanently reliant on Saudi Arabia. Probably a sense of panic, at its height in March and induced by the fall of the regimes in Tunisia and Egypt, explains the intensity of the repression in Bahrain. A price for this will be permanently to deepen the bitter hostility between Shia and Sunni.

Probably one should not be so surprised by the faltering of the mass movements associated with the Arab Spring. The surprise is rather that they should have succeeded so easily in Tunisia and Egypt. After all, socalled "velvet revolutions" do not have a high success rate. They may have worked in Eastern Europe when communism was displaced 20 years ago, but the communist leadership was not prepared to fight it out, was divided, massively unpopular and hoped to be part of the new order. A better parallel to the Arab Spring is the Green movement's attempt to stage a velvet revolution in Iran in 2009, which signally failed. Even if the election of that year was fixed by the Iranian government, it still had a core of committed supporters in the Revolutionary Guards. The urban poor never joined the protests en masse as they did in Tunisia and Egypt.

The lesson of the past six months 'Unless the protesters can split the armed forces, their chance of success is limited' in the Arab world is that unless the street protesters can split or guarantee the neutrality of the armed forces, their chance of success is limited. Their only option is to get full-scale foreign military intervention, as has happened in Libya. In practice, this means obtaining support from the US, even if the military action is carried out by the UK and France. It was the fear in Saudi Arabia and the Gulf monarchies this year that they no longer had a guarantee of support from Washington that panicked them into their violent onslaught on protesters in Bahrain.

The foreign media - notably al-Jazeera and satellite channels - played a central part in opening the way for the Arab Spring. Censorship, control of information and communications played an important role in the establishment of the police states that monopolised power in the Arab world from the 1970s. But this control has been weakened by the internet, satellite television and mobile phone. At the same time, not all the instruments of power have changed. Security forces remained. The spontaneous nature of the Arab uprising was at first an advantage because the police did not know who to arrest, but this lack of leadership became a disadvantage when the revolution faced opposition.

The moderation of the early protesters is turning out to be a crippling weakness as rulers fight for power.

Patrick Cockburn

PART 2

ARAB WINTER

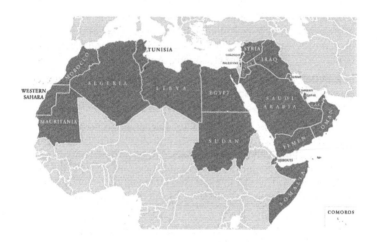

Saturday, 9 January 2016

THE NEW MAP OF THE ARAB WORLD

MOROCCO: Concessions by King Mohammed VI, including a referendum in July 2011 that led to changes in the constitution, helped ensure that protests fizzled out by end of 2012.

ALGERIA: Barely affected after an initial year-long state of emergency; some terrorist activity, including 2013 gas plant attack in which dozens of foreign hostages were killed.

TUNISIA: The birthplace of the Arab Spring is also its one success story. There were free elections in 2011 and 2013, and the country is largely peaceful - although up to 300 people died in the unrest that overthrew President Ben Ali in 2011. Terrorist attacks in 2015 have cast a shadow, and threaten to cause a disastrous fall in tourism.

LIBYA: Hopes raised by Nato-aided overthrow of Colonel Muammar Gaddafi in August 2011 were bitterly disappointed. An elected parliament, the General National Congress, took power in August 2012 but was forced to withdraw to Tobruk as a rival government seized Tripoli. Much of the country is now under control of neither, with Isis established in some parts.

EGYPT: Up to 900 people were killed in protests that led to fall of President Hosni Mubarak in 2011. His successor, Mohamed Morsi of the Muslim Brotherhood, was ousted by the army in July 2013. Nearly 1,000 people were killed in the protests that followed. A new President, General Abdel Fattah el-Sisi, was elected in 2014; hundreds of Muslim Brotherhood members have since been sentenced to death.

JORDAN: Moderate protests led to modest reforms, and a few changes of government, by King Abdullah II. The main effect of the Spring has been the arrival of a least 600,000 Syrian refugees (and a similar number of Syrians who are not classified as refugees).

LEBANON: The country has taken in more than a million Syrian refugees as a result of the Spring. Also at risk of violence spilling over from Syria. Sectarian violence in some cities, notably Tripoli.

SYRIA: A few weeks of hope in 2011. Since then, endless catastrophe, defined as a civil war by the UN since mid-2012. Up to 350,000 people have died, 4.4 million are refugees, swathes of the country are controlled by Isis, moderate rebels have been massacred, the Assad regime remains (partly) in place, and intervention by foreign powers - including Russia, Iran, the US, France and the UK - has not slowed the slaughter.

IRAQ: Minor protests in 2011 and major ones in 2012-13, aimed at corruption and anti-Shia discrimination. The electoral defeat of Nouri al-Maliki as Prime Minister in 2014 came too late to disperse the resentment; by then, Isis was running amok. Despite recent gains by the Iraqi army, large regions are under Isis control.

SAUDI ARABIA: Kept a lid on domestic discontent through a mix of authoritarianism and state largesse. Helped crush protest in Bahrain. Military intervention in Yemen has been bloody and inconclusive. Plummeting oil prices and a change of monarch have destabilised the regime.

KUWAIT: Protests in 2011-12 fizzled out after fall of one government. The Al-Sabah family continues to rule.

BAHRAIN: Around 30 people died when protests against the ruling Khalifa family were suppressed, with Saudi help, in early 2011. Thousands have since been jailed in the crackdown by the Sunni regime on its majority Shia population.

QATAR: Largely unaffected by domestic protests, but involved in upheavals elsewhere, notably by joining the Nato-led campaign that overthrew Colonel Gaddafi in Libya.

UAE: Calls for greater democracy fizzled out. Remains stable and, for now, prosperous.

OMAN: Protests in 2011 led to the creation of a Public Authority for Consumer Protection.

YEMEN: President Ali Abdullah Saleh was forced out of the country and office in, respectively, 2011 and 2012. An uprising by Shia rebels led by Abdul-Malik al-Houthi, which began in 2014, led to the flight of Saleh's successor, Abd Rabbuh Mansur Hadi, in 2015. The Iran-aligned Houthis now control the capital but are under attack from a Saudi-led Sunni coalition.

A SPRING THAT BEGAN IN HOPE BUT ENDED IN DESPAIR

Arab Spring was always a misleading phrase, suggesting that what we were seeing was a peaceful transition from authoritarianism to democracy similar to that from communism in Eastern Europe. The misnomer implied an over-simplified view of the political ingredients that produced the protests and uprisings of 2011 and overoptimistic expectations about their outcome.

Five years later it is clear that the result of the uprisings has been calamitous, leading to wars or increased repression in all but one of the six countries where the Arab Spring principally took place. Syria, Libya and Yemen are being torn apart by civil wars that show no sign of ending. In Egypt and Bahrain autocracy is far greater and civil liberties far less than they were prior to 2011. Only in Tunisia, which started off the surge towards radical change, do people have greater rights than they did before.

What went so disastrously wrong? Some failed because the other side was too strong, as in Bahrain where demands for democratic rights by the Shia majority were crushed by the Sunni monarchy. Saudi Arabia sent in troops and Western protests at the repression

were feeble. This was in sharp contrast to vocal Western denuncia-
tions of Bashar al-Assad's brutal suppression of the uprising by the
Sunni Arab majority in Syria. The Syrian war had social, political and
sectarian roots but it was the sectarian element that predominated.
Why did intolerant and extreme Islam trump secular democracy? It
did so because nationalism and socialism were discredited as the slogans of the old regimes, often military regimes that had transmuted
into police states controlled by a single ruling family. Islamic movements were the main channel for dissent and opposition to the status
quo, but they had little idea how to replace it. This became evident in
Egypt where the protesters never succeeded in taking over the state
and the Muslim Brotherhood found that winning elections did not
bring real power.

The protest movements at the beginning of 2011 presented
themselves as progressive in terms of political and civil liberty and
this belief was genuine. But there had been a real change in the balance of power in the Arab world over the previous 30 years with Saudi
Arabia and the Gulf monarchies taking over leadership from secular
nationalist states. It was one of the paradoxes of the Arab Spring that
rebels supposedly seeking to end dictatorship in Syria and Libya were
supported by absolute monarchies from the Gulf.

The West played a role in supporting uprisings against leaders
they wanted to see displaced such as Muammar Gaddafi and Assad.
But they gave extraordinarily little thought to what would replace
these regimes. They did not see that the civil war in Syria was bound
to destabilise Iraq and lead to a resumption of the Sunni-Shia war
there.

An even grosser miscalculation was not to see that the armed opposition in Syria and Iraq was becoming dominated by extreme
jihadis. Washington and its allies long claimed that there was a moderate nonsectarian armed opposition in Syria though this was largely
mythical. In areas where Isis and non-Isis rebels ruled they were as
brutal as the government in Damascus. The nonsectarian opposition
fled abroad, fell silent or was killed and it was the most militarised
and fanatical Islamic movements that flourished in conditions of permanent violence.

Patrick Cockburn

AN ABSURD ISIS DEBATE

"Watching them both yacking on about the Middle East as a pink dawn glowed from behind the Lebanese mountains above Beirut, I found the Trump-Clinton show a grimly instructive experience. In the few hundred miles east and south of Lebanon, hundreds are dying every week - in Syria, in Yemen, in Iraq - and yet there were the terrible twins playing "I can beat Isis better than you can beat Isis". Was this what the Arab world really meant to the reality show participants at the unpronounceable university campus on Long Island?

What was it Trump said to Clinton? "You've been fighting Isis your entire adult life!" And what did Clinton say? "Well at least I have a plan to fight Isis!" After an hour, I was praying that the Lebanese slept on amid the mountains. Please God there would be electricity cuts in Aleppo and Baghdad and Sanaa - just for these 90 minutes, you understand - so that the people enduring the Middle East tragedy did not witness how the next US president was using their homelands as a movie back-lot.

"He has no plan to defeat Isis," quoth Madame Clinton. But does anyone? It's a pity, for example, that they didn't outline "plans" for justice, freedom and dignity in the Middle East and an end to the policy of bombing, bombing, bombing and more bombing that now seems to equal political initiative in the Arab world. But of course they did not, for all this was slotted into the last bit of the CNN show, the climax which was - wearingly and predictably - entitled "American security".

There was a very brief mention by Trump of "Bibi Netanyahu" that must have left many American viewers completely floored - save for those supporters of Israel to whom, of course, it was addressed - but that was all we heard about another small conflict in the Middle East. Cliché and banality rubbed up against each other. Clinton claimed that Obama had stopped those "centrifuges that were whirling away" in Iran - I'm not sure that centrifuges do "whirl", though Clinton may have been talking about the "whirling dervishes" who also live in the region. And then Trump came up with his apple pie throwaway.

"The Middle East is a total mess," and Iran would soon be a "major power" - as if Iran was not already a major power in the region, as it has been for around 3,000 years. But what particular "mess" was he talking about? The "mess" in the hospitals of eastern Aleppo? The "mess" of Egypt's civil rights - though I do suspect that Brigadier-General-President al-Sisi's version would rather appeal to Trump - or the "mess" left behind by the bombing of the Médecins Sans Frontières hospital in Afghanistan? Or perhaps the "mess" of Palestine - another word that mercifully was not dwelt upon by the duo who both plan to rule America? Didn't "Bibi" mention that to Trump? Or the "mess" of Nato, whose killing of Serbs (and quite a few Kosovo Muslims) in 1999 was followed by the Alliance's support for the Afghan war but which, according to Trump, "does not focus on terror"?

"We have to knock the hell out of Isis - and we have to do it fast," the great man told the world. Well, sure, but haven't we all been knocking the hell out of Afghanistan, Iraq, Yemen, Syria, even Lebanon (a few years ago), and achieving the constant rebirth of ever more vicious warriors, of which Isis - heaven spare us the thought - may soon generate another, even worse progeny? Trump apparently believed that Isis would not exist if Obama had left 10,000 US troops in Iraq - a strategy Isis would surely have applauded - while Clinton moaned on about how the Iraqi government "would not protect American troops".

And there you have it, I suppose. It is the Arab world's job, isn't it, to "protect" America in its various military occupations, or - at the very least - the task (yes, this old chestnut was indeed produced) of "our friends in the Middle East". And who were they, I wondered? Those fantastic Saudis who gave us 15 of the 9/11 hijackers? About the only nonsense left unuttered by Trump and Clinton was that Isis was born outside the United States. There they would have been on safe ground. Or would they? For I suspect there may be a growing number of Arabs who believe that Isis is indeed a child born in America."

Robert Fisk

Friday, 21 October 2016

FREEDOM IS SCARCE FIVE YEARS AFTER ARAB SPRING

I was planning to visit Baghdad last summer and stay with my friend Ammar al-Shahbander, who ran the local office of the Institute for War and Peace Reporting. I had stayed with him for 10 days in June

2014, just after Isis forces had captured Mosul and Tikrit and were advancing with alarming speed on the capital.

Ammar was a good man to be with in a moment of crisis because he had strong nerves, an ebullient personality and was highly informed about all that was happening in Iraq. He was sceptical but not cynical, though refreshingly derisive as the Iraqi government claimed mythical victories as Isis fighters approached ever closer to the capital. He did not believe that they could successfully storm Baghdad, but that did not mean they would not try - and one morning I found him handing over a Kalashnikov to somebody to have its sights readjusted.

We shared a fascination with the dangerous complexities of Iraqi life and politics and I had been looking forward to resuming our conversations in 2015. I was just about to send him a message saying that I was coming to Baghdad, when I heard that I was too late and he was dead. He was killed on 2 May by a car bomb that exploded as he left a café in the Karrada district, where he had been sitting with a friend after attending a concert. A piece of broken metal entered his heart and he died, along with 17 other people killed by Isis bombs in Baghdad that night.

All too many journalist friends have been killed in Iraq, Syria and Libya since 2011, but most were doing dangerous things when they died and knew the risks they were taking. Simply by living in Baghdad rather than London, Ammar knew that he was taking a risk but, high though the level of violence may be in the city, it is not a battle zone. He was not personally targeted so there was a greater element of ill-luck in his death than that of other journalists and people working in the media, making his murder feel all the more poignant and unnecessary.

His death made me think about how much more difficult it has become to be a foreign or local journalist in the Middle East and North Africa over the past few years. The overthrow of Saddam Hussein in 2003 and the Arab Spring in 2011 were meant to herald greater freedom of expression and an end to censorship and the persecution of journalists. In reality, just the opposite has happened with country after country becoming highly dangerous for foreign journalists to visit and independent local journalism being stamped out by authoritarian governments and murderous Islamist opposition movements.

Journeys I took in reasonable safety a few years ago are now impossibly dangerous. In 2003 I drove from Damascus to the city of al-

Qamishli in north-east Syria in about 12 hours, passing through territory now divided up into hostile enclaves by the Syrian army, Isis, extreme Islamists and Syrian Kurds.

A year or so later, I went from Baghdad to Mosul and spent the night in Kirkuk before returning to the capital, a route that nobody would think of taking today.

In 2011, I travelled from Cairo to Benghazi in Libya without difficulty and later in the year, a little more problematically, from Tunisia to Tripoli, passing safely through territory now ruled by warring militias.

The figures for journalists killed in 2015 tell something of the story, with 110 reporters killed across the world over the year according to a report published last week by Reporters Without Borders. Unsurprisingly, the countries with the most journalistic fatalities are Syria, Iraq and Yemen. together with France - where the figure was boosted by the massacre of cartoonists, journalists and security staff on the Charlie Hebdo magazine. But the raw casualty figures do not really explain why so much of the wider Middle East and North Africa has fallen off the media map. Civil wars in Libya, Somalia, South Sudan and Yemen are barely reported because of the extreme danger of doing so and lack of interest in the rest of the world about what is happening there.

The fighting in Afghanistan has escalated sharply as the Taliban launch offensives across the country, but the foreign press corps in Kabul is very shrunken compared to a few years ago.

The war in Iraq and Syria is heavily covered by the international media, but much of the reporting is from other countries such as Lebanon or Turkey. Aside from a few brave exceptions, foreign journalists do not enter areas held by so-called Islamic State, deterred by the kidnapping and ritual decapitation of their colleagues. Areas controlled by non-Isis armed opposition have often proved equally dangerous.

Criminalisation is pervasive and local gangs know that a kidnapped foreign journalist is worth a lot of money because he or she can be held for ransom or sold on to Isis.

Even supposedly safe parts of Syria and Iraq are less risky only by comparison with the rest of the country.

In September, I was in the Kurdish held north-east corner of Syria that now extends from the Tigris to the Euphrates after a series of Syrian Kurdish victories against Isis. But front lines in this war are porous and it soon became clear that the threat from Isis had not wholly disappeared: in Tal Abyad, an important crossing point on the Syrian border captured from Isis in June, a local woman stopped our car to warn that a man dressed like an Isis fighter had just run through her courtyard. Police said there were still Isis sleeper cells around. In a Kurdish town, Ras al Ayn, there were two suicide bomb attacks in the brief period we were there.

The media-free zones that have opened up across the wider Middle East are worse than ever before because today both the region's governments and Islamist-dominated opposition are targeting journalists.

Patrick Cockburn

Friday, 21 October 2016

THE MIDDLE EAST BURNS

Maybe it's because I live in Lebanon, and return to Beirut from Aleppo and Damascus, that the place seems so "normal". While all around this little jewel, the Middle East burns - Syria, the occupied West Bank, Iraq, Yemen, Libya, increasingly Egypt and, alas, Turkish Kurdistan - Lebanon glistens brightly in the darkness, largely untarnished by the horrors on the other side of its borders. Or so it seems.

We might be forgiven for believing that this little paradise still exists in the Arab world. True, Lebanon has no president, no functioning government and constant power cuts (I currently have three electricity outages a day, sometimes totalling six hours, without a generator). Reading by candlelight might seem as romantic as Milton - preferably without its physical effect on him - but it gets a little boring after a while.

True, the Syrian war has stained Lebanon. Mosque bombings, the attempted destruction of the Iranian embassy by suicide killers, the brief capture of the Lebanese town of Ersal by Isis and the beheading of Lebanese soldiers who were seized there, seemed to foreshadow a replay of the country's old civil war.

Hezbollah fighters from southern Lebanon receive military funerals when they are driven home by the dozen from the Syrian battlefields. Sunni and Alawite (Shia) gunmen have fought in the northern city of Tripoli.

But the new Lebanese war didn't happen.

I have a few pet theories about Lebanon's survival. It has the most educated population in the Arab world and the most talented (in the literal sense of the word) people. Its own civil war, with its 150,000 dead - a little common grave compared to Syria today - taught the Lebanese that no one wins, although the Christian minority continued to hold the presidency and the Shia Hezbollah continued to keep their guns.

For their own safety, tens of thousands of Lebanese children - offspring of the middle classes and the elite, of course - were sent abroad by their parents during the 1976-90 war. They lived in Geneva, Paris, London, New York. They studied at Oxford, Harvard and the Sorbonne. They grew into adulthood in Western nations where dignity and freedom were natural rights rather than privileges.

They returned to their country appalled at its sectarianism, its corruption, the hatreds of the family "zoama", the seigneurs who believe they have a blood-right to power. The returning children loathed the stigma of mixed marriages and their self-righteous priests. Good on them, I used to say. They've even forced the government to accept civil marriages - to the meddlesome fury of both Muslim and Christian prelates.

Yet the old traditions persist. I recall a Muslim friend whose son attended a British university and whom I would meet in the UK from time to time. He enjoyed his freedoms - beer, girlfriends, the freedom to speak his mind - but in his final term he asked his mother back in Beirut to find him a Muslim bride. I was saddened. He enjoyed the good life, and then wanted mummy to find him a teenage bride of the right religion.

Almost every six months I encounter a Muslim or Christian friend whose parents threaten to disown them if they marry a man or woman from a different religion. Up in the Chouf mountains at Beit Eddine, I attended a conference on sectarianism at which a worthy Western academic suggested that the youth of Lebanon must be encouraged to marry whomever they love, whatever their religion. No, I said. It's their parents to whom they should preach.

And what do you do about corruption? It's a cancer in the Middle East (and a lot of Western countries, I might add). I regularly meet with men and women who have dodgy backgrounds. It's part of my job as a journalist. They defrauded a bank, or have civil war blood on their hands, or are trying to smear a rival politician. I used to frequent a vegetable shop whose owner had murdered another man in a family feud.

He kept a rifle beside the cauliflower stall. Last week, an internal security force officer used his service pistol to shoot his neighbours in the Kesrouan region over a dispute about their pit bull dogs.

Banks which levy outrageous charges on current accounts threaten their customers. My own bank in Beirut (its charges are not outrageous and it's owned by former prime minister Saad Hariri, of whom more later) used to send me a letter in which I was supposed to promise not to break US federal banking laws.

The bank was so frightened of US money-laundering threats - if a bank can't deal in dollars, it's out of business - that it went on sending me this wretched note year after year until I sent them a lawyer's letter which told them that they had no legal right to make this demand of a British citizen. At which point, the whole fandango immediately came to an end.

Every few years, the government commences an "anti-corruption drive" in which civil servants immediately refuse to take bribes (for a few weeks) to avoid being fired. But then what happens? Quite a while back, my landlord captured this nonsense rather well. When his phone line was cut in the past, the PTT man came right away. He received a few Lebanese pounds for his work and the line was fixed. "Now when my phone line is cut," my landlord moaned, "the PTT man won't fix the line because he's not allowed to take a gift. How do I get my phone back?"

Corruption, even small scale, oils the wheels. But what is Lebanon to do with Sister Syria next door? It's calculated that $10bn of Syrian money lies in Lebanese banks, apartment blocks, investments and cash.

You can imagine how the Americans - who've put around 80 Syrians on their economic blacklist - might roar with outrage at this statement. But it's true.

And thanks to the Middle East's former colonial masters (French, of course) who broke Lebanon off from Syria, many Lebanese families are also Syrian families - this might apply to about a third of the population of Tripoli, Lebanon's northern city - and many of these Lebanese also hold US citizenship and are, of course, perfectly entitled to hold accounts in Lebanese banks. And if they withdraw it and spend the money in Damascus, who is to know?

There is - thank God, say all the Lebanese - the army. Reconstructed after the civil war, it's the only totally non-sectarian force in the country. It's also the only institution that still works. Without it, that civil war may yet have reignited Lebanon. The Saudis were going to pay for its rearmament - three billion dollars' worth, the weapons to come from King Salman's chum Francois Hollande. But when the Saudis were angered by the Shia Hezbollah's attacks on the Kingdom, they pulled the plug — and so Lebanese soldiers are still protecting their nation with old British SLR rifles once used in Belfast and outdated Humvees and even more outdated Huey helicopters of Vietnam vintage.

In the absence of a president, the most powerful man in Lebanon is General Abbas Ibrahim, head of the country's internal security, a Shiite who is a good friend of Qatar - he has helped to negotiate the release of soldiers and nuns who were held captive by the Islamist Nusrah group - and a brave (some might say foolhardy) man. Whenever I see him (the last time was in Qatar) I always tell him to take care of his life because I fear he is the most endangered species in Lebanon: a very brave man whom an awful lot of people would like to kill.

If he is vain (as his critics claim), he is also courageous. When he was the senior army intelligence officer in southern Lebanon, it was his duty to maintain contact with all armed groups in the area. He would walk, at night, alone and unarmed, into the Ein el-Hilweh Palestinian camp to talk to members of Osama bin Laden's al-Qaeda. He deserves to survive.

So does Lebanon. But in the very latest bit of roguery to appal the Lebanese, it looks as if ex-General Michel Aoun might at last achieve his ambition of becoming president of Lebanon. Aoun was the Lebanese army general who in 1990 thought he was the president and went to war with the Syrian army. After hundreds of his soldiers were "martyred" by the Syrian army (and quite a few hundred Syrians "martyred" in a minefield by the Lebanese army), Aoun fled to the French embassy, set off to Paris in self-exile and then returned triumphantly to Lebanon to become (wait for it) a friend of President Bashar al-Assad of Syria and his Hezbollah allies. Quite a lot of Lebanese thought he was completely crackers.

None was more infuriated than Saad Hariri (yes, the owner of my bank), the former Sunni prime minister whose own ex-prime minister father Rafiq was assassinated - so Saad believed - by Syrian security personnel in 2005. Saad could not stand the sight of Aoun. He raged at his words. But now, to the shock of Lebanese Sunnis, Hariri is declaring himself (after visits to France and Saudi Arabia) in favour of Aoun's presidency.

In other words, Hariri is cosying up to support a man who is an ally of the regime which he believes murdered his father. Could this possibly be because Saad wants to become prime minister again - even Aoun's prime minister? In Lebanon, the president must be a Christian Maronite, the prime minister a Sunni and the speaker of parliament a Shia. But the Shia speaker of parliament is Nabih Berri who says he will not tolerate Aoun as president. So do at least 13 of Hariri's own top party supporters.

It's sectarianism again; the system in which every Lebanese Christian and Sunni and Shia Muslim lives in mutual love, suspicion and fear of each other, love always trumping fear if the people don't want another civil war. Politely, this is called the National Pact. And that's why Lebanon will always be a nation-inwaiting.

To be a modern state, Lebanon must de-confessionalise so that anyone, whatever his religion, can be president or prime minister. But if you de-sectarianise Lebanon, it ceases to exist. For the identity of Lebanon is sectarian. It's a Rolls Royce with leather seats, flat screen TV in the back, a cocktail cabinet - but square wheels. Beautiful, luxurious, coveted, it doesn't work. But thank God it's got the Lebanese people.

Which is why Lebanon will survive. Its people have what so few Arabs enjoy: relative freedom, education, a love of books (real books outnumbered e-books at the last Beirut book fair) and an abiding belief in their history: Roman ruins, Crusader castles, ancient mosques, the Phoenician love of travel and adventure (which is why the national airline is always packed, even if does show advertisements for medical facelifts).

The Lebanese are their own heroes.

Robert Fisk

A TERRIFYING CHOICE BETWEEN WAR AND PEACE AWAITS

Of course, it will be no change in the Middle East. The one thing which always united Hillary Clinton and Donald Trump - despite Trump's nonsense about Muslim immigrants - was that large area of land between Algeria and the Pakistani-Indian border. Or is it Morocco and the Pakistani-Indian border? Or the Iranian-Pakistani border? Heaven knows where the "Middle East" actually is in the minds of American politicians. Or Trump. Well, it's the large pond of Muslims, I guess, along with Israel whose majority population is Jewish, a Middle East which also has a smidgeon of Christians which we remind ourselves of when their churches are burned and their people enslaved because - long ago, in the days when Europe was called Christendom - we in the West used to call ourselves Christians as well. But that's about it.

So Trump's Middle East is likely to be pretty much the same as Hillary's Middle East might have been.

Uncritical support for nuclear Israel and its chaotic prime minister, constant bombast about terror, terror, terror, terror, terror, terror (delete when you get tired of the word) and support for "moderates"- be they rebels (of the Syrian variety), presidents and kings (of the Sissi of Egypt/Abdullah of Jordan variety) and our friends (Saudis/Qataris/Kuwaitis) whose dead kings will usually be worthy of a flag at half staff.

But we will arm them. Be sure of this. The Gulf states will continue to gobble up US weapons/missiles/tanks/aircraft and Trump will visit these dusty monarchies and be treated like a king - which, I suppose, he would rather like to be - and he will assure Israel of America's undying, constant, unquestioning support for the "only democracy in the Middle East". And, of course, he will speak of terror, terror, terror, of the Isis kind unless Obama has broken it by the time he walks into the White House, when Isis may have chosen another name for itself. And he can dust off the tired old State Department lie about how the parties to the Middle East - all-powerful Israel and occupied Palestine - must make the " hard decisions" for peace.

To be sure, there is that little Trump campaign promise to move the US embassy from Tel Aviv to Jerusalem. It's been lying around in the locker room for so many years that the lads in the White House can probably produce several old files, yellowing with age, as to why it would really upset the Arabs - and especially the Palestinians (who would like a US embassy in their half capital of Jerusalem) - if the American ambassador took the road to the Holy City. But I suspect that "security concerns" might push this little project onto the back-burner for a while.

And yet. There is always an "and yet" when new American presidents take over. A lot of them came to grief over the Middle East. Afghanistan, Iraq, Syria... Not a lot of White House flag-waving over those nations, is there? What does Trump actually do when these lands present a "threat" to the West? Dust off his anti-Muslim hatreds? Call up his mate Vladimir? Ask for an atlas? But remember, we used to say things like that about George W Bush - and we got Iraq. The Trump presidency cannot afford to go down that road. Can it? So I'll hazard a cruel prediction. The Middle East will reach out and grab Donald Trump when he least expects it, that it will present him with a terrifying choice (war or peace), and his administration - such as it is - will not be capable of dealing with it. That will be the ultimate responsibility of American voters, of course. But don't let's get on our high British horse. Remember a wildly popular prime minister not so long ago? Got caught up with Afghanistan, didn't he? And then Iraq? Tony whatshisname?

Robert Fisk

Friday, 11 November 2016

IT'S NOT TRUMP THAT MATTERS NOW – IT'S PUTIN

Predictable claptrap is being uttered about Trump and the Middle East. How can the Muslim world deal with a man who is an Islamophobe? For that is indeed what Trump is. He is a disgrace to his country and to his people - who, heavens above, elected the chap.

But here's a mollifying thought. US prestige in the region has fallen so low, the Arab world's belief (and quite possibly the Israeli belief) in American power so shattered by Washington's stupidity and ineptness, that I rather suspect little attention will be paid to Donald Trump.

I'm not quite sure when respect for American governance began to collapse. It was certainly at its height when Eisenhower told the

British, French and Israelis to get out of the Suez Canal in 1956. Maybe Ronald Reagan mixing up his cue cards and taking his presidency into the early stages of Alzheimer's had a larger effect than we thought. I did once meet a Norwegian diplomat who sat down to talk to Reagan about Israel and Palestine and found the old boy quoting from a paper on the US economy. Bill Clinton's Middle East "peace" couldn't have helped.

I guess it was George W Bush, who decided to attack Afghanistan even though no Afghan had ever attacked the United States, and who created a Shia Muslim state in Iraq out of a Sunni Muslim state - much to Saudi Arabia's disgust - who did more harm than most US presidents to date. The Saudis (from whom came 15 of the 19 killers involved in 9/11) launched their war on Yemen with scarcely a whiff of concern from Washington.

And Obama seems to have goofed every time in the Middle East. His "handshake" to Islam in Cairo, his Nobel Prize (for public speaking), his "red line" in Syria - which disappeared in the sand the moment he was rescued by the Russkis - is best forgotten. It's Vladimir Putin's Sukhois and Migs that are setting the pace in the terrible Syrian war. And amid lands where human rights count not a jot for most of the regional dictators, there's been hardly a whimper about the Kremlin. Putin was even taken to the opera in Cairo by Field Marshal President al-Sisi.

And that's the point. Putin talks and acts. Actually, in translation at least, he's not terribly eloquent, more businessman than politician. Trump talks. But can he act? Cast aside the odd relationship which Trump thinks he has with Putin. It's Trump who is going to need a translation of Putin's words, not the other way round. In fact, the Arabs and Israelis, I think, will be spending far more time during the Trump presidency listening to Putin. For the fact is that the Americans have proved themselves as unreliable and fickle in the Middle East as Britain was in the 1930s.

Even America's blitz on Isis didn't really get under way until Putin sent his own fighter-bombers to Syria - at which point, many Arabs were asking why Washington hadn't managed to destroy the cult. Go back to the Arab revolutions - or "spring", as the Americans pathetically called it - and you see Obama and his hapless Secretary of State (yes, Hillary) goofing again, failing to realise that this massive public awakening in the Arab world was real and that the dictators were going to go (most of them, at least). In Cairo in 2011, about the only decision taken by Obama was to evacuate US citizens from the Egyptian capital.

It is easy to say that the Arabs are appalled that an Islamophobe has won the White House. But did they think Obama or any of his predecessors - Democrat or Republican - had any special concern for Islam? US foreign policy in the Middle East has been a spectacular series of wars and air raids and retreats. Russian policy - in the Yemen war during Nasser's age and in Afghanistan - has been destructive enough, but the post-Soviet state seemed to have curled its claws until Putin moved his men into Syria.

No doubt we'll see Trump turn up in the Middle East before long, to fawn before the Israelis and repeat America's uncritical support for the Israeli state, and to assure the wealthy Gulf autocrats that their stability is assured. What he says about Syria will, of course, be fascinating, given his views on Putin. But maybe, he will just leave the region to his minions, to secretaries of state and vice-presidents who will have to second guess what the guy really thinks. And that, of course, is where we all stand now. What does Trump think? Or, more to the point, does he think?

Robert Fisk

CHAPTER 8

TUNISIA WINTER

Tunisian beach without tourists.

Sunday, 28 June 2015

ATTACKING ARAB SPRING'S ONLY SUCCESS

Vast stretches of sand were empty of people along the normally packed beaches of Sousse yesterday. There were still a few tourists around; they had taken the entirely correct view that the place was safer now than it has ever been in recent times, having a heavy security presence in the wake of Saturday's massacre.

But even these hardy visitors said they would be gone as soon as their holiday finishes, and the gloomy hotel and restaurant owners do not expect a new wave of custom to follow this summer, or indeed anything like the same numbers for the next season either.

It is perhaps surprising that there were so many Western tourists around for the dreadful slaughter. They obviously had not thought that the attack at the Bardo Museum in Tunis three months ago, in which 20 foreigners died, meant that they, too, were potential targets. Or perhaps they simply decided to come despite the risks involved.

The fact is that Islamist extremists have very specific targets in Tunisia. The killer, Seifeddine Rezgui, was extraordinarily careful in his choice of victims, picking on obvious foreigners, deliberately sparing locals when he could, urging them to get out of the way. This is not seen as visceral hatred of kafirs (unbelievers) and altruism towards fellow Muslims, but part of a deliberate plan to destroy the tourist industry, the biggest revenue earners and the biggest source of employment, in the country.

Tunisia has not suffered over much from the arbitrary massacres of suicide bombs. The internal targets have been civic society figures, the security forces and politicians. The aim, it is felt, is to undermine fatally the structures which have made the country, arguably, the only one of the Arab Spring with a fledgling democracy and an election in which the main Islamist party, Enhada, was edged out of power.

There are not many here who disagree with Prime Minister Habib Essid's assertion that the aim of the Islamist campaign is to sabotage the economy and undermine the democratic process. Nor are there dissenting voices, among non-Islamists, to the desperate reaction of the tourism minister Salma Elloumi, who had tried hard to present Tunisia as a safe destination for visitors from abroad, that what happened was nothing short of a "catastrophe".

So what is happening in Tunisia, compared to other jihadist arenas, does not point towards a "one size fits all" formula in the jihadist order of battle. One has to recognise, of course, that the Sousse attack took place on the same day as the beheading in France and the bombing of a Shia mosque in Kuwait, three very different attacks in three continents. The resultant huge publicity for Islamists was too much to be a coincidence, and something which must have been planned, a number of security analysts held. Among them was Bruce Riedel, formerly of the CIA now at the Washington think-tank, Brookings Institution, who said: "It appears to be an effort to launch and inspire a wave of attacks in different places, reminiscent of al-Qaeda's simultaneous multiple attacks in the past."

Western and allied intelligence agencies are trying to establish a link and evidence may yet emerge of a grand plan, but that has not happened yet. Islamic State (IS), locked in a deadly struggle for the soul of international jihad, is claiming credit.

Abu Mohammed al-Adnani, the spokesman for IS, declared in an audio message to the group's followers last week: "Muslims embark and hasten towards jihad. Oh mujahedin everywhere, rush and go to make Ramadan a month of disasters for the infidels." This, however, appears to be a general call to arms rather than the smoking gun. The 23-yearold Sousse murderer, Rezgui, also known as Abu Yahya, an electronics graduate, frequented a hard-line Salafist mosque in his home city of Kairouan, but there is nothing to suggest that he was a follower of IS.

There is, nevertheless, one international dimension to this. The Tunisian government has claimed that Islamists carrying out attacks had trained in Libya, in territories nominally controlled by the Tripoli government which is vying for control of the country with a rival internationally recognised government based in Tobruk.

I was in Libya a few weeks ago when a car packed with explosives blew up a checkpoint outside the northern port of Misrata. Libyan ministers were keen to tell me that the suicide bomber was a Tunisian, Abu Wahid al-Tunsi, and that it was Tunisia, not them, exporting terror. Soon after, Mokhtar Belmokhtar, a well-known Algerian jihadist commander was reported to have been killed in a US drone strike in eastern Libya. There is a burgeoning Salafist insurgency in Egypt's eastern border and intrinsic links between Islamist violence in the Sahel states and North Africa, buttressed by weapons and people smuggling.

All the grim indications are that this region will experience violent turbulence in years to come. And it is unlikely that what is left of the tourist trade in Tunisia will escape being a hunting ground for jihadists again in the future.

Kim Sengupta

TUNISIAN TERRORIST EXPORT

On 11 July Mohamed Lahouaiej Bouhlel rented a 19-tonne refrigerated truck, paying the required deposit.

He failed to return the vehicle, using it instead as a weapon in carrying out one of the deadliest terrorist atrocities ever seen in Europe, killing 84 people, including ten children, and injuring 202 others, 52 of them critically.

The 31-year-old former delivery driver and chauffeur, the father of three children, had followed instructions from Isis to use all means possible to conduct jihad, with the use of vehicles mentioned as one of the options. The devastating toll came from him mowing through Promenade de Anglais in Nice packed with 30,000 people celebrating Bastille Day, while firing an automatic pistol.

However, unlike the other Islamist killers who had wreaked havoc in France and Belgium in the past two years, there was no direct Syrian connection to this massacre. Instead, Lahouaiej Bouhlel's introduction to a cult of death may have come in Tunisia, the birthplace of the Arab Spring.

His family came from the town of M'saken, near Sousse, the resort where 38 tourists, 30 of them Britons, were gunned down by Seifeddine Rezgui, a student, on the beach last June. The killings had been preceded by an attack at the Bardo Museum in Tunis, resulting in 22 deaths, which also had links to the Sousse area.

Lahouaiej Bouhlel had, it appears, visited the Sousse on a number of occasions, the last time around eight months ago.

President François Hollande, arriving in Nice, declared: "We are facing a long battle because we have an enemy who will continue to hate all the people who enjoy liberty. The whole of France is facing the threat of Islamist terrorism."

The state of emergency declared after the terror attacks in Paris last November is being extended. But the French authorities are insisting that they had no reason to suspect Lahouaiej Bouhlel of having terrorist links. He was known to be a petty criminal and some of his arrests were drugs-and drink-related. He had lost his job after falling asleep at the wheel of a lorry and crashing into a row of cars. In January he was found guilty of assaulting a man and given a suspended jail sentence. Today, his victim at the time decried that his attacker had been left free to carry out the slaughter "where is the justice here. This is a small world, so stop allowing them to walk free", said Jean-Baptiste Ximenes.

Lahouaiej Bouhlel's flat at the Abattoirs district, near Nice railway station, has been searched by police who had taken away what was described as "digital material". They were also examining two mobile phones belonging to him. Neighbours and acquaintances of the killer held that there had been no sign of Muslim religious zeal in his behaviour; he seldom attended mosques, and consumed alcohol. He was also said to have been violent towards his wife, Hajer Khalfallah, from whom he was in the process of getting divorced. Her home, too, was searched by the police who are continuing to question her.

Walid-Hamou, who said he was a cousin of Lahouaiej Bouhlel's wife, claimed her husband "mistreated her, he beat her up. He was bad, bad man. I don't understand what's happened, this man drank, took drugs, he was no Muslim". Wissam, a neighbour, who came from the same town as the killer in Tunisia, said "he was even drinking just before he did this. He was heard arguing with someone who told him that he was worthless. Lahouaiej Bouhlel shouted back 'One day, you'll hear about me'".

Lahouaiej Bouhlel's slaughter spree has left behind profound loss and sorrow. Fatima Charrhi was among the first to die. Her son said: "All I can say is she wore a veil and practiced Islam the proper way: it was real Islam, not the version of the terrorists." Some of those who survived have harrowing memories.

Simon Coates, a lawyer from Leeds said: "I saw one woman on the ground talking to her dead child. I had been separated from my wife, I turned around and followed the path the lorry took checking the people killed to see if she was one of them. I had to check every body, they were so disfigured the only reliable way I could check was to look for her bike and her shoes as most people were simply not recognisable." Mr Coates's wife had managed to escape; both of them remain in a state of shock.

Others witnessed acts of courage. Richard Gutjahr, a German journalist, said: "People were celebrating and the truck drove through them. Surprisingly, the truck driver drove very slowly. He drove slowly and he was chased by a motorcyclist who attempted to overtake the truck and even tried to open the driver's door, but he fell and ended up under the wheels of the truck." The motorcyclist is believed to be in a critical condition in hospital.

More than 50 young boys and girls were injured, many of them severely. At the city's Foundation Lenval Hospital, two of the children died after being brought in. Many of the staff had been in tears while they worked without break. Frederic Sola, a paediatric surgeon, said: "There are very bad physical injuries but also great emotional hurt." The patients and their families are being offered psychological counselling.

Stephanie Simpson, as an official in administration, said: "Some of the grown-ups are in such shock that they cannot talk. But some of the children are talking, the psychologists have heard terrible things from the children, what they have been through has been so terrible, so terrible."

This is the third time that France had been visited by terror in the past 18 months and there are accusations and recriminations. Pierre Lellouche, a former French Europe minister who was part of a commission of inquiry into the Paris attacks, said: "We need much better intelligence, much better coordination of intelligence inside France, among Europeans, with our neighbours controlling our borders.

This is not happening fast enough."

Kim Sengupta

Thursday, 26 May 2016

THREAT OF ECONOMIC COLLAPSE

The Tunisian ambassador in London has asked the British Government to drop its warning to British nationals not to go to his country for anything other than essential travel. The guidance has led to a 90 per cent drop in British visitors to Tunisia so far this year - a crippling blow to its tourist industry.

The Foreign Office travel advice came after the massacre last summer at the beach resort of Sousse, killing 39 people. It has not changed since, despite the Tunisian government taking extensive security measures and no further major attacks taking place in the country. In fact, more people have been killed by terrorists in Paris and Brussels in the intervening period.

The Foreign Office, however, holds that further attacks in Tunisia are "highly likely". The terms used are chosen carefully, in line with structured intelligence assessments, but the fact remains that there are many countries where further terrorist attacks are, and have been, "highly likely" and even "imminent" without tourists fleeing.

MI5's assessment of the terror threat in the UK, for example, is "severe", which it explains means "an attack is highly likely".

The British Government has effectively imposed economic sanctions on Tunisia, the only country of the Arab Spring which has emerged without prolonged violent strife or sliding back under authoritarian rule.

Not so long ago, Western governments were praising Tunisia for this achievement. They were right to do so.

I was in Tunisia reporting on the fall of Zine el-Abidine Ben Ali five years ago. Compared to the mayhem my colleagues and I subsequently covered, as the Arab Spring turned into the bleak Arab winter, the country has coped remarkably well.

The tourist industry is Tunisia's biggest employer and foreign revenue earner. The lack of international visitors is leading to unemployment. This will sow dissatisfaction among those losing their jobs, who happen, mainly, to be young men. A rich seam is being created for Islamist extremists to exploit.

When covering the Sousse murders, I met many of these young men who feared tourism drying up and them losing their jobs. That is exactly what has happened to many of them now.

Some who have kept in touch speak of a sense of hopelessness and increasing bitterness, of friends and colleagues who may become attracted to violent Islam.

Seifeddine Rezgui, the young student who carried out the Sousse murders, lived with other members of his cell in the Islamic holy city of Kairouan. There, at the Great Mosque of Sidi Uqba, the Imam, Taib al-Gazi, spoke about clerics coming from Saudi Arabia and other Gulf states spreading intolerant Wahaabi doctrine.

"We were being infected by extremism, it was very damaging," he told me. "We have managed to put a stop to that, but these people will try to reappear and, given the chance, they will try to spread their poison again. We know the extremists are here, but in small numbers. Britain should help us get rid of them, not help them by taking away the livelihood of so many young people."

The terrible consequences of an economic collapse will not just be confined to Tunisia.

We know the scope of international jihad. Rezgui was trained across the border in Libya by Isis, as had those who carried out an attack on the Bardo museum in Tunis two months previously.

Britain is among Western states being drawn back towards military action in Libya. British, western European and American special forces are already on the ground. A UN-sponsored administration trying to establish itself in Tripoli will soon start receiving weapons and training for its troops.

The Western re-engagement is an attempt to combat Isis, which is spreading out from its base in Sirte, Muammar Gaddafi's home town.

During my last visit to Libya, officials were keen to stress that Isis in their country was run by Tunisians. This may not be true, but there are certainly quite a few Tunisians in their ranks.

There was a suicide attack while I was there, at the northern port of Misrata; the bomber, with the nom de guerre of Abu Wahid al-Tunsi, was from Tunisia.

So Britain is becoming militarily active in Libya to confront jihad while helping to create conditions next door in Tunisia for further jihad.

There have been mistakes in Western policies in the Arab Spring and its aftermath. This is one of them - and one which will have dangerous consequences.

Kim Sengupta

CHAPTER 9

EGYPT WINTER

"Truth Giulio Regeni" banner in Italy, October 28, 2016.

Sunday, 17 April 2016

MURDER OF GIULIO REGENI

We've all grown so used to the "Muslim terror" narratives trotted out by our favourite dictators - I'm talking about Nasser, Sadat, Mubarak and now, of course, Field Marshal-President al-Sissi of Egypt - that we're in danger of believing them. The Muslim Brotherhood and its campaign of "terror" (in fact, Egypt's violence has nothing to do with the Brotherhood) has allowed al-Sisi's thugs to beat up, lock up, torture, murder and otherwise execute thousands of his people who object to his outrageous police state behaviour.

But the real danger to his regime - indeed, to the Egyptian governments under British rule, to Sadat and finally to Mubarak - always came from the secular, socialist opposition, symbolised by the country's immensely brave, tough and independent trade union movements.

Secularism and real socialism, not "Muslim terror", was always the enemy of Egyptian dictators. A few weeks ago, a young PhD student wrote presciently that "the [Egyptian] unions' defiance of the state of emergency and the regime's appeal for stability and social order - justified by the 'war on terror' - signifies ... a bold questioning of the underlying rhetoric the regime uses to justify its own existence and its repression of civil society".

The Cambridge University student who wrote these words was Giulio Regeni, whose brutally tortured body - so mutilated that his mother could only recognise him by his nose - was found dumped close to the Cairo-Alexandria motorway in February. Over the previous nine days he had been beaten, tortured with electricity, stabbed and suffered a severe brain haemorrhage.

Al-Sissi's cops variously announced that Regeni had been the victim of a traffic accident; kidnapped and murdered by "a criminal gang"; even killed in a lover's argument. Italy, exploding in anger at Regeni's death - the British Foreign Office only clip-clopped into complaining about the Cambridge student's murder after it received 10,000 signatures of protest from within the UK - believed that the "criminal gang" were al-Sissi's own state security police.

The creepy excuses of the Egyptian government need not detain us here. Al-Sissi blames a "conspiracy" (of course) by "people of evil" (naturally) and the shortcomings of journalists who believe in social media - as opposed to the officially sanctioned Egyptian newspapers and television, which largely continue to fawn over the field marshal and the coup d'etat he staged against the elected Muslim Brotherhood government it once supported.

Far more attention, however, needs to be paid to the institutions which Regeni was studying in Cairo - the independent trade unions which represent, in the long term, a far more dangerous enemy of the al-Sissi government - as part of a PhD investigation which may have led directly to his murder.

Even under the British, Egyptian industrial workers protested their appalling conditions and poverty-line wages. Tobacco and printing workers, railway and tramway employees went on strike. The big cotton factories repeatedly closed down during the 1920s.

It became almost a national tradition; one of Nasser's first acts - before creating the inevitable "official" union, which still exists - was to execute two leading strikers, Mustafa Khamees and Abdel Rahman al-Baqary, from the Kafr al-Dawar spinning factories. Under Mubarak, police killed striking steel workers in 1989.

But the real source of fear for Mubarak's regime, and one of the principal reasons he was eventually overthrown, came from the cotton workers and spinners of Mahala, a grubby town north of Cairo in the Nile Delta.

A French colleague first pointed out to me the importance of Mahala, whose great cotton factories provided millions of dollars of exports for Egypt. The independent trade unions there staged an attempted coup against Mubarak in 2006 - seven years before the Cairo Tahrir Square revolution.

Cotton workers, led by women, occupied the centre of Mahala and held off riot police and plain-clothes cops for up to a week, calling in the country fellahin, labourers, to support them by using mobile phones and social media. Trade unionists were released from detention, they got pay rises - but did not destroy Mubarak. They tried again in 2008, and were savagely suppressed.

But the lessons were learnt. When Egyptians gathered in Cairo's Tahrir Square by the million in 2011, the first industrial workers to join them were the cotton factory employees of Mahala - which is one reason why the Mubarak regime immediately halted all railway traffic between the capital and the Nile Delta.

When I visited Mahala after the 2011 revolution, the workers were flushed with their success.

They felt safe. No one could ever accuse them of being pussy cats for the Brotherhood. It was one thing to use the Egyptian army and police to shoot down bearded Islamists, quite another to open fire at the workers.

But the official trade union has tried to destroy the independent unions; striking under the military regime was now "treason", according to its leadership - you can see how this fits into the al-Sissi story of plots and treachery against the state. Secular socialists were more dangerous than the Brotherhood; they could close Egypt down, destroy its economy, even overthrow its military leadership - unless they were suppressed.

Enter Regeni, whose last anonymous report for the Italian newspaper Il Manifesto has been reprinted by the British socialist magazine Red Pepper. Regeni wrote about the Centre for Trade Union and Workers' Services - "a beacon of independent Egyptian trade unionists", he called it - and of how al-Sissi's attack on trade union freedoms had caused "widespread discontent among workers".

He remarked on the large participation of women. He wrote about recent, unreported industrial strikes. He said that "in an authoritarian and repressive context under General [sic] Sissi", these events would "break the wall of fear..." Regeni must have had many contacts - with trade union "traitors", of course, who wished to "destroy" Egypt.

You can see how the cops work in Cairo. Who were Regeni's contacts, they must have asked? And in a country where foreign-funded organisations, even students, are now regarded as spies, who was Regeni "really" working for? Italian and other European newspapers have named the Egyptian police general, Khaled Shalabi - who was given a suspended sentence in Alexandria in 2003 for torturing and killing a detainee - as the man in charge of the CID in Gaza governorate where Regeni's body was found. It was Shalabi who stated the student had been killed in a road accident - surely the first traffic violation whose victim appeared to have been tortured with electricity.

But this is not the point. Regeni, like every good student and journalist, had spotted the greatest threat to a dictatorship - and almost certainly paid the price.

Robert Fisk

Tuesday, 26 April 2016

PROTESTING AL-SISSI'S RULE

Troops, armed police and armoured cars mobilised on the streets of Cairo yesterday following the arrests of dozens of activists and members of the media as Egypt's president, Abdel-Fattah al-Sissi, faced the most serious and sustained protests to his rule since coming to power nearly two years ago.

Witnesses reported security forces using tear gas to disperse protesters as jets and helicopters circled over the Egyptian capital. There has been rising popular discontent over a range of issues, with the president claiming his opponents were seeking to endanger national security. But the focal point of yesterday's demonstrations was nationalistic - anger over the decision to hand over two uninhabited islands in the Red Sea to Saudi Arabia.

The sheer scale of the security operation that blocked off Tahrir Square - the symbolic centre of protests and access to the headquarters of the journalists and doctors unions - and the presence of forces in their thousands on the capital's ring roads and the city centre illustrated the wariness of the authorities at what is unfolding.

Yesterday was also the anniversary of Sinai Liberation Day commemorating the withdrawal of Israeli forces from the peninsula in 1982. The military and the Interior Ministry stated that they were deploying to "protect peaceful citizens" who wanted to celebrate the occasion.

But, apart from a few dozen people waving flags on the streets of the affluent district of Mohandeseen, the mood was sombre with expectation of troubles ahead.

Police raids continued yesterday with three journalists detained, a member of the Press Syndicates Board, Khaled el-Balshy, confirmed. An activists' group, Freedom for the Brave, said that more than a hundred people were arrested last week.

President Sissi has been accused of "selling" national territory after saying that the two islands, Sanafir and Tiran, will come under Saudi sovereignty. He has sought to stress that the islands originally belonged to the Kingdom and had been put under Egyptian protection in 1950 to stop them being occupied by Israel.

Despite the "protection", the Israelis captured the uninhabited islands in both 1956 and 1982, returning them voluntarily to Egypt on both occasions. President Sissi's announcement came during a visit by King Salman of Saudi Arabia. The Kingdom announced a multi-billion dollar aid and investment package for Egypt at a time when the country is in dire financial straits.

The Saudis had been supportive of President Sissi's government ever since, as the head of the armed forces, he overthrew the Muslim Brotherhood government of Mohammed Morsi.

The Brotherhood, supported at the time by Qatar, had long been regarded with loathing by the Saudis.

Since President Sissi came to power in June 2014 more than a thousand people have been killed and an estimated 40,000 jailed in a clampdown against the regime's political opponents. Amnesty International has claimed that Egypt has reverted "back to being a police state".

Separately, the Egyptian authorities were reported to be investigating the Reuters news agency over its report that a 28-year-old Cambridge student, Giulio Regeni, whose torturemarked body was found on the side of a road in Cairo, was detained by police the night he disappeared. The agency stressed that it had based its report on six police and intelligence sources. The Egyptian government has strongly denied that its officials were involved in the death.

Kim Sengupta

CHAPTER 10

LIBYA WINTER

Friday, 1 January 2016

FATE OF THE GADDAFIS

He is one of the most soughtafter prisoners in the world. Since Hannibal Gaddafi was arrested in Lebanon's Bekaa Valley last month,

Syria has demanded his return to Damascus; and this week one of the two rival governments in his own country, Libya, has requested his extradition.

Both demands were rebuffed by the Lebanese government, which has questions of its own that it wants answered - aside from those raised by the kidnapping, freeing and arrest of Colonel Gaddafi's fifth son.

Who was the woman, Fatima Assad, who lured him from Syria to Lebanon to be seized? What was he doing in Syria? Could he now reveal what really happened to the Shia cleric Musa al-Sadr, who disappeared 37 years ago during a visit to Libya - at the time under the control of Hannibal's father.

There has been speculation that Hannibal had left the safety of Oman, where he had been living after fleeing Libya, to seek political help in Syria, despite the dangers of its civil war. He had, it is claimed, met officials of Bashar al Assad's regime, as well as Russians and Iranians. There is, however, no corroboration of this, or of what kind of help he was seeking.

More may be revealed about Hannibal's Syrian journey if he stands trial in Lebanon. Meanwhile, the dramatic episode has rekindled interest in what happened to Col Gaddafi's family after he was lynched and his regime of four decades fell.

Some of them are dead. The body of Mutassim Gaddafi was laid by his father's in a meat warehouse in Misrata, after both were captured and killed as they tried to flee the dictator's home town of Sirte. Another son, Khamis, who led a brigade named after himself in the conflict, was killed by a Nato air strike at the end of August 2011.

Saif al-Islam Gaddafi, the dictator's heir apparent, was also caught as he tried to flee Libya. He was sentenced to death by a court in Tripoli earlier this year. The International Criminal Court wants him to be tried in The Hague. Saif, however, remains in the custody of the city of Zintan, which shows no inclination to hand over its prisoner, a valuable bargaining chip in the power play between the country's competing militias and governments.

The same Tripoli court is trying Saif's brother Saadi, once a would-be professional footballer with his own football team in Libya who had tried unsuccessfully with clubs in Italy and Malta. He eluded capture during the war but was extradited from Niger, accused of crimes including the murder of a former footballer, Bashir Riani.

Mohammed, Colonel Gaddafi's son with his first wife, Fathia, the head of Libya's Olympic Committee, held the lucrative position of chairman of the company controlling Libya's mobile and telecommunications networks. He and Hannibal, who chaired a company which controlled the country's seaports and maritime trade, took their mother Safiya and sister Ayesha to Algeria as the rebels closed in.

Ayesha, a former UN goodwill ambassador and lawyer, once part of Saddam Hussein's defence team in Baghdad, gave birth to her fourth child, a daughter, in Algeria. Her husband, Ahmed al-Gaddafi al-Qahsi, an army colonel, had previously been killed in a Nato strike on Tripoli.

It was reported at the time that Ayesha, often referred to in the Arab press as the "Claudia Schiffer of North Africa" because of her dyed blonde hair, had set fire, more than once, to a villa near Algiers where they were being kept. As relations with the host government deteriorated, the Gaddafi siblings left for Oman and were granted political asylum in October 2012.

It is not known when Hannibal travelled onwards to Syria. His Lebanese wife, Aline Skaf, remains in Algeria with their children and the couple are now believed to be estranged. Hannibal, it is claimed, met the mysterious Fatima in Latakia, an enclave of the Alawite community, from where the Syrian elite are drawn, and travelled with her to Damascus before he disappeared.

He was taken across the border to the Bekaa Valley where he was abducted by gunmen from the Amal Movement, founded by al-Sadr. A video was posted of him, with bruises on his face, declaring that the truth about al-Sadr's fate must come out. "I am with people who fear God, people who have a cause," he said. Col Gaddafi has been long suspected of ordering the disappearance of the imam after becoming enraged during a theological debate.

A former Hezbollah MP, Hassan Yacoub, whose father Sheikh Muhammed went missing in Libya along with al-Sadr, was arrested in connection with Hannibal's kidnapping but has insisted he was not involved.

While Hannibal had supposedly been involved in political intrigue in Syria, there have been complaints in Tripoli that Saif has become too close to his Zintani captors. He has, more than once, stated that he would like his trial to take place in Zintan rather than Tripoli or The Hague. The head of the Zintan militia, Mukhtar al-Akhdar, a former colonel in the regime forces, has stressed that Saif is happy with his treatment in custody and gets on well with his guards.

After days of public display, Muammar Gaddafi's body was quietly buried in a secret desert location. With Libya in turmoil and many thinking nostalgically of pre-revolutionary stability, the question now being whispered is whether one of the dictator's sons may yet be in a position to revive the fortunes of the Gaddafi family.

Kim Sengupta

Friday, 8 January 2016

GADDAFI'S PROPHETIC WARNING

The Libyan uprising always contained more extreme Islamists than portrayed by its supporters inside and outside Libya. There is some truth in Muammar Gaddafi's claim to Tony Blair that the jihadis had "managed to set up local stations and in Benghazi have spread the thoughts and ideas of al-Qaeda."

His claims sound particularly prophetic since the transcript of the Blair-Gaddafi phone conversations were published on the day that a suicide bomber driving a truck packed with explosives killed an estimated 65 people at a Libyan police academy. The attack is likely to be the work of the Libyan branch of Isis, which today controls Sirte, Gaddafi's home region and last stronghold, and is battling to take over Libya's main oil ports.

But it is also true that protests that began in Libya on 15 February 2011 and turned into a general uprising had wide popular support among Libyans. By the time of the phone calls, protesters had seized Benghazi, Misrata and many other cities and towns, while part of the regular armed forces had defected to the opposition.

Gaddafi's repeated claim to Mr Blair that there was nothing happening in much of the country shows that he was either eager to downplay the swift spread of the rebellion or ignorant of what was going on.

The latter seems the most likely explanation, given Gaddafi's repeated invitations to Mr Blair, who was in Kuwait, to come to Tripoli, and his belief that once foreign journalists arrived they would see for themselves that accounts of violence had been exaggerated. "Send reporters and politicians," the Libyan leader says. "Talk to them [protesters] directly; see what kind of people they are and their connections to AQ [al-Qaeda]."

It would be interesting to know whom Mr Blair spoke to between the two conversations on the same day, because in the second he says: "If you have a safe place to go you should go there because this will not end peacefully." Later Mr Blair says: "I repeat the statement that people have said to me, if there is a way that he [Gaddafi] should leave he should do so now."

This may have been an attempt to panic Gaddafi into bolting the country, or it may be a sign that foreign military intervention in Libya, which began on 19 March, was already considered inevitable by some. Gaddafi appears to have interpreted the message as a threat of foreign military action. "It seems that this will be colonisation," he replies. "I will have to arm the people and get ready for a fight."

It was Nato air support for the opposition that was decisive in determining the outcome of the war. At the time of the phone calls, Gaddafi does not seem to have thought that his own rule was really under threat. Foreign governments and media exaggerated the military capacity of the rebels and underestimated their extreme Islamic and regressive ideology. Secular supporters of rebellion were taken back when one of the first proposals of the transitional government that replaced Gaddafi was to end the ban on polygamy.

Patrick Cockburn

Friday, 1 April 2016

NEW GOVERNMENT TAKES POWER FROM ISLAMISTS

Libya's Unity Government, set up by the UN and the West to supposedly bring stability to the fractured country, has begun its first days in Tripoli guarded behind barricades amid threats from Islamists who have been holding power in the capital.

The establishment of the new administration is meant to pave the way for the possible intervention by Western forces against Isis which has spread its territories after capturing Muammar Gaddafi's home town of Sirte, as well as traffickers taking hundreds of thousands of refugees to Europe.

Fayez Sarraj, the prime minister designate, arrived with seven colleagues by sea to a naval base in the city after Islamists closed the airspace in an effort to keep them out.

He said on arrival: "There are challenges ahead of us, including uniting Libyans and healing divisions. We will work for a ceasefire across Libya, for national reconciliation and the return of displaced people. And we will seek to confront Islamic State (Isis)."

But Khalifa al-Ghawi, the head of the Islamist Government of National Salvation, declared: "We call on these illegitimate infiltrators to either hand themselves over or go back to where they came from. The Salvation Government is working with judicial and legistlative estates, all state institutions and NGOs, as well as community leaders, to take the necessary steps to save the country from the threat of chaos and foreign intervention. We won't leave Tripoli as long as we are not sure of the fate of our homeland."

The fragility of the security situation was highlighted a little later when a group of armed men stormed the offices of the television station, al-Nabaa, cutting off its transmission and forcing out staff at gunpoint.

"Some of the men were in combat fatigues and some were in civilian clothes. They stopped all broadcasting," said one of the journalists.

Al-Nabaa has supported the Islamist administration and the armed group are believed to be supporters of the unity government. Misrata, the port city which emerged with power and influence in the chaotic aftermath of the fall of the Gaddafi regime, is backing Mr Sarraj and guarding him and his colleagues in Tripoli.

There were swift expressions of support for Mr Sarraj's Tripoli arrivals from international powers. The US Secretary of State, John Kerry, said "the crucial work of addressing the full range of Libya's political, security, economic and humanitarian challenges can now begin".

Philip Hammond, the British Foreign Secretary, promised that the UK would "stand ready to respond positively to requests for support and assistance" and Ban Ki-Moon, the UN Secretary-General, added "there are many countries who really wish that Libya now establishes this government so that we can help them, so that they can establish their country."

The European Union's foreign affairs chief, Federica Mogherini, said an aid packet of €100 million was on offer. The EU has also been drawing up military plans for strikes against Isis, although this is not expected to come into operation immediately and there is said to be no appetite, at the moment, to have troops, other than special forces, on the ground.

Kim Sengupta

CHAPTER 11

BAHRAIN WINTER

Financial district, Manama, Bahrain.

Saturday, 9 July 2016

ADOPTING THE 'EGYPTIAN STRATEGY'

Bahrainis are calling their government's intensified repression of all opposition "the Egyptian strategy", believing that it is modelled on the ruthless campaign by the Egyptian security forces to crush even the smallest signs of dissent.

In recent weeks, leading advocates of human rights in Bahrain have been jailed in conditions directed at breaking them physically and mentally, while others, already in prison, have been given longer sentences. The Bahraini citizenship of Sheikh Isa Qasim, the spiritual leader of the Shia majority in Bahrain, was revoked and the headquarters of the main opposition party, al-Wifaq, closed and its activities suspended.

Bahrain, once considered one of the more liberal Arab monarchies, is turning into a police state as vicious and arbitrary as anywhere else in the region. Mass protests demanding an end to the Sunni al-Khalifa dynasty's monopoly of power during the Arab Spring period in 2011 were violently suppressed with Saudi help. The authorities agreed to an international investigation into what had happened that revealed widespread use of torture, unjust imprisonment and killings of protesters. Repression continued but failed to eliminate entirely the protest movement, despite imprisoning at least 3,500 Bahrainis.

Brutalisation of these detainees has markedly increased in the past few months, a prominent example being the arrest of Nabeel Rajab, Bahrain's leading human rights advocate. He was arrested on 13 June on the grounds that he had made comments alleging torture in Jau prison and criticising air strikes by a Saudi-led coalition in Yemen. Rajab had been imprisoned in the past, but this time he was placed in solitary confinement for 15 days.

Conditions in East Riffa police station, and later in West Riffa police station, to which he was transferred, appear to have been deliberately geared to break his morale, forcing him to use lavatories so filthy and infested with insects that he tried to eat very little so he would not have to visit them.

He lost 8kg in weight over 15 days in solitary confinement before he was taken to hospital where he was diagnosed as having an irregular heartbeat. His wife, Sumaya Rajaab, says the police did not allow the doctor to complete his examination before taking her husband back to the same police station where he had previously been confined. "The authorities clearly intend to punish Nabeel Rajab by isolating him as if he were a dangerous criminal," said Joe Stork, deputy Middle East director of Human Rights Watch.

He is not the only victim of enhanced mistreatment by the Bahraini security forces. Dr Abdul Jalil al-Singace, another human rights activist in Bahrain, has been in Jau prison since 2011 after he was sentenced to life imprisonment for allegedly plotting to overthrow the government in the Arab Spring protests. A polio victim who can only stand on one leg, he was tortured at the time of his detention by beatings, sexual assault and being forced to stand upright for long periods.

The Bahrain authorities promised improved conditions for prisoners at the time of the Bahrain Independent Commission of Inquiry in 2011, but recently his family have become worried that the Bahrain security forces are depriving him of the medications he needs to treat his many disabilities.

What is striking about the Bahrain government's new campaign to suppress dissent is not only its cruelty but its pettiness such as, say Dr Singace's family, depriving him of the rubber pads for his crutches.

Bahraini opposition leaders in exile say that the final decision by the authorities to systematically stamp out any remaining opposition in Bahrain was taken about two months ago. The security forces were influenced by the example of Egypt, where there are an estimated 60,000 political prisoners. Ali al-Aswad, the director of advocacy at the Londonbased Bahrain Institute for Rights and Democracy, says: "We have been told that the security services wanted to take a tougher line based on that being followed in Egypt.

But the switch in Bahraini policy appears to have been triggered by a trip King Hamad bin Issa al-Khalifa (below) took to Saudi Arabia. Saudi Arabia considers Bahrain to be very much within its sphere of influence.

The event indicating that the Egyptian model had been adopted came at the end of May when Sheikh Ali Salman, the leader of al-Wifaq opposition party, who had previously been sentenced for inciting hatred, disobedience and insulting public institutions, had his sentence increased from four to nine years.

This was significant because the US and UK had been lobbying King Hamad to reduce the sentence or issue a pardon. US Secretary of State John Kerry visited Bahrain in April and had raised the matter with the King.

It is unsurprising that Saudi Arabia should look for more aggressive action against the Shia majority in Bahrain because it neighbours Saudi Arabia's Eastern Province where the population is also largely Shia. With Deputy Crown Prince and Defence Minister Mohammed bin Salman wielding political influence in Saudi Arabia, it has become more militant in repelling what it claims is an Iranian-backed Shia offensive against the Sunni.

The Bahrain government's crackdown on dissent has proceeded swiftly and ruthlessly over the six weeks since Sheikh Ali Salman's sentence was more than doubled. On 14 June the authorities issued an "expedited" instruction to close down the headquarters of al-Wifaq, seize its funds and end its activities. A day earlier, Nabeel Rajab had been arrested. On 20 June the citizenship of Sheikh Isa Qasim, the Shia spiritual leader, was revoked. Another advocate of peaceful dissent, Zainab a-Khawaja, has fled abroad because she had heard she was about to be rearrested.

The Bahrain authorities probably calculate that the response of the US and UK to the effective ending of political and civil rights will be mild. The US Fifth Fleet is based there and the UK is extending its naval facilities there with Bahrain footing the bill. The US lifted a prohibition on arms sales to Bahrain last year. The British Foreign Secretary, Philip Hammond, has praised the Bahraini government's "commitment to continuing reforms" and said it was "travelling in the right direction". Bahrain justifies repression by saying that civil rights and political activists are proxies for Iran but the 2011 independent inquiry debunked this. This week, the Iranian supreme leader, Ayatollah Ali Khamenei, went out of his way to say that "the Islamic Republic of Iran will not intervene in any way in the affairs of Bahrain".

Patrick Cockburn

CHAPTER 12

YEMEN WINTER

Old UNESCO World Heritage City of Sanaa, destroyed by the civil war.

Friday, 16 April 2016

AL-QA'IDA NOW HAS A MINI-STATE IN YEMEN

They have done it again. The US, Britain and regional allies led by Saudi Arabia have come together to intervene in another country with calamitous results. Instead of achieving their aims, they have produced chaos, ruining the lives of millions of people and creating ideal conditions for salafi-jihadi movements like al-Qaeda and Islamic State.

The latest self-inflicted failure in the "war on terror" is in Yemen, where Saudi Arabia and a coalition of Sunni states intervened on one side in a civil war in March 2015. Their aim was to defeat the Houthis

- labelled somewhat inaccurately as Shia and pro-Iranian - who had seized most of the country in alliance with the former President Ali Abdullah Saleh, who retained the loyalty of much of the Yemeni army. Yemeni politics is exceptionally complicated and often violent, but violence has traditionally been followed by compromise between warring parties.

The Saudi intervention, supported in practice by the US and Britain, has made a bad situation far worse. A year-long campaign of air strikes was supposed to re-impose the rule of former president Abd Rabbo Mansour Hadi, whose dysfunctional and unelected government had fled to Saudi Arabia. Relentless bombing had some success and the forces fighting in President Hadi's name advanced north, but were unable to retake the capital Sanaa. Over the last week there has been a shaky truce.

The real winners in this war are AQAP which has taken advantage of the collapse of central government to create its own ministate. This now stretches for 340 miles - longer than the distance from London to Edinburgh - along the south coast of Yemen. AQAP, which the CIA once described as the most dangerous protagonist of "global jihad" in the world, today has an organised administration with its own tax revenues.

Unnoticed by the outside world, AQAP has been swiftly expanding its own statelet in Yemen in 2015/16, just as Isis did in western Iraq and eastern in Syria in 2013/14. Early last year, President Obama contemptuously described Isis as being like a junior basketball team that would never play in the big leagues. Likewise in Yemen, the American and British governments misjudged the degree to which AQAP would benefit from Operation Decisive Storm, the ill-chosen Saudi name for its military intervention that has proved predictably indecisive.

The Saudi intervention turned a crisis into a catastrophe. Some 6,427 people are known to have been killed in the fighting, but these are only the figures for casualties known to the health authorities. Since the UN says that 14.1 million Yemenis, 54 per cent of the population, have no access to health care, this is likely to be an underestimate. Even before the war, Yemen was the poorest Arab nation and its people are now starving or malnourished. OXFAM estimates that 82 per cent of Yemen's 21 million people are in need of humanitarian assistance.

The disaster is not only humanitarian, but political, and does not only affect Yemen. As in Iraq, Libya, Syria and Afghanistan, foreign intervention energises and internationalises local difference as factions become the proxies of outside powers.

Yemen has always had Shia and Sunni, but it is only recently that sectarian hatred has begun to get anywhere near the level of Syria and Iraq. Saudi Arabia portrays the Houthis as pawns of Iran, though there is little evidence for this, so Yemen is drawn into the regional confrontation between Saudi Arabia and Iran.

A point seldom given sufficient weight is that AQAP is expanding so fast, not because of its own strength, but because its opponents are so weak. The Saudi-and Gulf-financed media often refer to pro-President Hadi forces as taking territory, but in reality the government-in exile remains in Saudi Arabia. It recaptured the port city of Aden last summer, but its few officials who are there dare not leave their heavily-defended compound except by helicopter.

Even where Saudi-backed fighters advance, they leave anarchy behind them, conditions in which the arrival of disciplined AQAP forces may be welcomed by local people.

I have been struck, ever since the US and British invasion of Iraq in 2003, by the extent to which their whole strategy depends on wishful thinking about the strength and popularity of their local ally who usually, on the contrary, is feared and hated. I seldom spoke to Afghans who truly supported the Taliban, but I was always impressed by the number who detested the Afghan government. Yet when one UN official stated publicly that the foreign powers fighting the Taliban, supposedly in support of the government, had "no local partner", he was promptly fired.

There was the same lethal pretence by Western powers in Libya and Syria that the rebels they backed represented the mass of the population and were capable of taking over from existing regimes. In reality, the weakening or destruction of central government created a power vacuum promptly filled by extreme jihadi groups.

The dire consequences of the Saudi intervention and the rise of AQAP has been largely ignored by Western governments and media. Contrary to their grim-faced declarations about combating terrorism, the US and UK have opened the door to an al-Qaeda mini-state.

This will have an impact far beyond the Middle East because what makes the atrocities orchestrated by Isis in Paris and Brussels so difficult to stop is that they are organised and funded by a real administrative apparatus controlling its own territory. If one terrorist cell, local leader or bomb expert is eliminated, they can be replaced.

As has happened repeatedly since 9/11, the US and countries like Britain fail to combat terrorism because they give priority to retaining their alliance with Saudi Arabia and the Gulf monarchies, even when their policies - as in Yemen - wreck a whole country and enable al Qaeda and Isis to use the chaos to establish safe havens.

Patrick Cockburn

Friday, 23 September 2016

DOUBTS ABOUT THE FUTURE

The Saudis step deeper into trouble almost by the week. Swamped in their ridiculous war in Yemen, they are now reeling from an extraordinary statement issued by around two hundred Sunni Muslim clerics who effectively referred to the Wahhabi belief - practiced in Saudi Arabia - as "a dangerous deformation" of Sunni Islam. The prelates included Egypt's Grand Imam, Ahmed el-Tayeb of al-Azhar, the most important centre of theological study in the Islamic world, who only a year ago attacked "corrupt interpretations" of religious texts and who has now signed up to "a return to the schools of great knowledge" outside Saudi Arabia.

This remarkable meeting took place in Grozny and was unaccountably ignored by almost every media in the world - except for the former senior associate at St Antony's College, Sharmine Narwani, and Le Monde's Benamin Barthe - but it may prove to be even more dramatic than the terror of Syria's civil war.

For the statement, obviously approved by Vladimir Putin, is as close as Sunni clerics have got to excommunicating the Saudis.

Although they did not mention the kingdom by name, the declaration was a stunning affront to a country which spends millions of dollars every year on thousands of Wahhabi mosques, schools and clerics around the world.

Wahhabism's most dangerous deviation, in the eyes of the Sunnis who met in Chechenya, is that it sanctions violence against non-believers, including Muslims who reject Wahhabi interpretation. Isis, al-Qaeda and the Taliban are the principal foreign adherents to this creed outside Saudi Arabia and Qatar.

The Saudis, needless to say, repeatedly insist that they are against all terrorism. Their reaction to the Grozny declaration has been astonishing. "The world is getting ready to burn us," Adil Al-Kalbani announced. And as Imam of the King Khaled Bin Abdulaziz mosque in the Saudi capital of Riyadh, he should know.

As Narwani points out, the bad news kept on coming. At the start of the five-day Hajj pilgrimage, the Lebanese daily al-Akhbar published online a database, which it said came from the Saudi ministry of health, claiming that up 90,000 pilgrims from around the world have died visiting the Hajj capital of Mecca over a 14-year period. Although this figure is officially denied, it is believed in Shia Muslim Iran, which has lost hundreds of its citizens on the Hajj. Among them was Ghazanfar Roknabadi, a former ambassador and intelligence officer in Lebanon. Iran's supreme leader, Ali Khamenei, has just launched an unprecedented attack on the Saudis, accusing them of murder. "The heartless and murderous Saudis locked up the injured with the dead in containers..." he said in his own Hajj message.

A Saudi official said Khameni's accusations reflected a "new low". Abdulmohsen Alyas, the Saudi undersecretary for international communications, said they were "unfounded, but also timed to only serve their unethical failing propaganda".

Yet the Iranians have boycotted the Hajj this year (not surprisingly, one might add) after claiming that they have not received Saudi assurances of basic security for pilgrims. According to Khamenei, Saudi rulers "have plunged the world of Islam into civil wars".

However exaggerated his words, one thing is clear: for the first time, ever, the Saudis have been assaulted by both Sunni and Shia leaders at almost the same time.

The presence in Grozny of Grand Imam al-Tayeb of Egypt was particularly infuriating for the Saudis who have poured millions of dollars into the Egyptian economy since Brigadier-General-President al-Sissi staged his doleful military coup more than three years ago.

What, the Saudis must be asking themselves, has happened to the fawning leaders who would normally grovel to the Kingdom? "In

2010, Saudi Arabia was crossing borders peacefully as a power-broker, working with Iran, Syria, Turkey, Qatar and others to troubleshoot in regional hotspots," Narwani writes. "By 2016, it had buried two kings, shrugged off a measured approach to foreign policy, embraced 'takfiri' madness and emptied its coffers." A "takfiri" is a Sunni who accuses another Muslim (or Christian or Jew) of apostasy.

Kuwait, Libya, Jordan and Sudan were present in Grozny, along with - you guessed it - Ahmed Hassoun, the grand mufti of Syria and a loyal Assad man. Intriguingly, Abu Dhabi played no official role, although its policy of "deradicalisation" is well known throughout the Arab world.

But there are close links between President (and dictator) Ramzan Kadyrov of Chechenya, the official host of the recent conference, and Mohamed Ben Zayed al-Nahyan, the Abu Dhabi Crown Prince. The conference itself was opened by Putin, which shows what he thinks of the Saudis - although, typically, none of the Sunni delegates asked him to stop bombing Syria. But since the very meeting occurred against the backcloth of Isis and its possible defeat, they wouldn't, would they? That Chechenya, a country of monstrous bloodletting by Russia and its own Wahhabi rebels, should have been chosen as a venue for such a remarkable conclave was an irony which could not have been lost on the delegates. But the real questions they were discussing must have been equally apparent.

Who are the real representatives of Sunni Muslims if the Saudis are to be shoved aside? And what is the future of Saudi Arabia? Of such questions are revolutions made.

Robert Fisk

Wednesday, 28 September 2016

FUNDING A WAR IN YEMEN WHILE OIL PRICES COLLAPSE

Almost exactly a year after Salman bin Albdulaziz Al Saud, king of Saudi Arabia, Custodian of the Two Holy Mosques and head of the House of Saud, hurriedly left his millionaire's mansion near Cannes with his 1,000 servants to continue his vacation in Morocco, the kingdom's cash is not flowing so smoothly for the tens of thousands of subcontinental expatriates sweating away on his great building sites.

Almost unreported outside the Kingdom, the country's big construction magnates - including that of the Binladen group - have not
been paid by the Saudi government for major construction projects
and a portion of the army of Indian, Pakistani, Sri Lankan and other
workers have received no wages, some of them for up to seven
months.

Indian and Pakistani embassies approached the Saudi government, pleading that their workers should be paid. Economists who
adopt the same lickspittle attitude towards the Saudi monarchy as the
British Government, constantly point out that the authorities have
been overwhelmed by the collapse of oil prices.

They usually prefer not to mention something at which the rest
of the world remains aghast: deputy crown prince and defence minister Mohamed bin Salman's wasteful and hopeless war in Yemen. Since
the king's favourite son launched this preposterous campaign against
the Houthis last year, supporting the internationally recognized Yemeni president against Shia Muslim rebels, aircraft flown by Saudi and
Emirati pilots (aided by British technical "experts" on the ground)
have bombed even more hospitals, clinics and medical warehouses
than America has destroyed in Serbia and Afghanistan combined
since 1999.

The result? A country with 16 per cent of the world's proven oil
reserves, whose Aramco oil company makes more than $ 1bn a day
and now records a budget deficit of $ 100bn, cannot pay its bills. At
first, the Yemen fiasco was called "Operation Decisive Storm", which -
once it proved the longest and least decisive Arab "storm" in the Middle East's recent history - was changed to "Operation Restore Hope".
And the bombing went on, just as it did in the pre-"hope" "storm",
along with the help of the UK's "experts". No wonder the very same
deputy crown prince Mohamed announced this year that state spending on salaries would be lowered, yet individual earnings would rise.

In Pakistan, whose soldiers make up a large number of the
"Saudi" armed forces, there has been outrage, parliamentarians are
asking why three Saudi companies have not paid salaries for eight
months, refusing even to provide food for their employees. In some
cases, the Pakistanis have paid their own nationals for food supplies.

In Saudi Arabia itself, the government seems unable to cope with
the crisis. The Arab News says that 31,000 Saudi and other foreign

workers have lodged complaints with the government's labour ministry over unpaid wages. On one occasion, the Indian consulate and local Indian expatriates brought food to the workers so that their people should not starve. The overall figure that the government owes the construction companies owed may be billions of dollars.

Overtly xenophobic comments have emerged in the Saudi press. Writing in the Saudi Gazette, Abdulrtahman Saad Al-Araabi said: "Many expats hate us and are angry because we are a rich country.

Some of them go so far as to say that we, Saudis, do not deserve these blessings and the money we have.

That is the reason why some of them become violent when they do not get paid on time."

Well, I suppose some people are paying a lot of cash to the Jabhat al-Nusra (recently re-named Jabhat Fateh al-Shamal-Nusrah) or Al-Qaeda or Isis lads out there in the line of fire in Syria.

Embassy staff from the Philippines, France and many countries in the Middle East, have raised the problems with the Saudi government. Typical of their responses has been that of Saudi Oger which said it had been "affected by current circumstances [sic] which resulted in some delays in delays in fulfilling our commitments to our employees".

The Saudi government insisted the company paid its employees. Many of them, it should be added, are Lebanese whose Sunni Muslims come from the Sunni areas of Lebanon who traditionally vote for the Sunni leader's son Saad.

An official of the company made the extraordinary statement that "the company's situation is unstable due to the scrapping [sic] of many of its projects it was to execute," Meanwhile, workers at United Seemac construction company are complaining they have not been paid for months - or even granted permission to leave the country. Some had apparently not been paid for more than a year and a half. Unlike the big companies such as Binladen and Oger, these men - and they are indeed mostly men - are consumed into the smaller employees. "All the attention is on the big companies - it's easy to ignore us because we are not so many people."

All in all, a dodgy scenario in our beloved monarchy-dictatorship, whose war against the Shia Houthis - and the Shia Hezbollah, the Shia/Alawite regime in Damascus and Iran - is unending. Wasn't there an equally dodgy Al-Yamamah arms deal with the Saudis a few years ago? No cash flow problems then. And what does "yamamah" mean in Arabic? "Dove"? Let us go no further.

Robert Fisk

Monday, 24 October 2016

WAR ON AGRICULTURE

The Yemen war uniquely combines tragedy, hypocrisy and farce. First come the casualties: around 10,000, almost 4,000 of them civilians. Then come those anonymous British and American advisers who seem quite content to go on "helping" the Saudi onslaughts on funerals, markets and other obviously (to the Brits, I suppose) military targets. Then come the Saudi costs: more than $ 250m (£ 200m) a month, according to Standard Chartered Bank - and this for a country that cannot pay its debts to construction companies. But now comes the dark comedy bit: the Saudis have included in their bombing targets cows, farms and sorghum - which can be used for bread or animal fodder - as well as numerous agricultural facilities.

In fact, there is substantial evidence emerging that the Saudis and their "coalition" allies - and, I suppose, those horrid British "advisers" - are deliberately targeting Yemen's tiny agricultural sector in a campaign which, if successful, would lead a post-war Yemeni nation not just into starvation but total reliance on food imports for survival. Much of this would no doubt come from the Gulf states which are currently bombing the poor country to bits.

The fact that Yemen has long been part of Saudi Arabia's proxy war against Shiites and especially Iran - which has been accused, without evidence, of furnishing weapons to the Shia Houthi in Yemen - is now meekly accepted as part of the Middle East's current sectarian "narrative" (like the "good" rebels in eastern Aleppo and the "very bad" rebels in Mosul). So, alas, have the outrageous bombings of civilians.

But agricultural targets are something altogether different.

Academics have been amassing data from Yemen which strongly suggests that the Saudis' Yemen campaign contains a programme for the destruction of rural livelihood. Martha Mundy, emeritus professor at the London School of Economics, who is currently working in Lebanon with her colleague Cynthia Gharios, has been researching through Yemeni agriculture ministry statistics and says that the data "is beginning to show that in some regions, the Saudis are deliberately striking at agricultural infrastructure in order to destroy the civil society".

Mundy points out that a conservative report from the ministry of agriculture and irrigation in the Yemeni capital Sana'a, gathered from its officers across the country, details 357 bombing targets in the country's 20 provinces, including farms, animals, water infrastructure, food stores, agricultural banks, markets and food trucks. These include the destruction of farms in Yasnim, the Baqim district of Saadah province and in Marran. Mundy has compared these attacks with figures in the Yemen Data Project, which was published some weeks ago. Her verdict is a most unhappy one.

"According to the Food and Agriculture Organisation, 2.8 per cent of Yemen's land is cultivated," Mundy says. "To hit that small amount of agricultural land, you have to target it." Saudi Arabia has already been accused of war crimes, but striking at the agriculture fields and food products of Yemen in so crude a way adds merely another grim broken promise by the Saudis.

The kingdom signed up to the additional protocol of the August 1949 Geneva Conventions which specifically states that "it is prohibited to attack, destroy, remove or render useless objects indispensable to the survival of the civilian population, such as foodstuffs, agricultural areas for the production of foodstuffs, crops, livestock...for the specific purpose of denying them for their sustenance value to the civilian population...whatever the motive..." In a lecture in Beirut, Mundy has outlined the grievous consequences of earlier economic policies in Yemen - cheap American wheat from the 1970s and the influx of food from other countries which discouraged farmers from maintaining rural life (terracing of farms, for example, or water husbandry) - and the effect of Saudi Arabia's war on the land. "The armies and above all air forces of the 'oil-dollar'," she said, have "...come to destroy physically those products of Yemeni labour working with land and animals that survived the earlier economic devastation."

There are photographs aplenty of destroyed farms, factories and dead animals lying in fields strewn with munitions - effectively preventing farmers returning to work for many months or years. Poultry and beehive farms have been destroyed. Even today, more than half the population of Yemen relies in part - or wholly - on agriculture and rural husbandry. Mundy's research through the files of other ministries suggests that technical support administration buildings for agriculture were also attacked. The major Tihama Development Authority on the Red Sea coastal plain, which was established in the 1970s - and houses, as Mundy says, "the written memory of years of 'development' interventions" - is responsible for a series of irrigation structures. It has been heavily bombed twice.

But I guess that one war - or two - in the Middle East is as much as the world can take right now. Or as much as the media are prepared to advertise. Aleppo and Mosul are quite enough. Yemen is too much. And Libya. And "Palestine"...

Robert Fisk

CHAPTER 13

SYRIA WINTER

Syrian refugees flee shelling, Latakia, Syria, 15 February 1016.

Monday, 14 March 2016

HIGH ON ARAB SPRING, WE FORGOT SYRIA WAS SHIA

Just before I left Syria last month, an eloquent Franco-Lebanese man walked up to me in a Damascus coffee shop and introduced himself as President Bashar al-Assad's architect. It was his task, he led me to understand, to design the reconstructed cities of Syria.

Who would have believed it? Five years after the start of Syria's tragedy - and within six months of this, remember, the regime itself trembled and the Western powers, flush with dangerous pride after destroying Muammar Gaddafi, predicted Assad's imminent fall - the Syrian government is preparing to rebuild its towns and cities.

It's worth taking that embarrassing trip down memory lane to the early spring and summer of 2011. The US and French ambassadors visited Homs to sit amid tens of thousands of peaceful demonstrators calling for the overthrow of the Assad government. EU diplomats were telling the political opposition not to negotiate with Assad - a fatal mistake, since the advice was based on the false assumption that he was about to be overthrown - and journalists were gathering with rebels in eastern Aleppo for the inevitable march of liberation on Damascus.

The Assad regime, came the message from the Washington think-tanks and mountebank "experts", had reached - a cliché we should all beware of - "tipping point". Hillary Clinton announced that Assad "had to go". French Foreign Minister Laurent Fabius declared that Assad "did not deserve to live on this planet" - although he failed to name the galaxy to which the Syrian President might retire.

Looking back, it's not difficult to see where we all got it wrong. We were high on Arab revolutions - Tunisia, then Egypt and then Libya - and journalists were growing used to "liberating" Arab capitals. We forgot that their dictators were all Sunni Muslims, that they had no regional super-power support - the Saudis could not save Hosni Mubarak in Egypt but Shia Iran was not going to allow its only Arab ally, Alawite-Shia-led Syria, to fall.

At first, the Syrian Baath party and the regime's internal security agents behaved with their usual inane brutality. Teenagers who wrote anti-Assad graffiti on the walls of Deraa were tortured, the local tribal leaders abused - and a deputy minister dispatched to apologise for the government's "errors". But torture was so much an instrument of state power that the intelligence apparatus knew no other way to resolve this unprecedented challenge to the regime's authority.

The government army was ordered to shoot demonstrators. Hence the brief but ultimately hopeless dawn of the "Free Syrian Army", many of them deserters who are now slowly returning to the ranks or drifting off home with the regime's tacit permission. But there were signs from the very start that armed groups were involved in this latest manifestation of the Arab awakening.

In May 2011, an Al Jazeera crew filmed armed men shooting at Syrian troops a few hundred metres from the northern border with

Lebanon but the channel declined to air the footage, which their reporter later showed to me. A Syrian television crew, working for the government, produced a tape showing men with pistols and Kalashnikovs in a Deraa demonstration in the very early days of the "rising".

The sectarian nature of Middle East civil wars has always been manipulated. For 100 years, the West has used the confessional nature of society in the region to set up "national" governments which were, by nature, sectarian - in Palestine after the 1914-18 war, in Cyprus, in Lebanon, in Syria - where the French used Alawites as their "force speciale" - and, after 2003, in Iraq. This not only allowed us to portray Middle Eastern people as essentially sectarian in nature but permitted us to forget the degree to which minorities would naturally lend their support to local dictators - not least the Christians (Maronites, Orthodox, Armenian Catholic, Melkite, and so on) of Syria.

And by constantly reminding readers and viewers of the Alawite "domination" of Assad, we journalists ourselves fell victim to our own reporting. We forgot - or did not care - that perhaps 80 per cent of the Syrian government army were Sunni Muslims who would, over the next four years, be fighting their co-religionists in the opposition militias and - by 2014 - struggling against them in the al-Qaeda/Nusra alliance and in Isis.

In Lebanon, the Syrian army was a deeply corrupting influence, its soldiers indisciplined, its officers often involved in dodgy business and real estate deals. But the Syrian army that found itself fighting for its life after 2012, especially when the Nusra and Isis suicide squads began to cut into their ranks - ritually chopping off the heads of their military prisoners by the dozen - became a different creature.

As ruthless as ever, its soldiers fought to survive - I suspect they even began to like fighting - and many of their front-line generals, when I met them, turned out to be Sunni Muslims as well as Alawites. In other words, the real backbone of the one institution that could save the Syrian state was not an Alawite-Christian alliance but a Sunni-Alawite-Christian military force - out-gunned and outmanned after 60,000 dead, to be sure, but still capable of holding the line if it was reinforced with new armour and air power.

Enter Vladimir Putin. The Syrians within Assad's current frontiers - less than half of the land mass, but including well over 60 per cent of the Syrian people - have adopted a phlegmatic approach to the Russians. Their Sukhoi jets strike at villages and towns beyond the front line - and Moscow has adopted exactly the same tactic of denying civilian casualties in air strikes that the Americans and British and French have for so long been using in their own "antiterror" war in Syria and Iraq.

I've even seen a new poster on the streets of Syrian cities. It shows Bashar al-Assad and, right alongside him, the face of Colonel Suheil al-Hassan, the "Tiger" as the army call him, the country's most successful military commander, the "Rommel" of Syria.

We should pay attention to these phenomena. The army expresses its loyalty for Assad. But, every time Assad speaks, he shrewdly begins with praise for the "martyrs" of the Syrian army.

On principle, I don't like armies - whomever they work for.

But that doesn't mean we can disregard them. Nor can President Assad.

THE FALL OF SYRIA TIMELINE

18 March 2011: Security forces open fire on a protest in Daraa, killing four people, in what activists regard as the first deaths of the uprising. Demonstrations spread.

June 2011: Police and soldiers in Jisr al-Shughour in north-eastern Syria join the protesters they were ordered to shoot, and the uprising claims control of its first town.

August-September 2013: A chemical weapons attack in Damascus kills hundreds.

October 2013: Under international pressure, Syria destroys its chemical weapons production equipment.

February 2014: Peace talks led by UN-Arab League mediator Lakhdar Brahimi in Geneva end without a breakthrough.

June 2014: Isis seizes much of northern and western Iraq and declares a self-styled Islamic caliphate.

30 September 2015: Russia begins launching air strikes in Syria in support of Assad's forces.

3 February 2016: Indirect peace talks between the Syrian government and opposition in Geneva collapse after a few days.

22 February: The US and Russia announce that a partial ceasefire in Syria will start on 27 February.

Robert Fisk

SHIITES ARE WINNING

The Shiites are winning. Two pictures prove it. The US-Iranian photo op that followed the signing of the nuclear deal with Iran last year and the footage just released - by the Russian defence ministry, no less - showing Moscow's Tupolev Tu-22M3 bombers flying out of the Iranian air base at Hamadan and bombing the enemies of Shia Iran and of the Shia (Alawite) regime of Syria and of the Shia Hezbollah.

And what can the Sunni Kingdom of Saudi Arabia match against this? Only its wretched war to kill the miserable Shia Houthis of Yemen - with British arms.

Poor, luckless Turkey — whose Sultan Erdogan makes Theresa May's political U-turns look like a straight path - is at the centre of this realignment. Having shot down a Russian jet and lost much of his Russian tourist trade, the Turkish president was quickly off to St Petersburg to proclaim his undying friendship for Tsar Vladimir. The price? An offer from Erdogan to stage Russian-Turkish "joint operations" against the Sunni enemies of Bashar al-Assad of Syria. Turkey is now in the odd position of assisting US jets to bomb Isis while ready to help Russian jets do exactly the same.

And Nusrah? Let's remember the story so far. Al-Qaeda, the creature of the (almost) forgotten Osama bin Laden, sprang up in both Iraq and Syria where it changed its name to the Nusrah Front and then, just a few days ago, to "Fatah al-Sham". Sometimes allied to Isis, sometimes at war with Isis, the Qatari-funded legion is now the pre-eminent guerrilla army in Syria - far eclipsing the black-costumed lads of Raqqa whose gruesome head-chopping videos have awed the West in direct proportion to their military defeats.

We are still obsessed with Isis and its genocidal creed. We are not paying nearly enough attention to Nusrah.

But the Russians are. That's why they are sprinkling their bombs across eastern Aleppo and Idlib province.

Nusrah forces hold almost all the rebel areas of Syria's second city and much of the province. It was Nusrah that fought back against its own encirclement by the Syrian regime in Aleppo. The regime kicked Isis out of Palmyra in a short and bloody battle in which Syrian soldiers, most of whom are in fact Sunnis, died by the dozen after stepping on hidden land mines.

But Nusrah is a more powerful enemy, partly because it has more Syrians among its ranks than Isis. It's one thing to be told that your country is to be "liberated" by a Sunni Syrian outfit, quite another to be instructed by the purists of Isis that your future is in the hands of Sunni Chechens, Pakistanis, Iraqis, Saudis, Qataris, Egyptians, Turks, Frenchmen, Belgians, Kosovars and British. Isis has Sunni Saudi interests (and money) behind it. Nusrah has Sunni Qatar.

As for Turkey - Sunni as well, of course, but not Arab - it's now being squeezed between giants, the fate of all arms smuggling nations, as Pakistan learned to its cost. Not only has it been pushed into joining Moscow as well as the US in waging war on Isis, it's being politically attacked from within Germany, where a leaked state intelligence summary - part of a reply to a parliamentary question by the interior ministry - speaks of Turkey as a "central platform for Islamist and other terrorist organisations". State interior secretary Ole Schroder's remarks, understandably stamped "confidential", are flawed since he lumps Erdogan's support for the Egyptian Muslim Brotherhood and Hamas with armed Islamist groups in Syria.

The Sunni Brotherhood, prior to its savaging by Egypt's President-Field Marshal al-Sissi, did indeed give verbal approval to Assad's Sunni armed opponents in Syria, and Sunni Hamas operatives in Gaza must have cooperated with Isis in its struggle against Sissi's army in Sinai. But to suggest that Turkey is in some way organising this odd triumvirate is going too far. To claim that "the countless expressions of solidarity and supportive actions of the ruling AKP [Justice and Development Party] and President Erdogan" for the three "underline their ideological [affinity] to their Muslim brothers" is going too far. "Ideological affinity" should not provide a building block for intelligence reports, but the damage was done. In the report, the Turkish president's name was written ERDOGAN, in full capital letters.

Someone in the German intelligence service - which regularly acts as a negotiator between Israel and the Shia Hezbollah in Lebanon, usually to exchange bodies between the two sides - obviously decided that its erring Sunni NATO partner in Ankara should get fingered in the infamous "war on terror" in which we are all supposed to be participants. So Erdogan offers help to Russia in the anti-Isis war, continues to give the US airbases in Turkey - and gets dissed by the German federal interior ministry, all at the same time. And the only

Muslim state in Nato, which just happens to be Sunni Muslim, is now being wrapped up in the Sunni-Shia war. What future Turkey?

Well, we better not write it off. Just as Erdogan has become pals with Putin, the Turkish and Iranian foreign ministers have been embracing in Ankara with many a promise that their own talks will produce new alliances. Russia-Turkey-Iran. In the Middle East, it's widely believed that Tehran as well as Moscow tipped Erdogan off about the impending coup. And Erdogan himself has spoken of his emotion when Putin called after the coup was crushed to express his support.

The mortar to build this triple alliance could well turn out to be the Kurds. Neither Russia nor Iran want independent Kurdish states - Putin doesn't like small minorities in nation-states and Iran's unity depends on the compliance of its own Kurdish people. Neither are going to protect the Kurds of Syria - loyal foot soldiers of the Americans right now - in a "new" Syria. Erdogan wants to see them crushed along with the dreams of a "Kurdistan" in south-east Turkey.

Any restored Syrian state will insist on national unity. When Assad praised the Kurds of Kobane for their resistance at the start of the war, he called their town by its Arab name of Ein al-Arab.

It is, of course, a paradox to talk of the Middle East's agony as part of an inter-Muslim war when one side talks of its enemies as terrorists and the other calls its antagonists apostates. Arab Muslims do not deserve to have their religious division held out by Westerners as a cause of war.

But Saudis and Qataris have a lot to answer for. It is they who are supporting the insurgents in Syria. Syria - dictatorial regime though it is - is not supporting any revolutions in Riyadh or Doha. The Sunni Gulf Arabs gave their backing to the Sunni Taliban in Afghanistan, just as they favour Sunni Isis and Sunni Nusrah in Syria. Russia and America are aligned against both and growing closer in their own weird cooperation. And for the first time in history, the Shia Iranians have both the Russians and the Americans on their side - and Turkey tagging along.

Robert Fisk

FAKE ANTIQUITIES

In the National Museum in Damascus are antique books of black magic and witchcraft listing curses and spells designed to dumbfound or destroy whatever enemy is targeted by the user. Alongside these tattered works lie a Bible made out of copper, religious works from the crusader period and, elsewhere in the museum, a striking stone statue of a falcon.

These look like impressive survivals from Syria's past, but in reality all are fakes for sale to foreign customers and dealers confiscated from smugglers on their way out of the country. Expertly manufactured in workshops in Damascus and Aleppo or elsewhere in Syria, these fraudulent antiquities are flooding a market full of unwary or unscrupulous buyers who find it easy to believe that great masterpieces are being daily looted in Syria in the midst of the chaos and war. "It started happening in 2015," says Dr Maamoun Abdulkarim, the general director of antiquities and museums in Damascus. "The looters had attacked all the ancient sites in 2013-14, but they did not find as much as they wanted, so they switched to making fakes."

There is a strong tradition of craftsmanship in Syria and, in addition, though Dr Abdulkarim does not say so, many unemployed archaeologists and antiquarians are prepared to give expert advice to fakers. The results are often magnificently convincing and come from both government and rebelheld areas. In rebel-controlled Idlib province, the speciality is making Roman and Greek mosaics, which may be then reburied in ancient sites to reinforce belief in their authenticity and so the buyer can be shown persuasive film of them being excavated.

The smugglers are able to take advantage of the dangers of conflict which ensure that few potential purchasers will risk entering Syria in the middle of a war to check exactly what they are buying. They suppose that they can get a bargain because Isis and other iconoclastic Islamic movements are stripping ancient sites for ideological reasons and to raise funds - which is true, but not on the scale they imagine. (It is not only fake artefacts from antiquity that are for sale, but modern documents bought by the foreign media that supposedly come from Isis but whose provenance and significance are dubious or exaggerated.)

Some of the fake antiquities can be swiftly detected as such by specialists, but others are so expertly made that only laboratory analysis can prove that they are of modern manufacture. Sometimes the real and fake are mixed to make detection more difficult. In the National Museum, its director, Yacoub Abdullah, scoops out of a bowl Abbasid, Roman and Byzantine coins and rapidly sorts them into two piles, muttering "fake, real; fake, real" as he does so. Some items, such as the black magic or witchcraft books made from the skin of bulls, are seized by the police without the museum staff knowing where they came from.

Dr Abdulkarim says that 80 per cent of supposed antiquities being smuggled out of Syria into Lebanon are fakes, compared to about 30 per cent a couple of years ago according to the Lebanese authorities. He adds that the smugglers know that if they are caught by the Syrian police they will get reduced sentences because they can show that they were not, though for entirely self-interested reasons, robbing Syria's heritage.

Smugglers benefit from Syria being the cradle of civilisation, containing many of the earliest agricultural settlements and cities in the world. Some sites are famous, such as the great Umayyad Mosque in Damascus with its wonderful eighth-century mosaics showing scenes of daily life at the time of the Arab conquest or Dura-Europos, the Hellenistic city called "the Pompeii of the Syrian desert", famous for the frescoes in the early Jewish synagogue, fortunately removed long ago to Damascus.

Unluckily, thousands of important sites are in the most war-torn parts of the country such as Ebla in Idlib province, a Bronze Age city from the second and third millennium BC. Others, such as Mari from the third millennium BC, are on Isis-controlled territory and are vulnerable to systematic destruction, looting and neglect. Pictures show deep holes dug by looters every few yards.

Many wars throughout human history have led to the loss of ancient masterpieces of art and architecture or the archaeological remains of past civilisations. The causes of destruction have usually been three-fold: damage due to fighting, looting for profit and ideological objections to certain types of art such as the representation of divinities or religious themes. Europe has seen all these forms of depredation, notable examples being the religious wars of the 16th and

17th centuries and the area bombing of cities during the Second World War.

The five-year-long Syrian civil war has combined these three causes in a uniquely destructive manner: there is warfare reaching every part of the country; a prolonged breakdown of law and order opening the door to looting; and the rule over much of eastern Syria of a religious cult in the shape of Isis that targets ancient remains as polytheistic in a way that may have no parallel in history.

The impact of all this has been devastating: Aleppo and Homs have been shelled and bombed for years at a time. Dr Abdulkarim warns that "if Aleppo goes on being a battlefield it will become like Warsaw in 1944." The al-Madina Souk, which had over 700 traditional shops, was burnt out and the Grand Mosque damaged. Damascus, Aleppo and Homs - the three largest Syrian cities - are full of "ghost districts" where every building is shattered and walls still standing are pitted with holes made by bullets and shrapnel. In Palmyra, Isis infamously blew up the Temple of Bel and vandalised or destroyed other buildings and statues.

This tale of destruction and violence might lead on to think that the story of the attempt to preserve Syria's heritage is one more depressing story of failure in the face of greed and fanaticism. So, to some extent, it is, but the stereotypical media picture of unstoppable triumph of evil in Syria is, on present evidence, not really true.

The news is not all bad and, when it comes to Syria's past, far more is being saved than has been lost. "We should not be pessimists," says Dr Abdulkarim, who was appointed director general of antiquities and museums in 2013, a job for which he takes no pay, and who regards himself as politically neutral. Of Armenian-Kurdish origin - his father was a survivor of the Armenian genocide in 1915 who was adopted by a Kurdish family - he revels in Syria's ethnic and cultural diversity and wants to do what he can to preserve it. He and his 2,500 staff, some of them in rebel-held areas, keep in touch with local communities who are often protective of archaeological remains in areas where they live.

Devastating though the losses have been, no major museum in Syria has lost its contents through looting or destruction, though some have come frighteningly close to disaster. Trucks carrying items from the museum in Palmyra left for Damascus three hours before Isis captured the city in 2015.

Some 24,000 objects were moved to safety from Aleppo and 30,000 flown out of Deir Ezzor on the Euphrates in the east of the country, including 24,000 cuneiform tablets. "I thought Isis were going to take the city at any moment," says Dr Abdulkarim. "I could not sleep for nights."

He adds that when he became an archaeologist he hoped he would spend his career "discovering treasures, but in the last three years I have spent all my time hiding them." Once rescued artefacts reach Damascus, they are placed in secret vaults, along with the contents of the National Museum, which is long closed. Its empty rooms are today stacked with old army ammunition boxes filled with broken sculptures from Palmyra, some shattered by Isis beyond repair but others in fragments that have all survived and can be painstakingly pieced together again.

Destruction of the antiquities of Syria has not been anything like as total as was once feared. It has been resisted by Syrian archaeologists and communities alike. Khaled Asaad, the 82-year-old former director of Palmyra antiquities, was publicly beheaded by Isis in the city on 18 August 2015 as a leading intellectual and because he would not tell them where treasures were to be found - though there may have been nothing to tell since they had been evacuated. The very fact that the great majority of antiquities being smuggled out of Syria today are fakes is back-handed evidence that the smugglers and their employers have failed to plunder as many original and irreplaceable artefacts as they wanted. The Syrian past, like the Syrian present, may be more durable than it looks.

Patrick Cockburn

Thursday, 8 September 2016

LIFE IN DAMASCUS

High on the upper slopes of Mount Qasioun, which towers over Damascus, is the Magharat al-Dam or "Cave of Blood" where Cain is believed to have killed Abel. The impression of a large hand on a rock inside the cave was supposedly made by Abel as his brother murdered him.

It feels appropriate that the site of the first fratricidal killing should look down on a city ravaged by civil war over the past five years. The cave is at the top of hundreds of steps that lead from a narrow and precipitous laneway winding steeply upwards through a poor neighbourhood in the Reku Aldeen district called Hajeh Anyseh, built into the side of Mount Qasioun. Despite the difficulty in reaching the mountain-top shrine, Mohammed Hatem, a 32-year-old Palestinian born in Syria, who took us there, says that Muslims of all sects - Sunni, Shia and Alawites - visit it because prayers there are believed to be particularly acceptable to God.

In the close-packed houses of Hajeh Anyseh, people are aware that they live near the place which saw the first murder in human history. They relate what happened then to their own lives, which are filled with violence. Mr Hatem drives a minibus with an especially powerful engine to negotiate roads which zigzag up the mountainside and are too steep for ordinary vehicles. He says that, earlier in the war, an armed opposition group broke into the district and 200 people were killed in three days of fighting. He did not say if they had support in the area, but many locals are Kurds who are unlikely to be sympathetic to the rebels.

Military conscription is one of the main topics of conversation in Damascus. Mr Hatem says: "I was lucky that I had just completed my military service when the war started in 2011 and so far I have not been called up again." Asked if many soldiers from the district had been killed or wounded in the fighting, he said that two had just been killed - probably by a mine explosion - in the district of Daraya, a rebel stronghold that surrendered on terms last week after a three-year siege under an agreement by which armed opposition fighters were taken to a rebel-held area of Idlib in the north of Syria. The political balance of power in Damascus is changing in favour of the government. After a rebel offensive in 2012 it became a patchwork of government and rebelheld areas, but many rebel enclaves have been besieged and pounded into submission.

Mr Hatem says that life in Hajeh Anyseh is tolerable, with the electricity supply three-hours-on and three-hours-off - as it is in the rest of the Damascus. The lack of electricity becomes more serious in winter when heaters are needed as the top of Mount Qasioun becomes blanketed in snow. Running water is plentiful, but there is a shortage of bottled gas for cooking. The inhabitants of Hajeh Anyseh have always been poor, so they may feel less shocked by the collapse in the Syrian standard of living which has seen prices soar while salaries stagnate, requiring employees to desperately search for a second job in an economy in which the unemployment rate may be as high as 65 per cent.

I was last in Damascus two-and-a-half years ago when security was worse than today in the government-held parts of the city. I stayed in Bab Touma, a Christian district in the Old City which was regularly mortared by a nearby rebel district called Jobar, producing a trickle of casualties every day. The thunder of government artillery on Mount Qasioun firing into besieged opposition areas boomed across the city every night. Even then people were getting used to this, but not as accustomed as they are now when many forget what it is like to live a normal life. The present mood in Damascus reminds me of Beirut half way through the 15-year-long civil war (1975-1989).

Earlier still in the conflict, people in Damascus were inexperienced in assessing the degree of danger they were in and would under- or over-react to each episode of fighting. I remember in early 2012 taking refuge from sniper fire in a shop selling wedding dresses in the Jaramana district, close to the airport road. The owner and I were both crouching down by the counter when three young women came into the shop, oblivious of the shooting outside, and excitedly discussed which of the flame-coloured dresses they would like to buy.

Four years later those same young women would be more likely to spend what little money they have left on food rather than dresses. After the Syrian pound plunged in value and salaries were raised by a much smaller margin, a family that had once lived on the equivalent of £300 to £375 a month must make do with £75. The definition of what is a luxury has changed radically since the start of the war. "Many families no longer eat chicken or lamb because they are so expensive," commented one friend. "And, if they do buy them, the quantity is a couple of hundred grams just to have a taste of the meat. They may buy locally grown fruit for their children, but not bananas, which are imported and cost too much." Holding a good job himself, the friend added that he has spent £225 to replace a broken car mirror which would have cost him £55 before the war.

As with almost every aspect of the Syrian crisis, not all the arrows point in the same direction. Mahir Jalhoum, a 22-year-old architectural student, says that while the real value of salaries may be well down and employment difficult to find there are now five million Syrian refugees, many of whom are working abroad and sending money back to their families. He says that "if somebody is remitting $100 [£75] a month to relatives that goes a long way in Syria." He adds that night entertainment in cafés and restaurants is expanding fast, with 20 bars opening in the Bab Sharqi neighbourhood in the Old City alone in the last couple of months. He was about to go off on a camping holiday with 40 other people in the mountains near Latakia on the Mediterranean coast.

People do adapt to new reduced circumstances, though they may not like doing so. In the bustling Bzoureyeh souk, a covered market in the Old City selling everything from perfumes and honey to dates and coffee beans, there is a row of small booth-like shops selling traditional medicines made from rare herbs and other more exotic compounds. Sitting behind a counter on which were neatly arrayed bowls of natural medication, was a middle-aged man named Abed. He explained that by profession he is a geologist specialising in oil and gas exploration and he had worked in Syria, Saudi Arabia and the Gulf for 27 years. But there is little work for geologists in Syria today - the oil and gas fields in eastern Syria were seized by Isis during their explosive advance in 2014, so he had switched to traditional medicine.

Asked how his business was doing, Abed said that he had few foreign customers, but that Syrians were buying more. He explained that because of the war and the economic collapse "most of the famous and experienced doctors in Syria have left the country and those that are left are second rate." Abed said that as a result Syrians do not trust the diagnoses of their illnesses or the medicines they are prescribed, so they prefer to turn to traditional remedies in the hope that they will be more effective.

This sounded convincing and many Syrians had complained to me about the decline in the quality of the health service and education system in the country. But Abed has a certain self-interest in badmouthing doctors and hospitals dealing in scientific as opposed to traditional medicine, so I went to see Dr Hashem Saker, the general director of the Al-Mousat University Hospital, which is the largest teaching hospital in Syria. He said it was difficult to get spare parts for medical equipment because of economic sanctions, but denied that the quality of care had gone down. "About 30 per cent of our professors and highly qualified staff have left," he said. "Most went to the Gulf where they were offered jobs and better money."

The 200-bed hospital was under great pressure, carrying out between 100 and 120 operations a day and treating between 600 and 1,000 emergency cases. Dr Saker admitted that conditions had got tougher but "we are getting used to the situation and the death rate has not gone up. We are still teaching as many hours as before."

There had been a shortage of medicines because many of Syria's pharmaceutical factories were in Aleppo and 90 per cent had closed. But several of these had reopened elsewhere and the UN was helping obtain spare parts and equipment. Some of the doctors who had gone to the Gulf were returning because conditions were "not as rosy as they had been promised".

It was encouraging that the health service in Syria was not in such a bad way as many in Damascus had claimed. But this more buoyant mood lasted only a few minutes until I started to meet the patients. I had asked to meet three people who had been wounded by an Isis suicide bomber on the Old Beirut Road the day before, but one was dead and the two others had been discharged. But then I saw a hospital bed on which lay the small body of 12-year-old Yazad Dahar, his head swathed in bandages, whose eyes had been torn out and his face disfigured by an explosion in the northern town of Manbij two days earlier. His father was standing by his bed and his mother in black traditional dress was crying loudly a few feet way. The parents had left their other five children in Manbij and somehow got their wounded son to Damascus, but doctors in the ward said they could do little.

Patrick Cockburn

Friday, 9 September 2016

COUNTRY OF SIEGES AND LONG CANYONS OF DESTRUCTION

A small triangular green flag with the words "there is no God but God and Mohammed is his Prophet" inscribed on it is stuck in a heap of smashed masonry half-blocking the street in the former rebel stronghold of Daraya, which fell to government forces two weeks ago at the end of a four-year siege. In a building nearby there is the entrance to a carefully-constructed tunnel said to be too dangerous to enter and somebody has written on the wall that "the martyrs of Syria are so many that they will build a new Syria in heaven".

The flag, the tunnel and the message are among the few signs of the fighters who fought for so long for this devastated ghost town in south-east Damascus, three miles from the centre of the capital. Its capture by the Syrian Army on 25 August was a decisive moment in the struggle for the Syrian capital, home to one third of the population, or at least five out of 16 million Syrians still in the country, full control of which is likely to determine who will emerge the victor in the civil war.

The Syrian government is confident it is winning: the resistance of Daraya was a highly-publicised symbol of rebel resistance though only 1,800 fighters and civilians were there at the end. International attention is focused on more distant battlefields in Aleppo or Palmyra, but the tightening government hold on Damascus is a more important development. Four years ago the city was a jigsaw puzzle of pro-government and pro-opposition areas with each side trying to expand their heavily-defended islands of authority. Today the government holds almost all the city and its outskirts aside from a single large opposition enclave to the east known as East Ghouta.

Isolated, starved, bombarded, divided among themselves and sensing that the war is going against them, the rebel townships are surrendering on terms that leaves the government in charge.

The Syrian army was eager this week to show off its latest success at Daraya, though concerned about booby traps and mines. "We have lost six soldiers dead and four injured defusing them," said General Ayman Saleh, a field commander in the 4th Brigade that has been besieging the town since 2012. "The devices are attached to doors into rooms, fridges and such like." Nevertheless, the army must be confident that its grip on the town is complete, since four soldiers without weapons walked past us.

The great majority of the 200,000 people who once lived in the town fled a long time ago, probably in 2012. The degree of visible destruction varies from street to street and neighbourhood to neighbourhood. It is total at the entrance to the town, close to what was once a municipal pound for cars confiscated by the police, where all the buildings are shattered with only the stumps of concrete supporting pillars rising a few feet above the debris. This was once the front line, but further into the town most of the modern apartment blocks are gutted but still standing, though often pitted with holes made by bullets and shrapnel. Every so often there is a tangle of broken concrete, window frames and furniture where a shell or a bomb has turned a whole building into a heap of wreckage.

There is complete silence, with no people or even signs of recent habitation. Daraya used to specialise in making furniture in small workshops and one occasionally sees the remains of broken woodcutting machinery. Shop signs are faded, though on one shop front there is a "for sale" sign, the desperate but doomed attempt of some shop owner to find a buyer before his neighbourhood was engulfed by violence. The streets are long canyons of destruction, where ornamental bushes have turned into trees 15ft high. In most towns and cities from which their people have been forced to flee, there are normally signs or smells of recent occupation, such as food scraps or garbage, but here there was none.

Standing beside a Muslim cemetery with white headstones near what used to be Daraya's Christian quarter, Gen Saleh told me that his unit had lost 286 dead and 276 wounded in the fighting here since 4 January 2012. He would not give the number of soldiers in his brigade, but pointed up at the wrecked apartment blocks whose windows had long disappeared, saying they were wonderful hiding places for snipers. He agreed that at the beginning of the siege the armed opposition had popular support in the township, but claimed this had diminished as time went on. Others recall seeing tens of thousands of anti-government protesters in the streets at the time, but there is not so much as an ancient slogan on a wall to show they ever existed.

Syria is full of sieges, which in some respects differ markedly from each other, but in others are very much the same. The government generally follows classic counterinsurgency strategy, made notorious by the French in Algeria and the Americans in Vietnam, which is to shell and bomb rebel areas to separate fighters from civilians. In Syria as a whole, there are an estimated 590,200 people encircled by hostile military forces. Most are in opposition areas, though Isis has surrounded an estimated 110,000 people in the government-held Deir Ezzor city in the east of Syria and there are another 20,000 in the Shia towns of Kefraya and Foua outside Aleppo.

The relief of these besieged areas is a main topic of international diplomacy and media attention, but the degree of deprivation varies from extreme malnutrition to something closer to the effects of an arbitrary economic blockade. For instance, the rebel towns of Zabadani and Madaya west of Damascus are entirely cut off with no food getting in. Zabadani is almost empty apart from 700 fighters, but there are 43,000 people trapped in Madaya. One woman, who had got out with her two daughters but did not want her name published, described how she had tried to make soup out of plants she found growing on waste ground. One of the girls had been shot through the leg trying to get water from a spring.

"You can see malnourishment in people's faces," said one observer who had recently visited Madaya. "There is no electricity so they burn plastic to cook and for heat in winter. Surprisingly, there is meat because there is no fodder for the sheep and they are slaughtering them, but this is too expensive for most people."

The nightmarish complexity of getting United Nations relief convoys into Zabadani and Madaya is further complicated because of the so-called "Four Towns Agreement" under which whatever is done for them also has to be done for pro-government Kefraya and Foua. Other towns cut off by rigorous sieges include Mouadamiya, with a population of 45,000, that is close to Daraya, which was even more closely invested (Gen Saleh said it was cutting the link between the two that finally led to the fall of Daraya).

The politics of food in Syria at war are contentious and the UN relief agencies find themselves caught in the middle of rancorous disputes. Outside Syria the true dimensions of the problem are little understood, because they are distorted by the unstated military and propaganda needs of both sides. Though 590,200 people are cut off and lack many things, those who are actually starving is about a third of this figure, or about 193,000. But even here there are great variations in levels of deprivation depending on political circumstances.

For instance, al-Waer, a Sunni Arab district in the west of the city of Homs with a population of 75,000, is entirely isolated from the rest of Syria most of the time. But every month or so, commercial traders are allowed in and people stock up, if they have the money, on food they can store like canned goods, chick peas and dried beans.

Almost half the total of besieged people - about 282,000 - are in East Ghouta, which is by far the largest pocket of anti-government resistance left in greater Damascus. Even so, the area has shrunk by a third over the last three years as government forces push in from the east and south. "Conditions are bad," says one observer familiar with the enclave. "But there is no malnutrition. The area used to be the garden of Damascus, growing much of its fruit and vegetables. You see small shops selling oil, sugar and biscuits that you would never see in Mouadamiya. Its most pressing need is seeds and agricultural machinery."

In Syria almost everybody is under siege to a greater or lesser degree. There are the encircled towns and districts, but there are also economic sanctions imposed by the US and EU that cripple economic life. As with UN sanctions on Iraq between 1990 and 2003, they hurt ordinary Syrians and have a negligible impact on the political leadership.

And, as with Iraq, everything to do with sieges, blockades and sanctions is at the heart of a propaganda battle in which everybody accuses everybody else of wilfully starving or killing the innocent. No doubt one reason why the Syrian government wanted to get the siege of Daraya over with, and bused rebel fighters to their stronghold in Idlib province in the north, was because the continued bombing of the town had become a damaging international political issue. The government protests vigorously that it was misled by the UN about the number of civilians still in Daraya, which the UN put at 4,000 but turned out to be less. But the true importance of fall of Daraya is military rather than political.

With its capture the long battle for the capital has turned decisively in the government's favour; and it is an old saying that whoever holds Damascus holds Syria.

Patrick Cockburn

Saturday, 29 October 2016

'THEY ARE JUST ANIMALS'

There is a problem with the story I am about to tell you. It is bloody. It is about the massacre of innocents - six of them, the youngest a little girl of two - blasted to death by shellfire in Aleppo.

Three of them were killed in their junior school, a teenage boy blown clean off the roof next to his classroom and then four storeys down into the street where he lay in a pool of blood. The shrapnel tore into his friends and when I reached the school, I was walking across floors swamped with crimson liquid.

But reader, bear with me. For the problem with my grim - some might say gruesome - and certainly tragic report is that the victims were slaughtered by the guns of the "rebels" of eastern Aleppo. These children were killed in western Aleppo, in the sector of the city held by the Syrian regime and its army. And that is why you will not know their names, nor have heard of their deaths in any news report. The suffering of the survivors, one of the wounded child survivors, groaning in agony as a doctor picked a piece of metal from his face with a scalpel in the Al-Razi Hospital, will be quite unknown to you.

None of what I shall describe excuses the savagery visited upon the people of eastern Aleppo by Syrian and Russian bombs. Indeed, when I asked the senior Syrian police officer at the wrecked school - he was standing on the rood beside a bloody puddle - if this might be some sort of revenge by the armed groups in the east, he sidestepped the question. "No, no, no, no, no - No!" he shouted. "They have hit other schools before now - they are just animals, they don't even know the meaning of childhood. When we opened the crossing points for the people of eastern Aleppo last week, we even cleared these schools as a reception place for them."

The first shell crashed into the corner of the roof of the privately run National School of Aleppo at almost exactly 11am, blasting part of the parapet into the street below, along with one of the pupils who was taking a class break on the patio outside his classroom. By the time I arrived, they were taking the corpses out of the school door in blue sheets. One of them was 15-year old Omar Deiry. Another was Imad Sabbagh who was also 15. The third was still unidentified when scores of parents - being a private school in an urban area of tree-lined streets of semi-detached stone apartments, they were well dressed and quite unused to the idea that violence might touch their families - ran toward the building, weeping and shrieking.

Given the world's understandable - and justified - horror at the suffering of eastern Aleppo's people, and its apparent inability to grasp that its defenders also kill indiscriminately, I suppose we must add that the pattern of mortar fragment marks around the impact point on the school roof left no doubt that the projectile was fired from the east. This was no devilishly designed hidden bomb placed by the authorities to kill children for propaganda purposes. Fired by the Islamist Jabhat al-Nusra group or its allies - the same name-changed al-Qaeda of 9/11 infamy whose ranks are now referred to respectfully as "rebels" by the rest of the world - it was directed into a residential district of western Aleppo, just like the second shell which landed on an apartment in the Hamdamiyeh district.

By the time I reached the University Hospital a mile from the Razi medical centre, this attack's three victims - all killed just after breakfast in their home - had just arrived. Khanom Fallaha was two-years-old and I found her lying on a trolley, her face grey with dust, slightly turned to the right as if sleeping, her clothes and tiny shoes black from the shell blast, although a bright, shiny earring remained in her left ear.

Behind her were the bodies of her two brothers, 10-year old Khalil and 11-year old Khaled.

One of them - I don't know which - lay with his face turned toward the ceiling in an unnatural, ungainly way. And of course, being human, familiar thoughts crept into one's mind. Yes, that is how her mother dressed Khanom this morning on her last day on earth, that is what she was wearing when she had breakfast with her brothers, and... Well now, like tens of thousands of other children in Syria, she was gone, departed from the world she scarcely knew, part of the past, a mere figure in the grotesque and massively abused casualty statistics of the dead, whose real total we shall never know or, one day, much care about. By tonight, she will be in the earth.

Is this sentimental? I don't think so. We weep over the dead children of eastern Aleppo, under siege by the Syrian regime. But Khanom is equally worthy of the world's sympathy. Neither she, nor her brothers, nor the three children at the school, chose which side of Aleppo they would live in. But of course, as always, there is astonishment as well as shock when you talk to the children who survived.

Although in great pain and with blood on his feet, 14-year old Ahmed Skeifeh, told me that he was still in the classroom beside the roof when the shell exploded. I had seen English textbooks and a half-eaten bun on the floor and on the broken desks and - incredibly, amid his pain - Ahmed chose to speak in perfect English. "I fell on to the floor and my friends were all with me and I saw my friends fall down and I saw my friends die with my own eyes," he said. "I can't remember anything more. I ran out of the room." The boy was propped up on his hospital bed, one of five boys seriously injured, his teacher standing beside him, his arm around the boy's head.

A younger boy lay on a hospital trolley, a doctor picking metal out of his face, all his limbs heavily bandaged. He was writhing in agony, moving his legs wildly, comforted by the director of the school, Sayed Kadayer. Outside, the street was lined by men and women, their heads and arms shaking in loss and mourning and disbelief. One middle-aged man was carried by two Red Crescent rescue workers - they wear orange suits and are of course less known than their opposite numbers who wear white helmets in eastern Aleppo - into the hospital, his legs collapsing beneath him as he realised his loss.

There was a bleak, frightening moment when a wounded man arrived, carried by his armed comrades, dripping blood and obviously in terrifying pain, crying out, bandages hanging off him but his camouflage clothes visible and bloody beneath a sheet. The other soldiers pushed the families aside. "He's from the front line," a doctor shouted. And so the dead children of western Aleppo were joined by a still living but gravely wounded soldier of the Syrian army of Bashar al-Assad - a man whose name, I noticed, was carved in white marble on a wall opposite the lift. He had, long ago in the days when no one could have imagined the war - least of all him - officially opened this hospital.

Robert Fisk

Wednesday, 2 November 2016

ALEPPO'S AGONY

They're keeping open the eight passages to western Aleppo, just in case. There have been no more air strikes on the surrounded east of the city by either Syrian or Russian jets - despite the anti-government bombardment by Jabhat al-Nusra and its largely Islamist allies. The Syrian army has pushed its enemies nine miles further north of the city, in which more than 80 civilians have been killed over the past six days and the militia offensive has predictably failed.

Not that the United Nations could be left out. "Shocked and appalled" it was, of course, and Staffan de Mistura, the UN envoy, has churned out the old "war crimes" threat, this time directed at the West's friendly 'moderates' in eastern Aleppo - whom he was keen to talk to a couple of weeks ago - rather than the Bashar al-Assad regime. But the UN's bleatings will make no difference. Nor will John Kerry's oddly Gaelic fears of Aleppo smashed to "smithereens" - originally an Irish word - have the slightest effect.

Yet the Syrian government still hopes more civilians - militiamen, too - will leave the besieged east and allow it to reabsorb the enclave without another war. Everything depends right now on three people: the commander of the Syrian Aleppo garrison, the head of the Baath party in the city, and the boss - whoever he is - of the Jabhat al-Nusra militia and their Ahrar al-Sham allies and other outfits who are defending or imprisoning (delete as appropriate, as usual) the 200,000 to 300,000 civilians in eastern Aleppo.

So we'll start with the bespectacled general in charge of the evacuation whose office I found adorned with vast operational maps of Aleppo - in which the east of the city appears as a grey, bent sausage with a circle to the left (the ancient citadel, still held by Syrian troops) pierced by eight large red arrows. Whether the arrows represent planned attacks or the crossing points which the government opened on 20 October from 8am to 4pm each day - with only 48 takers so far - was unclear. But the four large banners hanging from flagstaffs behind the general's desk told their own story: Hezbollah's green and yellow, the red, white and blue of Russia, the black, white and red of Syria and the green white and red of Iran.

A multicoloured coalition, then, with a lot of firepower - and an intriguing set of military video clips of the crossings as they opened on 20 October. Each shows a Syrian armoured vehicle with a loudspeaker calling on "the people of Aleppo" to "take out the wounded and civilians from the east of Aleppo along the routes that have been planned by the government", adding revealingly that "the Syrian government, in cooperation with the Russian forces, will guarantee safety for you and your family". Russian officers were indeed at the crossing points on the three first days. Two of them were wounded by snipers. One of the video clips shows a shell, apparently fired from eastern Aleppo, exploding in the background as two men run from the east to the Syrian army lines.

The general thought there were only 75,000 civilians left in eastern Aleppo, an intriguing figure since the number of trapped families in the enclave have moved between 70,000 and 300,000 according to various "experts". The UN believes the higher figure, a Syrian army officer on the front line suggested 200,000, another far more senior Syrian intelligence officer thought 250,000, the Ba'ath party guessed between 112,000 to 115,000. All of which proves that no one - neither the UN, the Syrians or journalists - has the slightest idea of just how many souls are waiting to be saved or to die.

"We promised to take care of the injured," the general announced. "We did. The people who came across were free to go and live with their relatives in the west of the city or to apartments which we had reserved for them. They chose their relatives." Then he added, almost without hesitation: "Now the decision is that we must enter the battle and put an end to the Nusra and other terrorist groups to help the people themselves to get rid of them."

Did this mean that the halt in Russian and Syrian bombing of eastern Aleppo would resume? A telephone rang on the general's desk and a flurry of staff officers ran into his office with aerial photographs - presumably the work of a drone - and his attention suddenly turned to more pressing matters. "There are armed men crossing from Turkey through the Bab al-Howa border point to the north of Lattakia" - which showed just how far the general's remit ran in northern Syria - "and they are driving a lot of vehicles with explosives and ammunition. Look! We search for a political solution and they are ready to attack and fight."

But would the Syrians and Russians bomb east Aleppo again? "There are orders that the planes cannot bomb within 10km of eastern Aleppo," the general replied. An interesting remark, since the general is the man who orders the air strikes - along with his Russian colleagues, of course - and he followed up with a slightly ambiguous remark when I asked for his feelings when he saw the wounded children of east Aleppo on television. "I see them as like my kids," he replied. "I have a very high sense of humanity with civilians.

But with terrorists, I have to do my national duty - to defend the civilians and protect them. The terrorists" - and the general thought there were 15 separate armed groups in eastern Aleppo - "are the same wherever they exist - in Syria, Iran, Britain, Russia, Lebanon..."

Perhaps. But the general also made a remark about "medical facilities for terrorists", which suggested that hospitals who treated militiamen in east Aleppo were targets for the Syrian-Russian coalition, whomever else the hospitals treated. Which also tells its own grim tale. So now to the Baath headquarters in Aleppo, bathed in generator light and sudden power cuts, where the local party head,

Ahmed Ibrahim Saleh, described how he talked to east Aleppo civilians by phone, claiming that - through these interlocutors - he has contact with 12,000 civilians in the enclave.

And negotiations were continuing, he said. The Ahrar al-Sham group had indirectly received a message from the government via text and they replied by recorded phone calls: the government's message was that they could send over a group of their men if they wanted to cross to the west of the city as a test - just two if they wanted - and these two could telephone when they arrived through the government lines and reached a safe place.

"They said: 'We trust you, but we don't trust the [Syrian] government or the [state] security apparatus'. I said, 'just find four or five armed men to cross'. They said they would discuss this. The problem is that the leaders of these armed groups, the foreigners, make them afraid and tell them that the security apparatus will execute them. But all the armed men who have come to this building have been well-treated." This appears to be perfectly true. But the constant reference to the 'security apparatus' was telling; everyone in Syria fears the mukhabarat security police.

When I asked Mr Saleh about hospitals in the east of the city, I heard a familiar story. "This is war. Maybe there are some mistakes. Maybe the plane cannot see women and children. One hospital shelled by a plane was a base for the leaders of the terrorists and was full of arms and weapons." This was quite an admission.

When Nato found soldiers hiding in a hospital during the 1999 war on Serbia, its bombs killed all the civilians in the building but none of the soldiers. No one spoke of war criminals. A different morality is in play in Syria, of course, where the bombing of hospitals is immediately - and legally correctly - referred to as a war crime.

As for the conflict, "war ends when foreign support stops", Mr Saleh said. "If America says 'Stop the war', the war will stop." So now to a young Syrian army captain on the front line who guards one of the crossing points. During the truce, he received two armed men who had contacted him earlier to arrange the crossing. "They came right here to my office," he said. "One of them was from Ahrar al-Sham, we let them come with their guns. We had vehicles ready for them with covered windows so that no one could shoot at them. I told them which road to use to come out. They were checked by our people in case they carried booby traps. We could see them but the two men could not see our soldiers.

"They told me that their life stopped when the war began and did not advance any more in the following years. One of the men said his dream was 'just one more night of sleep and one more day of life for me and my family'. The two men knew each other and they complained that the armed groups were uneducated and illiterate. Yes, when we shell east Aleppo, we are defending ourselves - just as they will defend their side of the city when we rocket them. How many people are there? I myself think the UN's figures might be exaggerated. When the passages were opened, eight wounded men from Ahrar al-Sham came out and we offered them health care and they refused and said they wanted to join the other terrorists in Idlib province. Because they were wounded, they were friendly to the army. I met the eight of them. We allowed them freely to go to Idlib."

And this is also true. The armed men who surrendered in Homs were allowed to go to Idlib. So were the armed opposition in the Damascus suburbs, including those of Mouadamiya. Idlib seems to be the favourite dumping ground for all varieties of Islamist fighters. For the Syrian government, the armed men of Aleppo should either agree to go home or head for Idlib themselves, along with their families. But will they? The captain had heard of 40 executions by Ahrar al-Sham of armed men who wished to leave eastern Aleppo. Propaganda? Maybe. But the commanders of the Islamist groups there give no interviews to visiting western reporters - because western journalists have wisely decided not to turn up in east Aleppo and have their heads cut off.

So was the recent offensive against western Aleppo the answer to the Syrians' "passageways" to freedom, to the "corridors" of safety that were opened for the civilians? Perhaps. But given the amount of weaponry the militias deployed in recent days, they may have decided that they still have no need to negotiate another truce or take the bus to Idlib. Then we are left with the general's remark about how "the decision is to enter the battle". In other words, Aleppo's agony is far from over.

Robert Fisk

Thursday, 3 November 2016

BODIES AND BLOOD

We arrived so soon after Jabhat al-Nusra's retreat from the village that one man and his family had only just buried the remains of four Islamists at the bottom of their field. "We found them at the back and they stank so much that we had to get rid of them," Mohamed Kenjo said. "So we took the remains and put them under a covering of earth away from our home."

But the house he once shared with his wife and six children had been looted - everything, from the washing machine and the water tank, to cups and saucers and kettles - and the homes of Kenjo's neighours lay in ruins, broken open by shells and rockets. This was the front line north of Hama, a city whose history lay in the blood of insurrection more than 34 years ago.

So close to the front line, in fact, that the fighter bombers were still howling over our heads to attack the Islamists - Ahrar al-Sham, Nusra, all the usual suspects - in the next village to the north-west. The Syrians say you can only see their jets, that the Russian fighter-bombers are so fast it's impossible to catch them with the naked eye. You could make out the spray of anti-missile flares that the aircraft released, four or five bright stars that drifted through the imperial blue sky like fireworks.

But then, as the planes turned one after the other from their bombing runs, you could just see them as the sun caught their swept-back wings, daggering up into the heavens to the south before their bombs exploded with a loud, hollow sound like two giant wooden planks banging together on the ground. Amid the soldiers, sweating, tired, a general turned up, steel helmet over his eyes, marching briskly with his officers through the ruins. I wanted to know how many of the Nusra men had died.

"Many, many," he replied. But when I asked how many of his Syrian soldiers had been killed in the broken, smashed village of Soran, his answer came without hesitation. "We had 42 martyrs,' he said bleakly. I didn't doubt the figure. And when soldiers tell the truth, it means they are winning. But that's a lot of men to lose for one dust-covered hamlet. The Syrian army's death toll in six years of war is a state secret. But I've been given a reliable figure for the government army's fatalities in this terrible war: around 75,000.

These are the dead, not the hundreds of thousands of wounded. Soldiers expect to die. They live by the sword.

Civilians on both sides are the innocents whose lives should be spared. Their mortality statistics come from all sides, including the United Nations. Is it 250,000 or 300,000 as the UN now states? Or 400,000 as the "experts" in faraway cities now claim? Whatever the figure, add another 75,000 to it.

The Nusra men and their allies had only captured this place two and a half months ago. House after house in what had been Soran had been blown apart. Some remained, their doors ajar, the bougainvillea still spilling over their concrete walls. But always, when I walked inside, there were cupboards torn open by the retreating Islamists, piles of children's clothes and toys and clocks and family snapshots scattered across the floor. One picture showed a baby smiling from a cot, another a husband and wife surrounded by their children. The Islamists had probably been looking for money hidden in the cupboards. But why did the looters want a washing machine? Did they plan to lug this rubbish away in their retreat? What happened to those who lived here?

There was no doubt of the tragedy of one middle-aged man. He stood forlornly in the street beside a huge bomb crater surrounded by heavy, jagged pieces of steel casing that lay at his feet. "I am a policeman in Hama," he said. "My father stayed behind. He was an old man. And on the day they left, the killers murdered him. They shot him at the back of his home." And he led me into his father's blackened house and pushed open the door to a small, darkened closet. "We found him there, on the floor," he said.

Other Syrian villagers, returning now that the Islamists had fled, told similar stories, of missing women, of bodies in the wreckage. Highways seem to survive wars, as if history insists that the basic geography of a society should remain mapped out amid the ruins for a village's later reconstruction. So on the main road, those who had fled the invaders last August had turned up in pick-up trucks and old cars to see what remained of their homes, to collect what detritus was left.

In the neighbouring village of Maardes, I found a woman and her daughter - her name was Qamar, which means "moon", and they had returned to a real moonscape. She and Qamar found part of a wardrobe and a mat carpet which they loaded pathetically onto a pick-up which a relative had brought up from Hama. In a different age, in 1982, the Muslim Brotherhood - a pale ghost compared to the Islamists of today - had staged a fearful insurrection in the city, put down with more than equal ferocity by Hafez al-Assad's army all those years ago.

The statistics of those long dead civilians who had died in the government's reprisals are as slippery as today's death toll. Was it five or six thousand? Or 20,000 as we journalists claimed at the time?

Many of the ruins of Hama's old city were bulldozed away to make room for new apartment blocks and a luxury hotel. But a few ancient houses remain beside the ancient "nouriah" water wheels that still wail and creak away in this haunted city. Its Sunni Muslim citizens are quiet now. Maybe they have learned their terrible lesson. Or maybe the government learned to treat them with respect, leaving new generations with their new-found trade and wealth and schools. Today, its market packed with shoppers, it feels like a memory of the old, dubiously "safe" dictatorship that dominated Syria before this war; content, subdued, careful, aware - to use an old British wartime maxim - that "careless talk costs lives". Brotherhood prisoners back in 1982 were later slaughtered in a prison massacre at Palmyra.

The Ibrahim mosque still displays a three-decade old shell hole in its minaret. But Nusra has not let the city forget its past. Less than a month ago, a suicide bomber set off a truck load of explosives outside the Baath party headquarters. One governor has been assassinated. It's a relief to drive north again to a wooded hillside whose burned trees and massive earth revetments show that it was an artillery position until a few days ago. Two 120mm guns stand on a parapet above the plain of Hama.

On top of the hill, there stands the almost untouched shrine of Ali Ibn Hussein al-Abdin, the fourth Imam who survived the seventh century battle of Kerbala, a Shiite holy place - the Alawi sect to which the al-Assads belong is Shia - and soldiers had arrived from the battlefront to pray and kiss the black marble shrine beneath its cupola of antiquity. A major later stood outside the courtyard and pointed to the horizon. You could see 30 - perhaps 40 - miles across the flat, featureless countryside where around 7,000 armed opponents of the Assad regime are still fighting to retake the lost villages and cut the desert military supply road to Aleppo. Are they all Nusra men? A few Isis members, no doubt. Perhaps they were the 'moderate' rebels whom David Cameron, a former British prime minister seemingly invented.

And how long before the Syrian army could recapture all those lands which ran seventy miles to Aleppo and linked up to the Turkish border north of the city? The major looked across this vast expanse of territory. Then he pointed to the sky and opened his hands. The gesture said it all. God knows.

Robert Fisk

Saturday, 5 November 2016

SURREAL WAR FROM THE GOLAN HEIGHTS

From Colonel Saleh's forward position on his front line north of Quneitra, he has a unique and exclusive view of the Syrian war. To his west and south is a vast area of his country which is occupied by Jabhat al-Nusra Islamist fighters - their earthen ramparts and supply roads are scarcely half a mile away. Then, another couple of miles away, Israeli soldiers are inside their concrete positions on the occupied Syrian Golan Heights, above the old and Nusra-held Syrian city of Quneitra.

"You see that mosque over there, just to the right of the water tower?" the colonel asks. "Well, Nusra is there. And you see the triangular hill beyond? The Israelis are there." It's what you call a politically intriguing battlefield - yes, shells do come whizzing in towards the Syrians from Nusra and also from the Israelis. The Syrians concentrate their fire on Nusra but Nusra's casualties are often taken through the Israeli lines for hospital treatment in Haifa.

So whose side is Israel on? Baath City is a concrete conurbation created back in pre-civil war days to defy the vandalisation of the old Quenitra. It was occupied by the Israeli army during the 1973 Middle East war and then - before they abandoned it under the Kissinger agreement - totally destroyed with explosives by Israeli troops. Nusra now occupy these 43-year old ruins. As for Baath City, its university, banks, fire station, schools, police force and hospitals are defiantly maintained by the Syrians under the eyes of their two enemies: the Nusra Islamists and the Israelis.

According to the Syrian army in Baath City - their forward lines and tanks are positioned in unfinished apartment blocks on the edge of the town - their intelligence department's Hebrew speakers constantly monitor conversations between the Israelis and between

Israeli and Nusra fighters. They know - and the Israelis have made no secret of the fact - that wounded Nusrah fighters are taken to Haifa for hospital treatment. On one occasion, a Nusrah man travelling in an Israeli ambulance on the Golan was dragged from the vehicle and lynched by a crowd of enraged Druze men who are largely loyal to the Syrian government and regard Nusrah as their mortal enemies. Reports of the man's murder highlighted the highly ambiguous relationship between Israel and the Islamists, whose name-changing cannot conceal their al-Qaeda roots.

Druze towns inside Syria and close to Baath City have taken the side of the regime - this does not apply to other Druze areas - but it makes the geography of the front line here all the more surreal. One Syrian lieutenant described to me how he directed his artillery fire onto an Israeli jeep in the Nusra-occupied town of Al-Hamidiya inside Syria and destroyed it. The jeep might have been a gift or borrowed from Israel - whether there were any Israeli personnel inside it if it was hit is another matter. The Syrians, however, also say that Israeli bulldozers were used to build a new supply route for Nusrah between Quneitra and Golan - again, inside Syria's frontiers.

All of which raises a compelling question. The Nusra-controlled territory between the Syrians and the Israeli lines on Golan - and other Islamist groups and a few remnants of the old "Free Syrian Army" allied to them in this location - stretches all the way south to the edge of the Syrian city of Deraa and right down to the Jordanian frontier. And beyond that frontier is the so-called "Military Operations Centre" - the "MOC" of which both the Islamists and the Syrian army refer - where Western intelligence officers maintain a liaison and weapons supply depot for the anti-government Syrian forces.

So what is the relationship between the MOC and its Western backers - who maintain contact with Nusra - and the Israelis who treat Nusra's wounded in their hospitals? The Jordanian border and the Israeli lines on Golan are at their most only about 70 miles apart and opposition fighters hold all the land in between.

Littered around the front lines outside Baath City are the wreckage of past battles and the abandoned UN posts from which Filipino UN soldiers were kidnapped en masse more than a year ago; the Syrian army now occupies several of these positions, the UN logo still painted on the walls although several of the "igloo"-type UN accommodation huts have migrated to Syrian compounds in the rear lines.

The UN force on Golan now operates only inside Israeli-occupied territory.

Only a few hundred yards away from Nusra-held territory, we found Abu Hashem, a farmer who fled from his village, now held by the Islamists, living today in family property close to one of the old UN posts. He fed us tea and coffee and walnuts from his orchard. His wife and six children now exist in this unfinished, cold house along with a small library of books - the speeches of Imam Ali (the "Najul Blagha") and a collection of medical books of Aleppo herbal cures for headaches and kidney infection, published in Beirut.

He says the people in his Nusra-occupied village are divided. Some are sympathetic towards the Islamists - they are not fighters - while others are sometimes permitted by Nusrah to cross the front lines for treatment in Syrian government hospitals. They are Bedouins and farmers, the unsettled and the landowners, always prey to the wolves of civil war insurgents.

Colonel Saleh, who is 50 years old, has been guarding his echoing and weed-strewn apartment blocks on the edge of Baath City for three years, noting wearily that the Israelis attack his army but never attack Nusra who - being al-Qaeda - might logically have earned Israel's enmity. But no. "I know every stone here," the colonel says. "I can see if a rock or a vehicle has moved across the fields in front of us - and I can immediately see if one vehicle has become two vehicles. We know when they are going to attack - they always precede their offensives with a big artillery and mortar barrage."

Sometimes the voices of Nusra men shout insults at the Syrians on their own radio sets, calling them "kafirs" - '"infidels" or "unbelievers". "If I am in a good mood, I invite them for coffee," Colonel Saleh says. "If I'm in a bad mood, I am silent. Their accents are very similar to the Jordanians. They come from the south of Deraa, along the Jordanian border."

As we spoke, further down the line, the Syrians and Nusra were fighting with tanks, artillery and mortars.

The Syrians claimed that their enemies arrived in several directions in a convoy of at least 13 vehicles.

They spoke, too, of a Nusra female officer called Souad al-Qatahani (nicknamed "Al-Nood"), the 30-year old sister of a Nusrah general called Qais al-Omani who commanded 1,200 fighters. She was, they pointed out rather remarkably, a former first lieutenant in their own Syrian government army.

And one further feature that the Syrians have noted about their enemies outside Baath City. Whenever Nusra fire a missile, they have to take a photograph of the rocket leaving its launcher - presumably to prove to their suppliers that they have not sold the weapon to someone else. Trust, as usual in the Syrian war, is in short supply.

Robert Fisk

AFTERWORD

A DANGEROUS NEW WORLD

Even before Donald Trump's election victory it was becoming clear that we are living in an age of disintegration. Nation states are returning to relationships based on rivalry and friction when the trend was meant to be in the opposite direction.

The internal unity of country after country is under stress or has already broken down. Governments and universities used to set up institutions to study greater integration and cooperation, while in fact they might have been better looking at how things fall apart.

The phenomenon is most obvious in the wider Middle East where there are at least seven wars and three insurgencies raging in the swathe of countries between Pakistan and Nigeria. But in Europe and the US, foreign and domestic antagonisms are also becoming deeper and more venomous. In this more rancorous political landscape, the election of Donald Trump as US President feels like part of a trend, toxic and dangerous but wide-ranging and unstoppable. Distinct though the political and economic situation in the US, Europe and the Middle East may be in many respects, there is the same dissatisfaction or rejection of the status quo without much idea of what should be put in its place.

Political shocks like the election of Trump can produce apocalyptic forebodings that in retrospect turn out to be misplaced or exaggerated. But, in this case, grim expectations about the future may be all too justified and unlikely to evaporate. Trump's promises of radical change may be phoney or opportunistic, but they have a momentum of their own which will be uncontrollable.

For all his demagoguery, there was a sense that Trump was often nearer to the issues that concerned voters than Hillary Clinton. In the final election rallies of Trump in Michigan and Clinton in North Carolina, he was promising voters the return of factories and well-paid jobs while she was repeating kindergarten waffle such as "love trumps hate" and "build bridges not walls". He will find it difficult to retreat from these pledges and this is bound to bring confrontation with other trading nations. Overall, the high days of liberal capitalism since the fall of the Soviet Union in 1991, which continued despite a battering from the financial crisis of 2008, are finally finished.

It is an age not just of disintegration but of extremes, with proponents of the status quo either weakened or discredited, as shown by the Brexit vote in Britain. The beneficiaries are mostly on the right: from the 1980s on, the mainstream left in Britain, France and Germany abandoned socialism for liberal free market capitalism as the proven recipe for human happiness, which meant that after 2008 they had no alternative system to advocate and could no longer provide a credible vehicle for protest. The political beneficiaries of disillusionment with things as they are have almost invariably been on the right as with Trump who, along with other rightist insurgencies, can plug into resurgent loyalty to the nation state in the wake of discredited globalisation.

There are similarities - so long as the analogies are not overstrained - between the forces behind the Arab Spring protests of 2011, the Brexit vote and Trump's electoral victory today. In all cases, the ruling establishment was weaker and more unpopular than even the most critical observers had imagined: the triumphant protesters were astonished by the extent of their own success. More ominously, it swiftly emerged in the Middle East that the proponents of change had little idea what it should be and had relied wholly on demonisation of their opponents as the source of all evils.

There is another parallel between what happened in the Arab world five years ago and events in the UK and the US this year. The old regimes were battered or discarded but there was nothing to replace them with. There is no consensus on what to do. Travelling to Britain from the Middle East, it is striking how the political, social and geographical divisions expressed by the Brexit vote have only deepened with time, whatever pretences there are to the contrary. Political commentators in the UK and US who endlessly proclaimed that, whatever the rhetoric, elections were won by those who seized the centre ground turned out to be wrong because there was not much centre ground to seize.

These are not the only political shibboleths which should be discarded. Shocks like these usually provoke jeremiads from the "commentariat" about how all is chaos and the centre cannot hold. Such dire warnings are swiftly followed by more hopeful commentary about how things have not changed as radically or dangerously as first feared. But, unfortunately, in the case of the US election, the first gloom-filled predictions may be the most accurate.

It is true that Trump's authority will be thwarted by the division of powers laid down by the US constitution - though this is somewhat contradicted by Republican control of both Houses of Congress as well as the presidency. Presidential powers are also diluted by those of other state institutions such as the Pentagon and the Treasury. But these comforting thoughts are probably wishful thinking. The extent of the rejection of the American establishment - Democrats, Republicans, celebrities, media - by US voters underlines its weakness. The US media in particular is so much part of the political class that it had become an echo chamber in which it heard only its own views.

Leaving aside these dangerous historical trends, there is another more immediate menace stemming from election of Trump in the US and the Brexit vote in Britain: it empowers and legitimises the crackpots and the cranks, those who want to roll back the verdict of past elections since the New Deal if not the Civil War. Those around Trump are not just the Team "B" of American politics but the Team "C" or even lower down the alphabet. They may not want to blow up the world but, out of sheer idiocy, they could do just that.

I am writing this in the Iraqi Kurdish capital Irbil which is 60 miles from Mosul, where rival armies are fighting their way into Isis's last great stronghold. Nobody expects this to be the end of the wars in Iraq and Syria or the multiple crises tearing the region apart. The experience is evidence of the fragility of states and how easily they can be capsized, not just by domestic divisions and foreign enemies but by avoidable political errors. With Donald Trump soon to be in the White House, it is difficult to avoid the feeling that the world has just become a lot more dangerous place.

Patrick Cockburn

ARAB SPRING — ARAB WINTER TIMELINE

2010

17 December: Tunisian street vendor Terek el-Tayeb Mohamed Bouazizi sets himself on fire, becoming a catalyst for the Tunisian revolution and Arab Spring.

2011

14 January: After several weeks of protests in Tunisia, President Ben Ali resigns.

25 January-25 February: Protests in Egypt and Lebanon (25 Jan); Yemen (3 Feb); Bahrain and Jordan (14th); Libya (15th); Morocco and Iraq (20th); Algeria (22nd); Jordan (25th.)

11 February: Hosni Mubarak resigns as President of Egypt.

6 March: Unrest in Deraa, Syria.

14-15 March: Bahrain unrest crushed with Saudi help.

19 March: Nato intervenes to support Libyan rebels.

3 June: President Ali Abdullah Saleh flees Yemen.

July: Syrian defectors form the Free Syrian Army.

20-22 August: Libyan rebels take Tripoli.

20 October: Muammar Gaddafi killed in Sirte.

23 October: Islamist Ennahda party wins elections in Tunisia.

2012

27 February: Abd Rabbo Mansour Hadi elected Yemen's President.

24-30 June: Mohamed Morsi elected President of Egypt.

7 July: Elections in Libya.

11 September: Islamists attack US diplomatic compound, Benghazi.

2013

9 May: Isis formed.

3 July: Morsi ousted as Egypt's elected President.

21 August: Chemical attack in Damascus; US and UK vow "serious response".

29 August: Commons votes against anti-Assad action.

2014

4 January: Isis takes Fallujah, Iraq.

14 January: Isis takes Raqqa, Syria.

28 May: Abdel Fattah al-Sisi elected Egypt's President.

29 June: Isis declares "caliphate".

8 August: US-led coalition starts air strikes against Isis in Iraq.

19 August: Isis beheads its first Western hostage, James Foley.

22 September: US-led coalition starts air strikes against Isis in Syria.

21 December: Beji Caid Essebsi wins Tunisia's presidential election.

2015

7 January: Charlie Hebdo terror attacks in France; 12 die.

26 January: Saudi-led air strikes on Yemen's Houthi rebels.

1 April: Isis takes Palmyra.

26 June: 38 killed in beach attack in Sousse, Tunisia.

14 July: Iranian nuclear deal.

21 October: Russian airliner brought down in Sinai; 224 killed.

30 September: Russia starts strikes against Syrian rebels.

12 November: Mohammed Emwazi ("Jihadi John") killed.

13 November: Paris terror attacks.

20 November: UN backs anti-Isis action; UK follows suit (2 Dec).

28 December: Iraq retakes Ramadi.

2016

3 January: Saudi Arabia executes 47 alleged "terrorists".

6 January: images of starving people emerge from Madaya, Syria.

17 February: At least 28 dead in Turkish capital explosion.

26 February: Temporary truce in Syria.

13 March: Ankara car bomb kills at least 32.

30 April: Iraqi Shia protesters storm Baghdad parliament.

12 May: Top Hezbollah commander Badreddine killed.

22 May: Falluja assault begins.

15 June: EgyptAir crash wreckage found in Mediterranean.

15 July: Turkish coup attempt.

23 August: Turkey begins anti-Isis campaign in Syria.

17 September: US air strikes kill dozens of Syrian government troops.

17 October: Liberation of Mosul begins.

1 November: Iraqi special forces break front line in Mosul.

11 November: Syrian President Bashar al-Assad extends gesture of cooperation to President-elect Donald Trump.

PHOTO CAPTIONS AND COPYRIGHTS

ALSO AVAILABLE FROM THE INDEPENDENT

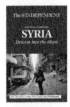

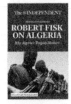
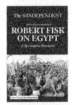

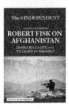
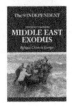